MW00977011

A Dozen Ways to Build an Affair-P

1. Stay interested and pay attention to what's going on in your partner's life and in your relationship together.

2. Make intimate moments a priority.

3. Treat your partner like a lover in your day-to-day life.

4. Take time to really listen to what your partner has to say.

5. Clear the air between you, even if it means scheduling time to argue.

6. Tailor your relationship to meet both of your needs.

7. Honor your commitments by doing what you agree to do.

8. Continually renew your love by keeping romance alive.

9. Establish mutually agreed upon boundaries about key issues, including relationships with others.

10. Regularly revisit these boundaries and revise them if necessary.

11. Build trust in each other by acting consistently.

12. Keep your eye on the prize—strong, long-lasting love!

alpha
books

tear here

The Warning Signs of an Affair

➤ A feeling of tension in the air.

➤ Changes in routine, including the amount of time you and your partner spend together.

➤ A general sense of sadness or disappointment.

➤ Increased irritability.

➤ Acting too nice or too happy.

➤ Changes in sexual routine and frequency.

➤ Distancing behavior, such as going to bed early, staying in bed longer than normal, overeating or overindulging in alcohol.

➤ More frequent criticisms of you, your kids, your family, your life together, or a general lack of interest in all of the above.

➤ Long telephone calls at inappropriate times, or hours spent on the Internet.

➤ More time out with "the boys" or "the girls."

➤ Changes in work schedules, including earlier or later hours, more late nights, possibly more travel.

➤ Changes in the mail; perhaps certain bills are no longer coming to the house.

➤ Changes in diet or exercise programs.

➤ Increased or new-found interest in appearance.

➤ New clothing, accessories, or jewelry that seems to appear out of nowhere.

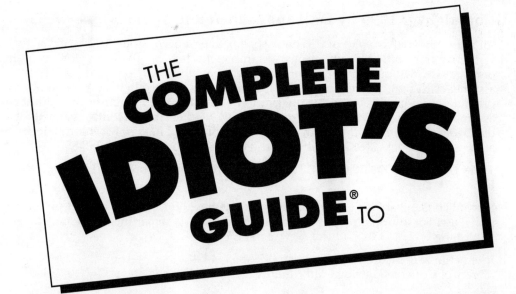

THE COMPLETE IDIOT'S GUIDE® TO

Affair-Proof Love

by Dr. Lana Staheli
with Sonia Weiss

alpha books

A Division of Macmillan General Reference
A Pearson Education Macmillan Company
1633 Broadway, New York, NY 10019-6785

International Standard Book Number: 0-02-863414-4
Library of Congress Catalog Card Number: 99-60973

01 00 99   8 7 6 5 4 3 2 1

Interpretation of the printing code: the rightmost number of the first series of numbers is the year of the book's printing; the rightmost number of the second series of numbers is the number of the book's printing. For example, a printing code of 99-1 shows that the first printing occurred in 1999.

Printed in the United States of America

Alpha Development Team

Publisher
Kathy Nebenhaus

Editorial Director
Gary M. Krebs

Managing Editor
Bob Shuman

Marketing Brand Manager
Felice Primeau

Acquisitions Editor
Jessica Faust

Development Editors
Phil Kitchel
Amy Zavatto

Assistant Editor
Georgette Blau

Production Team

Development Editor
Carol Hupping

Production Editor
Tammy Ahrens

Copy Editor
June Waldman

Cover Designer
Mike Freeland

Photo Editor
Richard H. Fox

Illustrator
Jody P. Schaeffer

Book Designers
Scott Cook and Amy Adams of DesignLab

Indexer
Craig Small

Layout/Proofreading
Angela Calvert
Mary Hunt
Julie Trippetti

Contents at a Glance

Contents

Foreword

Odds are that you or your partner will have a "hands on" experience with an affair at some point in your relationship. While an affair can sometimes be a springboard for growth, more often than not both partners find themselves emotionally flattened by the experience.

When I think about how devastating an affair can be, I recall a former client of mine named Maureen. When she entered my office for her first appointment, her young face was etched by lines of defeat and despair. Her eyes were red and puffy from days of crying and her mascara was smudged in black pools beneath her eyes.

Before she could even tell me her story, the tears began again. As she sobbed into her handkerchief, she mumbled that she couldn't understand where her marriage went wrong. Maureen described a near-perfect courtship and a blissful marriage, until the end of the second year. Then, without warning, the relationship took a sharp nose dive. Her husband Bob began spending less and less time at home. He usually worked late, and didn't make it on time for dinner. On weekends he was often out of town on business trips. And when he was home, he was always tired and impatient, criticizing her for minor mistakes. Maureen chalked his behavior up to stress from overwork and turned the other cheek.

One day, as Maureen was tidying up some papers on Bob's night table, she found it: a receipt from a lingerie shop. Bob was having an affair! Her heart felt skewered. She collapsed on the floor, literally blind-sighted by the discovery. How could she have been such a fool?

Why didn't Maureen suspect that her husband was cheating? Had she been living in denial? Or was Maureen, like most people, simply unschooled on the subject of infidelity?

Thanks to Dr. Staheli's invaluable book, readers will acquire an encyclopedic knowledge of the anatomy of affairs. They will learn what makes a couple ripe for an infidelity and howto recognize when an extramarital liaison is brewing.

Staheli also provides vital information on how to prevent an affair. In clear and practical language, she shows how to create an affair-proof love—by customizing the relationship so that both partners' emotional and sexual needs are met, establishing mutually agreed upon boundaries, listening and paying attention to each other, resolving differences, and keeping romance, laughter and magic alive.

This book is also a life saver for couples who are in the throes of an affair. Dr. Staheli offers sound advice on how to deliver the death blow to an ongoing affair and shows how to reestablish trust and faith, steer clear of new temptations, and rebuild a relationship on stronger foundations.

I highly recommend this book to any couple who wants to do everything possible to immunize their relationship against affairs, as well as those who want to repair a relationship that has been ruptured by an infidelity.

If I had my way, I would see a law passed requiring that this book be handed out with every marriage license.

—Dr. Jamie Turndorf

Jamie Turndorf, Ph.D., is an internationally known psychologist and relationship expert, advice columnist read by millions throughout the world, regular guest on national television, and author *of The Pleasure of Your Company: A Socio-Psychological Analysis of Modern Sociability*.

Introduction

There's a good chance that you've bought this book because you suspect that your lover or spouse is having an affair, or you know for sure that some extramarital fooling around is going on and you want to know what to do about it. If this is the case…well, welcome to the club. As you probably know by now, you've got lots of company.

Affairs are dangerous liaisons. They can bring joy, intensity, adventure, love and lust, and they also can be accompanied by unbearable pain, sorrow, regret and hope. But there are ways to prevent affairs from happening in the first place. And there are ways to emerge from affairs in better shape than before, should they occur. This is what *The Complete Idiot's Guide to Affair-Proof Love* is all about.

From twenty-five years of counseling couples, I have seen it all: the hopes and joys of new love and the devastation of betrayal that affairs can bring. I have seen marriages destroyed by an affair and I have seen marriages become stronger and more fulfilling after an affair. Sometimes the relationships that seemed most likely to come through intact didn't, while the ones I thought would never make it defied all logic and survived.

I began my research on affairs in 1992 after realizing that many of the couples I was working with either knew very little about affairs or had skewed perspectives on what they were really all about. Much of what they did know had been gleaned from novels, movies or television, where affairs are rarely portrayed realistically or with much depth. Relying on this knowledge alone could indeed destroy even the best of relationships.

After pouring through the many different reports and studies that touched on affairs in some manner, I came to believe that knowing more about affairs is important, not only when trying to prevent them but also when coping with them when (or if) they do occur. Generals on the battlefield know the chances are slim of overcoming their adversaries if they don't know much about whom and what they're fighting. The same holds true for anyone battling an affair.

Putting this knowledge to work is also essential to what I have come to call affair-proof love.

What is affair-proof love? It means basing your relationship on fact, not fiction. It means coming to agreement on life goals and deciding to work together to achieve them. It means paying attention to what is happening in each other's life and meeting each other's needs on a consistent basis, not just when certain issues arise. It means deciding, no matter what, to face together the curveballs that life can throw. And, perhaps most importantly, affair-proof love means making the firm commitment to do whatever it takes to help your relationship not only survive, but thrive.

When to Read This Book

Maybe you've picked up this book before there's even a glimmer of an affair in your life, and if so, congratulations! You've taken the first step toward defying the odds. In the pages that follow you'll discover how to recognize an affair and prevent one from happening.

If there is already an affair threatening your relationship, take heart—and read on. You'll find a good deal of insight and advice for getting through this difficult time—just the kind of guidance and perspective I give to people I counsel every day. Whatever is on your heart, regardless of what it is, this book can help. Are you wondering how you ever got into this mess to begin with? Maybe you're afraid of losing everything that's near and dear to you. Do you want to begin reconciling with your spouse right away but you don't know where to start? The answers are here. And, most importantly, so are many, many encouraging words, often spoken by people just like you who have gone through it, too.

How to Use This Book

Knowledge, as they say, is power. One of the best defenses against an affair is understanding all the elements that can cause one—and all that you can do to prevent one.

For this reason, it's a good idea to read or at least browse through *The Complete Idiot's Guide to Affair-Proof Love* from cover to cover. This is because each chapter builds on the information that precedes it, to give you a solid understanding of what affairs are, why they happen, how they can be prevented, and how to mend things and move on once they're over. That said, you can, of course, go directly to the sections that you feel are appropriate for your specific situation right now.

Part 1, "Until Death Do Us Part?," delves into what affairs are and why they happen, as well as what an affair can mean—both good and bad—for a relationship. There's also an overview of the scientific and societal reasons behind infidelity, and a survey of the different types of affairs and what makes them tick.

In **Part 2, "Secrets to Affair-Proof Love,"** you'll read about why it's so important to develop a relationship that keeps you interested in each other and how to create one by doing such things as establishing boundaries that are comfortable for you both, maintaining an enjoyable sex life and keeping the romance alive.

Affairs can be stopped in their tracks, and the best time to do it is before they ever happen. In **Part 3, "Danger: Affair Ahead!,"** you'll find key information on recognizing the patterns in your relationship that might lead to an affair someday and spotting the signs that an affair is just ahead. This is also where you'll find specific information on confirming the existence of an affair, should you need to do so.

Part 4, "When an Affair Happens" is a must-read for anyone who either suspects or knows that his or her spouse or partner is involved with someone else. Designed to help whether the affair is out in the open or not, it's full of information that will answer your most burning questions about the affair and what you should do, both to cope with it and to take care of yourself while it's happening.

One of the key themes that you'll find emphasized over and over in this book is that an affair doesn't have to mean the end of a relationship. In **Part 5, "Creating an Affair-Proof Future,"** you'll gain a clearer understanding of the work that's ahead of you—of what you and your loved one need to do to get your relationship moving forward again and become stronger than ever.

A note on the terminology: Affairs can happen at any time, whether you're married or not. For this reason, you'll find such terms as "marriage" and "relationship," and "spouse" and "partner" interchanged throughout the book. In the interest of fairness to both genders, and because women are just as capable of having affairs as men, specific gender references are interchanged as well.

Extras

Sprinkled throughout the chapters that follow are many stories of people just like you who have weathered affairs and lived to tell their stories. In addition to all the stories and guidance, you'll find other bits of information that will give you even more insight on what affairs are all about and how you can prevent them, arranged in boxes like these:

Affair Facts

Ever wonder how many people have affairs? Look to these boxes for tidbits of news, views, statistics and more.

Affair Speak

What's the difference between infidelity and adultery? Look here for definitions of these words and others.

Bumps Ahead

This is where you'll find out how to recognize the wrong turns and potholes to steer around while navigating relationship roads.

Dr. Lana's Secrets

The doctor is in! These boxes are where you'll find specific help on the problems you're facing...direct from the counselor's office.

In closing, I'd like to offer a special word of encouragement. You'll find that much of the material contained in *The Complete Idiot's Guide to Affair-Proof Love* is presented in a positive manner, and sometimes a little lightheartedly. Don't misunderstand this. An affair is a serious matter, and it shouldn't be taken lightly. But it doesn't have to destroy your life unless you let it. Stay alert, be positive, and protect your love. It can last a lifetime if you do.

Acknowledgments

From Lana:

My husband, L. Taylor Staheli, M.D., is the center of my world and I am eternally grateful for his unwavering love, devotion, and his willingness to consult with me on computer and soft-ware use as well as research interpretation.

When Jessica Faust, our editor, approached me about this project I was hesitant because I had other commitments. She suggested partnering with Sonia Weiss, a talented professional writer in Denver. Working with another writer was a new adventure and a valuable learning experience. Her writing improved the flow of the book.

Jessica Faust is a gifted and skillful editor, who created this project. Carol Hupping, our development editor, is articulate and offered a valuable perspective. Our production editor, Tammy Ahrens, and our copy editor, June Waldman, were efficient and effective. It takes a lot of people to get a book from conception through production and into your hands, and we are fortunate to work with this incredibly competent team.

My agent, Patti Brietman, is always a source of good advice and encouragement. Juli Verdieck takes care of our personal life allowing both my husband and I freedom to write books. Christy Alexander added creativity and perspective. Thank you!

I appreciate the love and affection I enjoy from our family, Todd Staheli, Linda Staheli and David Abramowitz, Diane and Peter Demopulos, Letha Staheli, Bruce, Kim and Dalton Ribble, and Mildred Ribble. I am inspired by my friend Natalie Mosca's unbridled enthusiasm.

And, of course, I am indebted to my clients who reveal the most intimate details of their lives to me and allow me to share their lessons with you.

From Sonia:

It was a blessing to work with such a talented team on this book. Lana Staheli's ever-present wit and positive attitude made her a joy to write with. Many thanks also go to Jessica Faust, who brought me in and kept the wheels going more than once; to Carol Hupping, an extremely gifted editor who managed to tread lightly while making things better; and to my husband Jim, who always reminds me of what is truly important.

Almost ten years ago Dr. Ed Chua put *The Road Less Traveled* in my hands and showed me what my life could be if I wanted to work hard enough. Ed, you always said I could do it. This one's for you.

Part 1
Until Death Do Us Part?

Great concept, isn't it? Staying together until the bitter end. Living under a covenant that lasts a lifetime. Too bad the odds are against it.

Until Death Do Us Part...these five words are the cornerstone of traditional wedding vows, and if you're married, more than likely you spoke them at your ceremony. But many couples today are parting well before the Grim Reaper shows even a flicker of his shadow. And, those partings are often aided and abetted by some extramarital fooling around.

Affairs have been part of the human condition since the world began, but never before have they received as much attention—nor raised as many questions—as they do today. Why are they so prevalent? Are some people more affair-prone than others? Are we biologically predisposed to needing more than one mate? Are affairs, as some folks claim, such a basic fact of life that we should accept them as such and not pay them much attention?

In Part 1, you'll learn what affairs are all about, why they happen, and why they can pose a threat to virtually all relationships, regardless of how strong the relationships are. You'll discover that there are as many different types of affairs as there are reasons to have them. You'll gain a clearer understanding of the effects—both good and bad— that an affair can have on a couple. And, you'll gain new insight into what "happily ever after" really means.

Chapter 1

Unfaithfully Yours

In This Chapter

➤ Defining an affair

➤ Understanding why affairs happen

➤ Playing the odds

➤ Who has affairs?

To be thy loving and faithful wife/husband, in plenty and in want, in joy and in sorrow, in sickness and in health, as long as we both shall live.

—Traditional Protestant wedding vow

Loving and faithful, as long as we both shall live. It's a great concept.

Unfortunately, not a very accurate one. Just ask Bill and Camille Cosby. Kathy Lee and Frank Gifford. Kevin and Cindy Costner. And a whole host of other not-so-famous people. Your aunt and uncle, or maybe the couple next door.

Odds are, even one of your parents has been involved in an affair as either the affairee, the spouse, or both. Some couples have weathered the storm, staying together despite the odds. Others…well, you know the rest.

They, like you, entered into their relationships with the best of intentions. But something happened along the way.

Always Means Forever, or Does It?

Yours could be a match made in heaven. You're very much in love, and you get along better together than any other couple you know. If you're married, you took your vows very seriously. You're committed and compatible. But beware! None of this ensures that you'll live together "happily ever after." There is a good chance someone will come between you and your spouse at some time in your life.

Regardless of how committed you are, how well matched you are, even how much you love each other, the simple truth—no matter how much you may want to believe otherwise—is that your relationship is much more likely to fail than it is to survive…and, more often than not, it's an affair that will bring it down.

Affair Facts

The well-publicized Kinsey Report in 1948 revealed that 50 percent of the men and 26 percent of the women interviewed admitted to an affair. Infidelity is not an invention of modern times; it has been part of life throughout the millenniums.

Affair Speak

The *affairee* is either of the individuals involved in an affair.

The *spouse* is the individual married to the affairee, not the partner involved in the affair. In this book, a "spouse" can also be a partner in a long-term, committed relationship.

Does an affair have to happen? Not necessarily. Understanding what affairs are and why they happen is essential to preventing them. Although the odds are against you, there are ways to work against the probability of hearing the five most dreaded words in any relationship:

"Honey, I've been seeing someone."

Why Affairs Happen

In today's world, most relationships, and especially marriages, are based on a commitment to fidelity—an explicit agreement that neither partner will become intimately involved, physically or emotionally, with anyone else.

With that said, here's the unfortunate truth. Belief in fidelity has very little to do with a successful marriage. We demand a great deal from our marriages these days, and quite frankly, they often crack under the pressure. When things break down in a relationship, for any reason, physical and emotional needs often go unmet…and relationships become vulnerable to affairs. Simply put, most affairs happen when physical or emotional needs, or both, are not being adequately fulfilled within the context of the relationship.

The reasons for this failure can range anywhere from spouses being separated from each other for long periods of time to a reevaluation of a relationship during a mid-life crisis. Regardless of the reason, we feel our needs aren't being met or can't be met, and we look outside of our primary relationship for fulfillment.

When Do Affairs Happen?

Maybe the better question is, When don't they? Affairs can happen as early as the first year of marriage or to couples who have been together for thirty, forty, even fifty years. They can be as short as a one-night stand, or they can endure for many years.

The exact point at which an affair might crop up varies from couple to couple, but one thing is for certain: An affair is more likely than not to take place in a relationship or marriage.

Many affairs are opportunistic. The motivation may be curiosity, a longing for variety, or a yearning to experiment. It is common for affairees to begin an affair with little forethought. Many say, "We were just in the same place at the right time, we were attracted to one another, and we were confident no one would find out. It was no big deal."

The needs that affairs fulfill are often more related to the age of the affairee than to the quality of his or her marriage relationship. Interestingly, older wives and younger husbands often seek affairs for the same reason, emotional intimacy. They are often feeling lonely and dissatisfied with their marriages.

Younger wives and older men are usually looking for sexual variety or sexual adventure and do not want to destabilize their marriages.

Affair Facts

Most people who have affairs say they are happy in their primary relationship and that sex within that relationship is good, but still they stray. Typically, affairees don't believe they will get caught, and most don't. But in spite of their intentions to keep their affair from affecting their family life, Annette Lawson, author of *Adultery,* found affairees are much more likely to divorce than people are who do not have affairs.

Just What Is an Affair, Anyway?

What actually constitutes an affair, or as President Clinton calls it, "an inappropriate relationship," depends a great deal on what you think it is. Men and women tend to define affairs differently. Chances are, anyone not in an affair will take a harder stand on where lines should be drawn than someone who is. People raised in families where affairs were common will have broader views of them (and generally be more accepting of them) than people who weren't.

The simplest definition of an *affair,* according to *Webster's New World Dictionary,* is that it's an amorous relationship or episode between two people not married to each other.

Affair Facts

Disapproval of infidelity is widespread throughout the world, but in the United States prohibition is stronger than in most other first world countries. According to a 1996 *Newsweek*/Princeton poll, 70 percent say an affair is always harmful to a marriage.

Affair Speak

In this book, *affair* means an amorous relationship with someone other than your spouse or partner, whether it's a one-night stand or an ongoing series of encounters.

Affair Facts

Men worldwide distinguish between sex with a prostitute and sex with anyone else. Generally, they do not consider sex with a prostitute as an affair or an infidelity.

Affair Facts

Some couples interpret fidelity as a primary commitment to one another, and the emphasis is on emotional intimacy, not sexual exclusivity. Continued intimacy and self-disclosure are their sacred vows. These couples are the most likely to survive a sexual affair with their commitment intact.

Beyond this, just about anything goes. Some people define affairs by their duration. In their book, the relationship has to be ongoing. A one-night (or afternoon) stand doesn't qualify. For others, any move beyond marital fidelity—no matter how slight or fleeting—signifies an affair. In some relationships, just associating with the wrong people can constitute a marital betrayal.

Love Versus Sex

Some affairs are casual with little or no emotional involvement, while others are emotionally consuming. Think of them as being two different types of affairs, sex affairs and love affairs. Sex affairs, as the name implies, are strictly about sex. These affairs may be as simple as a one-night stand or as complex as an annual rendezvous, but the motivation and emphasis is sex.

Love affairs, on the other hand, are emotionally based and the focus of these relationships is emotional intimacy with sex being secondary. It is love affairs that are most likely to be discovered and to threaten the existing primary relationship.

How Men Versus Women See Affairs

Men, especially, classify affairs as sexual relationships. They separate their desire for sex from the feelings of love they have for their wives and see no conflict between their commitments to their wives and their affairs. Women, who have a more difficult time segmenting emotions and physical desire, tend to cast the net more broadly. To many women, going outside a marriage for either emotional or physical gratification constitutes an affair, whether it's their own affair or their husband's.

"It drove me crazy when I found out about Phil's affairs," says Lise. "He kept telling me that they didn't mean anything to our marriage, but it did. I had always looked at our relationship as something that should meet most of our needs, as much of the time as possible. I couldn't imagine that Phil didn't feel the same way. He felt that seeking sex outside of our relationship was perfectly natural."

Setting Boundaries Together

You and your partner are in the best situation to determine what an affair is and isn't. And it's not a bad idea to come to some agreement on that…and the earlier in your relationship the better.

Deciding on boundaries to protect your relationship is important. Men are more reactive to a perceived sexual threat, while women are more upset when their primacy in the relationship is threatened.

Jealousy is a feeling that arises when we sense a threat to our interdependence. It is like a flashing yellow caution light, warning us that our boundaries are being threatened. Jealousies arise when we are feeling neglected or excluded by our mate from an important part of our private relationship that is being opened to someone else.

Affair Facts

An affair doesn't have to be up close and personal. Sexually explicit telephone talk, sexually arousing Internet chat, and letters describing lovemaking can all constitute an affair.

The Difference Between Adultery and Infidelity

Two terms, *adultery* and *infidelity,* are often used to describe relationships that are being conducted outside of marital boundaries. Traditionally and legally, however, there are differences between them. If you're one of those people who likes to parse meanings, you'll want to know the difference. Traditionally, adultery described extramarital affairs in legal or religious terms, addressing certain acts that were deemed sinful or unlawful. Infidelity was, and still is, the term used more often to describe acts that take place outside of a relationship that are lied about, denied, or covered up, constituting an emotional betrayal of the marital agreement.

Affair Speak

The term *adultery* is used to describe sexual intercourse between a married man and someone other than his wife, or between a married woman and someone other than her husband. *Infidelity* describes the unfaithfulness of a husband or wife, or an unfaithful or disloyal act.

Does an Affair Always Mean the End?

It doesn't have to. There's no denying that an affair can endanger a marriage and, discovered or not, have a lingering negative effect on a relationship. A one-night fling can cause years of guilt for a spouse that severely diminishes the vitality of a relationship. On the other hand, affairs can revitalize sagging sexual relationships and rekindle couple communication.

Affairs send a powerful signal. They tell us that it's necessary to reevaluate things, make some changes, renew a commitment, take the relationship to a different—and higher—level. They can signal the beginning, for many, of a mature relationship that *will* last. For others, they are the end.

Dr. Lana's Secrets

The effects of an extramarital affair are not always destructive. It is very unusual, in fact, for an affair to break up an otherwise healthy relationship. A major factor in determining the impact of an affair is the duration of the marriage and the depth of trust the partners have in each other. Newer marriages are most likely to end because of an affair because the partners have not had time to develop a repertoire of coping mechanisms. Additionally, they have not experienced years of trustworthy behavior to measure this violation against.

It Can't Happen to Me...or Can It?

Survey after survey shows that we believe in fidelity. The concept of sexual exclusivity is easy to grasp, and, in fact, it's maybe a more important component of today's relationships than ever before. However, as much as we believe in the concept, we find that actually walking the walk is significantly tougher than talking the talk.

It's difficult to pin down exact percentages when talking about the number of marriages that are affected by extramarital affairs. Why? The easy answer is because most people don't want to admit that they've had an affair, so they sure don't want to talk to some pesky researcher about it.

Do Numbers Lie?

One of the questions I am most commonly asked by reporters who are doing stories on affairs is, "Why is there so much difference in the statistics on how many people have affairs?"

Their observation that the gap between studies and surveys is vast is correct. For example, the "Sex in America" study (1994) claims that only 25 percent of men and 10 percent of women were ever unfaithful to

Affair Facts

Researchers report that anywhere from 25 to 88 percent of married men have some type of an affair during their married life. Studies dating back to the 1950s report 29 percent of married women admitted to straying, and current studies reveal that more than 50 percent had an affair. Shere Hite's 1989 study of younger affluent women reported that 70 percent of married women had been unfaithful to their partner.

their partner, while a similarly constructed study, the Janus Report (1993), conducted during the same time period reported 33 percent of men and 25 percent of women admitted to infidelity. Additionally, the Janus Report found that for those who divorced, 44 percent of men and 41 percent of women admitted to at least one affair.

Even more disparate numbers are reported when surveys are focused on younger, more affluent populations. For instance, Shere Hite reported that 70 percent of women and 72 percent of men were unfaithful (Hite 1989).

There are two possible explanations for the differences. One is socioeconomic: Younger people who are affluent and mobile have a higher incidence of affairs than either older people in the same situation or middle-class people who have little or no opportunity.

The other major factor is that more people are likely to lie about this question than about any other. In counseling situations, it often takes many sessions before a client will admit to infidelity, even though they have revealed many other private details about themselves.

I believe more marriages than not—some 50 to 60 percent of them—are affected by extramarital affairs. Although most people don't believe they or their spouse would have an affair, the facts say otherwise. Anyone can be a casualty of an affair. Anyone. No one is immune.

The bottom line is: If it happens to you, it's probably one too many.

It Can Happen Anywhere

You might be more likely to enter into an affair if you live in a large city on the East or West coasts, but affairs are also common in rural America. Although successful people, especially men, are more affair-prone, you don't have to be a top executive pulling down a multimillion-dollar salary to develop an eye for the vice president of finance down the hall. And as much as we might like to believe the opposite, church attendance and belief in God do not eliminate the risk of extramarital relationships.

Affair Facts

In their book *American Couples,* Blumstein and Schwartz report that 29 percent of married people younger than twenty-five years old admitted to an affair.

Affair Facts

Times are changing, and young women are now just as likely as young men to have an affair. However, when a young woman has an affair, especially if it is in the first couple years of her marriage, her husband will probably divorce her if he finds out. On the other hand, if a wife finds out her mate has strayed, she will try harder to rebuild the relationship.

Welcome to the Club, Guys...and It's a Big One!

Traditionally, men have had more affairs more often than women have. But, things are changing. Easy access to birth control, a greater percentage of women working outside the home, and multiple premarital sexual partners are all factors that have contributed to a much higher percentage of women having affairs.

Money *Can* Buy You Affairs

Financial success plays a key role here, with affluent men, both married and unmarried, having more affairs than the guys at lower socioeconomic levels. Not only can money buy you a certain level of security, it can also increase your opportunities outside of your marriage. Affluent men can make sexual fantasies happen. For example, to spend time with their lovers, wealthy men can arrange to send their wives away for a week on a dream holiday to a health spa. And, bottom line, if you have a thick wallet and a fat portfolio, you'll find yourself more appealing to women—even if you aren't the most attractive guy out there.

Women everywhere, literally from continent to continent, living in capitalism or socialism, committed to monogamy or polygamy, value one thing in a man more than any other characteristic: his ability to secure financial resources. It's the guy with the money that gets the gals (sorry, guys, but it's a fact of life).

The Male Take on Affairs

At one time, researchers thought that American men were more sexually faithful than their European or Asian counterparts, but recent studies have challenged that notion. A 1988 study in which 4,100 professionals, business executives, and salesmen were interviewed revealed that 88 percent had at least one affair.

Dr. Lana's Secrets

Family attitudes about sex are powerful predictors of whether you or your mate will be unfaithful. If either of your parents or one of your grandparents had an affair, you will be more affair-prone. Many people compartmentalize their affairs and believe they are "relationships" that enhance their marriages and give them stability, thus avoiding divorce. Certainly, the many reports of the Joseph and Rose Kennedy family suggest this attitude. The marriage would continue and the family would be protected, but affairs were a separate issue.

According to at least one study, men often start their extramarital sexual relationships early in their marriages. Ask these fellows why, and they'll say such things as, "Well, I really didn't want to be married anyway" or "Hey, my dad and granddad did. It is no big deal."

These men often see marriage in terms of a role or responsibility and not as an intimate liaison. Sometimes, their affairs are an extension of their pre-marital behavior. Sadly, the earlier they start having affairs, the less likely they are to stay in their marriage.

Affair Facts

More than two-thirds of the men who had an affair during their first two years of marriage were divorced before their tenth anniversary.

Men's affairs early in their marriage are almost always driven by one thing: sex. Love or affection are rarely factors, since most men think of sex as being separate from their emotional commitment to their wives. This rationale explains why many men are capable of having trysts or even longer sexual relationships without feeling that they've been unfaithful to their partners.

Younger Versus Older Men

Early in their marriage, men who have affairs rarely form emotional attachments, despite what they tell their lover(s). When they do bond emotionally with a lover, the chances of their maintaining a long-term marriage plummet. When men are in love with the affairee, they nearly always report that they feel lonely at home, either because their wife is busy with her job or with their kids.

Older men—those who have been married for ten years or more—are more likely to become emotionally involved with their affairees then younger men and are more likely to dissolve their marriage because of the affair. Most of these men also complain that their emotional needs were not being met at home.

Almost Any Time, Any Place

Many women find it hard to believe that their husbands or partners can find the time to have an affair…but they sure can, and they sure do! In today's somewhat boundary-less society, where you can choose to answer or ignore that cell phone call or pager beep, accountability is only a concept. Slipping away is much easier than you think.

Richard explains it this way:

"Every time they come up with a new communications advance, it makes it easier for me to find time away from my relationship. I can set up my office phone so that calls to it roll over to my cell phone, and my voice mail picks up on that if I don't answer it. It's never been that difficult to get away for a few hours during the day. Now, it's even easier."

Jack, an avid outdoorsman, uses his "weekends away with the guys" for time with his lovers. "My wife is great, but she'd rather spend time with the kids or with her friends than in a duck blind. I have a nice little cabin, which she's never seen, but my girlfriends have. She spends the weekend doing what she wants, I get the variety I need…and I even bring home a few ducks every once in a while."

It's Not Just a Guy Thing

For those of you who believe that women are just made to be more faithful than men, you've got a big surprise coming. Study after study has shown that women are having affairs as readily as men do, when they're given the opportunity.

Helen Fisher, in her book *Anatomy of Love,* reveals explanations of why humankind seems to have the need to stray. She explains that commitment wasn't an unfamiliar concept in prehistoric times, but it didn't keep cavewomen from sneaking into the bushes with fellows from foreign tribes. Such ancient trysts helped introduce better genes and more varied DNA into what were often somewhat limited gene pools, perhaps assuring the successful development of modern man and woman.

Affair Facts

Women are more cautious about entering into an affair than men are, usually taking at least a month to think about it and generally talking it over with a friend.

Women typically enter into affairs to satisfy emotional rather than sexual needs. For many women, the positive physical and emotional feedback they can gain from an affair helps them approach their primary relationship with renewed energy and interest.

Simone is a good example. Involved in a long-term relationship with Mark, she found out that he had had two affairs during the same period. In a tear-filled, emotional confession, Mark told her he loved her but found her lacking in passion. His words devastated Simone, who had believed that all was well in their relationship.

While visiting friends in her old hometown a few weeks later, she ran into Phil, with whom she had had a multi-year relationship some time ago. The relationship had ended when Simone met Mark, yet Phil was always someone who touched her heart in a very special way, and she felt her old emotions stirring once again.

Phil, although now in another relationship, was delighted to see Simone, and the two decided to meet for lunch the next day. At lunch Simone told Phil what had happened with her and Mark. Phil's response was to put a hand to her cheek and tell her that she was still a very beautiful and sexy woman. It was the first time Simone had ever thought of being unfaithful. All the way back home she thought about Phil, and a week later she called him. Over the next few weeks, they talked and then decided to meet. They met at the airport and went to a nearby motel. They spent the rest of the afternoon in bed.

For Simone, that afternoon and the weekly rendezvous that followed with Phil were exactly what she needed. "It broke through the impasse I had reached with myself," she says. "I was beginning to believe that Mark was right, that I was passionless. Phil showed me that the opposite was, in fact, true." Although she would have entertained a new relationship with Phil, he made it clear that it wasn't a possibility for him. Simone was disappointed, but also remembered why they broke up in the first place.

"I really needed someone at that exact moment to tell me that I wasn't lacking, that I was a passionate lover. I'll always be glad that Phil was the one who was there." The emotions Simone felt that day with Phil made her realize that she had been withholding physically and emotionally with Mark. She admits, "Even when he tried to be romantic with me, I would tell him I was too tired or busy to be interested," she says. "No wonder he felt the way he did." She renewed her commitment to her relationship with Mark, and the two started to address the issues that had arisen in their relationship.

Affair Facts

Women's interest in extramarital relationships is nothing new, and it's on the increase. The percentage of women who have extramarital sex has more than doubled during the last three decades, rising from 29 percent in 1953 to 70 percent in 1989. And they're having affairs at earlier points in their marriages. During the 1950s and 1960s, women often had their first affairs in their thirties and early forties. Now the starting age has dropped to the early twenties.

Now for Some Good News

Despite everything you've read up to now, there is hope. Admittedly, the odds are against your loving relationship with your spouse being totally affair-proof. But an affair doesn't have to happen, and if one does, it doesn't have to mean the end of a relationship or marriage. Yes, an affair—disclosed or not—will almost certainly upset your relationship as it currently exists. But the new relationship that lies ahead can be better and stronger than either of you ever dreamed.

Any couple that has weathered the storm of an affair will tell you that the affair wasn't the worst thing that ever happened to them, although it may have seemed like it at the time. Sure, feelings of betrayal, hurt, and anger will surface if the affair is disclosed or gets discovered. There's no getting around the fact that affairs stir up deep emotions. Even if the affair goes undisclosed and no one ever finds out about it, it will still be something that you haven't shared with your spouse and it will carry a significance and meaning of its own that can shape your behavior—both positively and negatively—for the rest of your life.

We live in a world where infidelity has always been and will most likely continue to be a reality. Those who are best informed and emotionally equipped to handle this invasion will be most likely to either prevent or survive an affair.

Success in dealing with an affair depends on how the two of you—both separately and together—approach the issue, whether it is something you can talk about openly or whether you can at least stay emotionally connected to each other during the crisis. Couples who are committed on a day-to-day basis to creating intimacy in their relationship, improving their communication, and having more fun in and out of bed can affair-proof their relationship.

The "Affair-Prone" Quiz

Are you wondering just how "affair-prone" your relationship might be? The following quiz describes situations and behaviors that are part of almost everyone's life. Circle the answer for the behavior that most accurately describes each situation if it took place in your relationship.

1. At a party, you:
    a. Search out someone new and spend time with that person for the majority of the evening.
    b. Spend the majority of your time talking to other people, not each other.
    c. Keep a close eye on each other.
    d. Spend some time together, some time apart as you like to mingle.

2. When you're out to dinner with your partner, you:
    a. Pay more attention to the action around you than at your table.
    b. Eat your meal with very little conversation between you, if any.
    c. Call your babysitter every fifteen minutes.
    d. Engage in lively communication with each other.

3. Your partner surprises you with a gift out of the blue. Your first thought is:
    a. It's about time.
    b. Gee, did I miss our anniversary?
    c. He's feeling guilty about something.
    d. What a nice gift! And what a sweetheart he is!

4. Your sexual relationship could be characterized as:
    a. Perfunctory at best. You know you should spend more intimate time together, but there's no time or little interest.
    b. Virtually nonexistent. Passion flew out the door years ago.
    c. Uptight because you're worried about those ten pounds you've gained.
    d. Enjoyable and fun. We look forward to our intimate moments together.

5. A couple close to you calls you at the last moment for a burger and a movie. What would your reaction be?

   a. Sure. You'd much rather spend time with your friend's husband anyway, even if it's only social.

   b. Why not? It will be a lot more exciting than staying home together.

   c. Nope, you'd rather stay home because you're pretty sure your friend's wife has an eye on your husband.

   d. Thanks, but you'll take a rain check as you had planned on a quiet night home together.

6. Your spouse is away on an extended business trip. When it comes to keeping in touch, you:

   a. Are too busy to really think much about it.

   b. Don't expect much more than a phone call letting you know when he'll be home.

   c. Expect a call every night so you can keep tabs on what he's doing.

   d. Look forward to his regular calls, even if they're just to say "I love you."

Scoring: Total up the answers you gave for each letter:

a ___   b ___   c ___   d ___

What Your Answers Mean

Mostly *a* answers: A high total in this category signifies a relationship that is fairly high on the affair-prone meter. For some reason, you're not paying a lot of attention to each other, and the time you spend together is often not very enjoyable or comfortable. There may be unresolved issues or a general lack of focus concerning your relationship, which if allowed to continue may seriously undermine your future together. Read on for suggestions on how you can repair things before it's too late.

Mostly *b* answers: Relationships in this category may not appear highly affair-prone, but that's often more due to laziness or lack of desire than the quality of the relationship. Couples in this category take each other and their relationship very much for granted and tend to drift away from each other emotionally while staying together physically (though often not intimately). These are lonely relationships, and they can spur long-term affairs that may not ever be disclosed. The following chapters will help you re-energize your relationship and bring you closer together.

Mostly *c* answers: High scores in this category denote relationships that are affair-prone due to unhealthy behavior. Often, there are trust and boundary issues present that lead to feelings of jealousy and mistrust. There may also be self-esteem issues; there may even be problems related to an unrealistic belief of what a healthy relationship should be. Turn to the chapters ahead to learn how to identify the issues affecting your relationship and what you can do to work toward a healthier relationship model.

Mostly *d* answers: If the majority of your answers are in this category, give yourself a pat on the back. Your relationship is in pretty good shape and you're clearly working at it. There's always room for improvement, though. This book will help you be even better at doing what it takes to affair-proof your relationship.

The Least You Need to Know

➤ Affairs happen, but they can be avoided.

➤ Opinions vary widely as to what constitutes an affair.

➤ Younger women are just as likely to have affairs as men.

➤ Solid relationships can and do survive an affair.

What Makes Us Affair-Prone?

I've looked on a lot of women with lust. I've committed adultery in my heart many times. This is something that God recognizes I will do—and I have done it—and God forgives me for it.

— Jimmy Carter, 1976

Jimmy Carter's well-publicized *Playboy* interview caused somewhat of a morality mini-riot when it appeared in 1976. But the peanut farmer from Plains was just giving voice to something that many people know is all too true. It's more in our nature to lust after something we don't have than it is not to do so. Maybe that's why, instead of condemning Carter for his remarks, we applauded his honesty by electing him president. And it could be that Carter's recognition and understanding of this simple fact is the reason that his marriage has stayed together all these years.

Still, many people found Carter's remarks hard to take. One of the reasons they caused such an uproar was that they highlighted a facet of human behavior that most of us have been conditioned to sweep under the rug. We're supposed to be faithful, aren't we? Looking at others with lust in our hearts is wrong, isn't it, especially when we're married? This is what conventional wisdom would have us believe...but it ain't necessarily so.

Made to Lust

Lust is not a feeling that should end when the wedding ring goes on or when vows of commitment are made. To do so would be to deny a part of human behavior that is firmly embedded within us...and frankly, the marriages that do deny such feelings are often the ones in which the participants are the least satisfied.

Basic human nature has a lot to do with why we couple together and why our attention occasionally gets pulled off-center by a member of the opposite sex. Regardless of how you believe our world came into being, one fact is indisputable: Human beings were put on the earth to procreate. Even our chemistry was developed to ensure that procreation would happen.

The Long and the Short of It

Scientists suggest that humans have a dual mating strategy, one long-term and the other short-term. Researcher David Buss, author of *The Evolution of Desire*, found that when women look for short-term lovers, they're mainly interested in good-looking guys. But when it comes to choosing a long-term mate, women are pickier, with a far longer list of qualities they're looking for.

The same is true of men. When they're playing the field, they're much less choosy about whom they're sexually involved with than when they're selecting a mate. In fact, one criterion that shifts dramatically is promiscuity. In short-term relationships men prefer women who are sexually experienced and accessible, but for long-term relationships they choose women who are virgins.

Biological Urges

Our human tendency toward extramarital liaisons, writes anthropologist Helen E. Fisher, seems to be the triumph of nature over culture. Our brains are

Affair Speak

Lust is a desire to gratify the senses; to feel an intense desire.

Affair Facts

The desire to enhance one's attractiveness dates back to ancient times. Some of the earliest artifacts from twenty thousand to thirty thousand years ago are body ornaments—in other words, jewelry.

Affair Facts

When women are looking for a short-term mate, they prefer a man who is extravagant, presuming he will share his resources with her and not save them for the exclusive benefit of his and his long-term mate's offspring.

programmed to recognize infatuation when we feel it, and we're driven to find the one perfect being with whom to bond. Still, Fisher says, philandering is part of our reproductive game.

Why this is so has more to do with deep-seated biological urges than a lack of morality or an inability to toe the line of propriety. Primitive man strove to mate with as many specimens as he could to ensure that his genetic coding would carry through to future generations. By choosing more than one mate, a man potentially improved his chances by tapping into more than one gene pool. Women also strove to improve the genetic makeup of their offspring by accessing different DNA strings. Or they would take lovers to ensure a consistent source of support in case their mate met a premature death.

How does this behavior translate in current generations? One theory is that the men who feel the strongest urges to stray are heeding their ancient calls to procreate. Women who stray may be interested in building better offspring, but are more often working to secure other resources, such as a secure home or a steady source of financial support.

What's Jealousy Got to Do with It?

Jealousy is like built-in radar scanning the horizon to protect us from the threat of interlopers who can take away what we value most. Since ancient times, male jealousy has been most acute when there is a threat that their mate will be sexually intimate with another man. A woman, on the other hand, is most jealous when her mate shares emotional intimacy with another woman.

The same holds true today. When couples are confronted with an affair, women seldom divorce if the relationship was strictly sexual, with no emotional bond. But men will more often divorce a mate who's had sexual relations with another guy.

There's No "Off" Switch

Although we're programmed to find a special someone with whom to bond, we don't have a little lust switch that we can turn off when we do find that person. For this reason, the same chemical reaction that causes us to engage in the courting rituals that lead to marriage can also trigger our infidelity rockets. When and where and how they get triggered is governed by a variety of factors that come together in the most important of all human body parts—the brain.

Affair Facts

Human beings aren't alone when it comes to straying. According to new studies, only about 10 percent of the birds and mammals that seem to mate for life are actually faithful to their partners.

The Brain Reigns

For being such an undistinguished, almost funny-looking thing, the human brain is the most remarkable machine on the face of this planet. It is unsurpassed in its ability to process, store, and generate information, even when compared to the most powerful computers. And the brain has something that all computers, no matter how advanced, can only pretend to have: the ability to use emotion as a basis for reasoning. A computer can only mimic the process that a human goes through when making a decision that's not based on yes-or-no logic. That's why intelligence, when it comes to machines, is artificial at best.

Our senses of sight, sound, hearing, touch, and taste are all processed by a part of the brain called the cortex—the gray, spongy matter that most of us visualize when we think of a brain. But if all the brain did was process this information, our response to everything would be the same. We wouldn't favor one brand of hot dogs over another or be attracted to a certain person's look or smell.

It's up to the cortex to combine what it sees and hears with other parts of the brain that control instinctive and emotional behavior. Our most basic behaviors are governed by an area known as the reptilian brain. Emotional responses, such as hate, fear, joy, sadness, happiness, and love are governed by electrical and chemical processes in a part of the brain known as the limbic system. When they all come together, they form an emotional response.

The Elements of Attraction

But something still has to happen to key sexual and emotional responses when we see one person but not when we see another. This is where the elements of attraction come into play. What each person finds attractive is special to a certain degree, but much of it is indelibly etched into our psyches. Some responses are shaped culturally and formed at a very early age. Men have been shown to respond to a woman's physical appearance. Women tend to be more attracted to a man's status than his looks.

What characteristics do men prize the most in a mate? Physical attractiveness gets top billing. Specifically, a small nose, big eyes, and luscious lips.

The evolutionary explanation is that finding a young, healthy female would ensure fertility. The most powerful and timeless sign of a woman's fertility is not how fat or thin she is, but her waist-to-hip ratio. The magic number is 0.7 (meaning that her waist is 70 percent of her hip measurement).

Affair Facts

Surprisingly, breasts aren't as high on men's lists as women think. When researchers asked men to identify specific parts of the female anatomy in terms of importance to them, only 50 percent mentioned breasts, and half of these guys preferred small ones. Yet each year more than seventy-two thousand women in the U.S. have breast augmentation surgery.

Women are no less original in their priorities. Dominance, maturity, and good health rank at the top of their lists. Physically, this vision translates into above-average height, prominent cheekbones, large jaw and strong chin, broad forehead, muscular body, wrist and ankle symmetry, and a slim waist and hips.

Again, the evolutionary explanation is that she needs to find a guy who can provide resources for her and for her offspring, and he has to be strong and healthy. The ideal hip-to-waist measurement for him is 0.9 (meaning his waist is 90 percent of his hip measurement).

The Sixth Sense?

What we see, hear, touch, smell, and even taste leads us to favor one person over the other. Our sense of smell in particular plays a major role in the attraction arena, thanks to the powerful human scents known as *pheromones*, whose role in the attraction process are only now beginning to be fully understood. Researchers believe that these unique human scents, constantly secreted through the skin, are a key element in fueling attraction—or lack thereof—between human beings.

Affair Facts

Researchers suggest that if your lover smells too much like your dad or brothers, it is best to sniff out someone new. They report that smelling the same is indicative of gene pool similarity, which produces a greater number of birth defects in offspring.

Some scientists now believe that pheromones are the basis for our deepest intuitions and gut feelings—that "sixth sense" that we sometimes refer to when we're not quite sure why we choose to do something or not. Why do opposites attract? Again, researchers think it might be due to deep, intuitive bonds fueled by compatible body chemistries.

Chemical Reactions

Most of us, when we give our brains any thought at all, consider their organic characteristics. What we don't often realize is that the brain is also a gland, containing essential hormones that govern its mood as well as the body to which it's attached. One of them—phenylethylamine, or PEA—seems to be the key to attraction.

Affair Speak

The word *pheromones* derives from Greek and means "to convey" or "I carry excitement." They are powerful human scents that play a large role in attracting human beings to each other.

Recent research has shown that PEA has stimulating qualities similar to amphetamine. Because it sits at the end of some nerve cells, it also helps translate nerve impulses from one nerve end to another. PEA is a permanent resident in the brain in small doses, but its levels rise when we feel stressed or excited. As the levels increase, the brain literally speeds up. In some people, it goes into overdrive.

Combine the effects of PEA with other neurochemicals such as dopamine and norepinephrine, and you get the classic symptoms of infatuation or "being in love." You feel giddy and happy, and you have energy that doesn't end. You can't eat, you can't sleep, and being with your lover is about all you can think about clearly. Anything and everything seems possible, and the world is a beautiful place. Oxytocin, the chemical that bonds mothers to their newborns, also increases during this period, stimulating our desire to cuddle.

(It's interesting to note that the physical sensations we feel when we're in love are nearly identical to those we feel when we're under stress or fearful. Such sensations as a dry mouth, an upset stomach or lack of appetite, trembling, and a fluttering heart are all caused by hormonal and nervous stimulation brought on by stress or excitement.)

Affair Facts

PEA is one of the chemicals present in chocolate, which is another reason why a box of chocolate truffles is such a romantic gift. Roses—another classic gift of love—also contain PEA.

When Infatuation Ends

The sheer joy of being in love is something that almost everyone experiences at least once, and it should be at the beginning of our emotional journey with whomever we eventually settle down with. For most people, however, there's a limit to how long our brains can function on overdrive. They either start to ignore the chemicals that are stimulating them or PEA levels drop.

This is the time when we settle into long-term relationships, get married, and start to cocoon. We smooth out and get mellow, thanks to endorphins, natural opiates that the brain releases to soothe its overstimulated nerve endings.

Dr. Lana's Secrets

Some people are hooked on love, or rather, on PEA. They crave the amphetamine high, and when the newness of the relationship passes, they move on to someone else. Generally, their relationships last anywhere from a few days to a couple of years.

But our basic instincts never go away. While it's always preferable to feel primary attraction to our mates, we would have to be totally deprived of our senses to not have an emotional and physical response to someone else that we find attractive. Being married or involved in a long-term relationship won't cancel out those feelings. However, the traditions and morals reflected in these institutions do have a great deal to do with how we respond to those urges.

Great Expectations

Most of us have been taught to expect fidelity in a marriage and have been led to believe that marriage has always been based on being faithful. But it just isn't so. Marital fidelity has been far from the norm throughout recorded history, and it is by no means unilaterally accepted or practiced even today. If you are a member of an Amazonian tribe in Brazil, you might have a number of lovers outside of your marriage and be proud of it. Head up to the Arctic Circle, and you'll see the custom of wife lending practiced among some Inuit peoples.

Psychologist and researcher David Buss found that the Western ideal of monogamy—that is, one marriage, one spouse—also isn't the norm in other cultures. It's estimated that 84 percent of the world's cultures allow polygamy, including societies in Africa, northeastern Asia, the New Hebrides, and Papua New Guinea. In the United States, some Mormon-related sects openly condone the practice, although the church itself no longer supports it.

Affair Facts

Demographers estimate that even in America, where polygamy is not legal, there are between twenty-five thousand and thirty-five thousand polygamous couples.

Polyandry—the practice of women having multiple husbands—is rarer but is still found in areas of the Philippines, Tibet, and Africa. It is often adopted in cultures that suffer a shortage of women, possibly from the practice of female infanticide.

Tradition...Tradition?

Even the notion of being sexually faithful to one spouse is relatively new. In ancient cultures, sexual behavior was largely governed by legal rights rather than a moral code. Most early societies didn't expect fidelity from their male members, but a strong double standard prohibited wives from the same behavior. Men were actively encouraged to pursue multiple sexual partners as a way to produce heirs who would ensure the survival of their line. Women, however, were generally expected to be faithful to their spouses. In many societies, women could be executed for being unfaithful.

The Egyptian Double Standard

In early Egypt woman was a partner to man. She had her duties and responsibilities and also her rights. The rules for marriage and divorce were detailed and concise. So were the rules and punishments for infidelity. Infidelity on the part of a man involved no punishment unless his wife decided to divorce him; then he had to return her dowry. But an unfaithful wife, who was caught with her lover, could be thrown (unbound) into the Tigris or the Euphrates River. Good swimming lessons were important for any wife considering an affair!

Jewish Law

Ancient Jews followed a set of sexual mores that were developed more to encourage their survival than to keep them faithful to a spouse. While marriage was recognized, its primary purpose was reproduction. If a child wasn't produced, the marriage could be dissolved, but it didn't have to be. If a husband died before a son was born, the husband's brother was obligated to marry the widow, even if he were already married. Of course, the brother wasn't limited to just one wife. Although Jewish law prohibited adultery (remember the seventh commandment?), such prohibitions governed a woman's activities more than a man's. Men were still permitted to have sex with women other than their wives and to take multiple wives—although the rabbis encouraged them to limit their conquests to four—in fulfillment of God's command to "Be fertile and multiply; fill the earth and subdue it." Only married women were off-limits. And again, women were expected to remain faithful to their husbands.

Affair Facts

European Jews allowed the practice of polygamy until it was banned in the mid-eleventh century. However, Sephardic Jews, who primarily lived in Spain and Portugal, continued the practice until the mid-twentieth century.

Japanese Custom

The Japanese, concerned about who fathered the children, adopted a strict code of fidelity for women. It was quite a different story for the men. Once a man was married and lineage was established, having a geisha or a mistress was a sign of prosperity. Geishas—entertainers, talented musicians, storytellers, and hostesses—were willing to offer pleasure to their clients in a variety of ways, physically, emotionally, and spiritually.

Fidelity, Hindu Style

Hindu women have endured terrible cruelty—from self-sacrifice to being thrown atop a dead husband's funeral pyre. However, during the fourth and fifth centuries, women of southern India were treated to some new pleasures when Vatsyayana, author of *The Kama Sutra,* wrote what is probably the most famous treatise on love.

He insisted that the art of love is designed for the pleasure of both men and women equally, and described in exacting detail courtship rituals, the ten possible kisses, and sixty-four possible variations preceding coitus. Sexual intercourse itself was described in detail with specific rules and alternatives.

Vatsyayana wrote *The Kama Sutra* to encourage fidelity within marriage by keeping sexual acts from becoming routine or boring. Most likely it worked—if you had a good memory!

Marriage Among the Greeks and Romans

The Romans thought of sex as a natural force to be enjoyed freely by both men and women. If a man and woman were married and not content with one another, they were free to find different partners. Rome was not particularly concerned about marriage vows or fidelity. The priority was good sex and lots of it.

The Greeks regulated sex for economic reasons. During good times, Greeks could have multiple partners, but because of the lack of arable lands there were a lot of bad times and several brothers would have to share a single wife. The important issue was controlling population growth, not sex.

Toward the end of the fifth century, Plato, a bachelor, advocated a law forbidding sexual intercourse with any woman except his lawful wife. Plato's dictates were humorously rebuffed by the Greeks, and free love prevailed. Ultimately, he concludes in the "Laws," "During marriage extra-legal connections may be allowed, provided the necessary discretion is preserved and scandal avoided."

The ancient Romans practiced polygamy for many centuries. Even after it was proclaimed a punishable offense, the great ruler Mark Antony ignored this ruling and took two wives for himself.

Adultery as Sin

The belief that adultery was a sin for both men and women wasn't widely accepted until some four centuries after the death of Jesus Christ. Prior to that time, sexual codes remained somewhat undefined for Christians, although Jesus certainly seemed aware of extramarital dalliances when he

Affair Facts

According to the book *A History of Social Customs,* the word *sex* was invented by the Romans, who used it to denote the natural differences between men and woman. It was probably first used in jokes referring to the bisexuality of the Greeks. According to an ancient fable, human beings possessed all the sexual organs of both men and women until the Greeks made Zeus mad. It was then that Zeus punished man and woman by severing half from each (ouch!), making two sexes out of one.

Affair Facts

The Journal of Social Sciences reported Roman Emperor Augustus tried to discourage rampant infidelity by fining the infidels one-half of their inheritance and prohibiting transgressors from marrying each another. Reportedly, the revenues were enough to fund the construction of the Temple of Venus!

expanded Jewish tradition and taught that a husband's dismissing his wife and marrying another woman was adultery against the first wife and a violation of their covenant commitment.

Marriage as Protection from Evil

In his first letter to the Corinthians, the apostle Paul further amplified Jesus' teachings when he stated that it was better for each man to have his own wife and for each woman to have her own husband, and that doing so would help protect them from sexual immorality.

Paul also counseled Christ's followers to not deny each other, except by mutual agreement for such specific activities as prayer, and to be sure to return to each other so that "Satan does not tempt you because of your lack of self-control." Celibacy was urged for anyone who wasn't married. Another forbidden activity: going to a prostitute, which Paul believed was a desecration of Christ, since the body belongs not to the person but to God.

Affair Speak

According to Christian theology, *original sin* is humankind's tendency to sin. This inherent depravity is a direct result of Adam and Eve's sin of rebellion.

Affair Facts

Saint Augustine was perhaps the first great leader to be influenced by a woman named Monica. In the saint's case, the influential gal was his mother, who urged him to cast aside his mistresses (he had several prior to his conversion) and to marry a woman of the appropriate caste and legal standing.

Blame It on Saint Augustine

The Roman monk Augustine—later, Saint Augustine—gave a great deal of thought to the notion of *original sin* as he wrestled with issues of the flesh prior to his own conversion to Christianity. He believed celibacy to be the purest state. But he eventually concluded that three good elements in marriage justified the sinful nature of sex: fidelity, offspring, and the marital sacrament itself. And it was his beliefs that would largely shape the Western view of marriage and infidelity for the next thousand years.

Chastity outside of marriage was a given, as far as Augustine was concerned. But he even advocated it for married couples, insisting that marriage became more holy when passion was subdued or denied. Procreation was a necessary evil. And enjoying it was a sin.

Augustine's beliefs marked the beginning of the Christian doctrine of sex as sinful. His writings strongly influenced early church leaders, who used them as the basis for new rules pertaining to sexual behavior. Still, the concepts of adultery and celibacy were not part of church doctrine until much later. By the eleventh century, marriage became sacred and divorce was forbidden.

And Then Comes Mohammed...

The prophet Mohammed, the founder of Islam, took a diametrically opposite view from Augustine and other Church leaders of the time. Mohammed saw sex as some-thing that should be enjoyed, and he encouraged his followers to marry so they could fully enjoy it. He rejected the idea of sex without responsibility because he was concerned about the survival of children. Mohammed required his followers to provide food and protection for their women and their offspring. However, he didn't think it practical to limit a man to one woman, so he allowed any man to have as many as four wives at a time, as long as he could provide for them equally. To avoid jealously, the man was required to rotate between his wives on consecutive nights. He could also have a few temporary marriages—he just had to agree on a fee to be paid to his temporary wife. Polygamy is expensive!

Polygamy is still practiced by many Muslims today, but the Islamic world still considers adultery a serious crime, punishable by death in some Islam countries.

Affair Facts

Most modern cultures have rules governing infidelity, but no culture in the world has found a way to stop humankind from consummating new sexual relationships. Even when the punishment for infidelity is deten-tion, expulsion from society or even death, both men and women find a way to have sexual relations outside of marriage.

Where We Are Today

Western civilization has traditionally held with the Judeo-Christian belief in one wife for each hus-band, one husband for each wife, and one marriage for both of them. Infidelity is generally not consid-ered a sin for either gender, especially among people who aren't actively involved in any particu-lar religion or faith, but most people believe that it's wrong.

These beliefs persist today in sheer defiance of basic human nature and are at the root of the double standard that exists when it comes to infidelity. We know we're supposed to be faithful—society's mores and our own beliefs dictate it. But we also know that many, many people still step outside of their relationship boundaries.

Affair Facts

As a country, we may not agree on how we define "inappropriate rela-tionships," but we sure know how we feel about infidelity. According to a recent Time/CNN poll, 86 percent of respondents said they believed that adultery committed by men is morally wrong; 85 percent similarly condemned women for adulterous behavior.

Freedom for All

Colonists fled to the New World to escape religious persecution. They found religious freedom, and they found other freedoms as well. The official stance on sex may have been to deny that it existed at all, but many early inhabitants of this country found new opportunities to couple up. More than one of the founding fathers of this country had extramarital relationships.

Some grand experiments with the marital model took place in the United States during the years that followed. The Shakers decided to practice celibacy. Mormons went in the opposite direction and decreed that it was perfectly acceptable for a man to take more than one wife. A form of free love was practiced in the mid-1800s in the Oneida Community, an experimental commune based on economic and sexual openness and equality for both genders.

Affair Facts

What do Benjamin Franklin, Michael Jordan, Marilyn Monroe, and Frank Lloyd Wright have in common? All had extramarital affairs—some more than one.

Affair Facts

Evolutionary behavior expert Stephen Emlen believes that true monogamy in the animal kingdom is rare. Among the animal order that includes humans, only two monkeys, the marmoset and the tamarin, are truly monogamous. What is the most sexually faithful animal? According to researchers, it's the California mouse, which by all indications really does mate for life.

Sexual Revolutions

There has been more than one sexual revolution in the United States since then, and our views of relationships and marriage changed as researchers learned more about what made us tick. Although we still professed belief in traditional models, studies—including the historic Kinsey Reports—revealed an amazing sexual double standard. We may have been preaching fidelity, but we sure weren't practicing it. For a country that prided itself on morality, we weren't moral at all.

Some 83 percent of the men who responded to Kinsey's studies in the late 1940s and early 1950s confessed to sexual intercourse before marriage. Half of them also said they'd had extramarital sex. The numbers weren't much different for women: Half said they'd had premarital sex; a quarter reported infidelities.

The following two decades were characterized by more open displays of sexual freedom and experimentation, as both men and women sought to redefine traditional relationship models that would better suit the needs of a new generation. Divorce rates soared as people realized that they now had socially acceptable options to staying in unsatisfying marriages. Marriage became almost a disposable commodity; some questioned the viability of the institution itself. What could marriage give you that you couldn't have without it?

Striving for Fidelity?

Interestingly, we're now living at a time when traditional marriages and faithful relationships are encouraged and welcomed more than most of us can remember them being in the past. It took the AIDS virus and the disintegration of the nuclear family to put the skids on our swinging lifestyles.

Today's relationship model is based on the notion that marriage or committed relationships should be all-inclusive entities that meet all of our needs as much as possible. That's a lot of pressure to put on one institution. And, again, although this is what we say we believe, we haven't lost the basic urges that might cause us to look somewhere else when our relationships fail to meet our expectations.

The Least You Need to Know

➤ Lust is a natural feeling.

➤ The biological need for variety and excitement drives many men to seek multiple partners.

➤ Powerful chemicals in our brains govern how we respond in all situations.

➤ Our beliefs and our actions concerning marriage often contradict each other.

Chapter 3

Is "Happily Ever After" Just a Myth?

In This Chapter

➤ Identifying successful relationships

➤ The importance of paying attention

➤ Why boundaries are important

➤ Being separate yet together

And they lived happily ever after.

—Traditional children's story ending

By now you're probably wondering if the notion of two people living happily ever after is just a remnant from children's stories of old or a silver-screen myth. Take heart. It's not. Loving, committed relationships are not figments of our imaginations. They do exist, but they're often not what we think they are. Nor are they what they appear to be. The couple in your monthly gourmet group that you've nicknamed the "Bickersons" might be a whole lot happier with and committed to one another than the Ken and Barbie duo at your health club who act so sickeningly lovey-dovey every time you see them.

Although it's fairly easy to identify examples of relationships that don't work, there are also many, many relationships that do. Why they aren't readily apparent to us is because we tend to rush to judgment, both when we try to identify what good relationships are and when we try to define them.

What Sets Successful Couples Apart?

A major difference between those who divorce and those who don't is sheer determination. Couples who stay together weather storms just as turbulent and torturous as those who split up. Many long-term marriages survive simply because the couple is unwilling to give up. For many of these lifetime partners, divorce is not an option regardless of hardship, disappointments or even infidelity.

As Jake recounts, "When Emma and I married, we made our commitment. We promised till death do us part. Once we made the decision, that was that. Don't see a reason to keep making it." Jake's sentiments were typical of these long-term happily married couples. When they made a commitment, it was made. It was not a decision they kept remaking. And it fuels their willingness to do whatever they need to do to keep their relationships intact.

Dr. Lana's Secrets

A happy marriage may not be what you think. The popular belief that people who are happy with each other get along and don't fight much is wrong. Marital strength and endurance are determined by your ability to fight it out and end up with agreements that satisfy both of you.

Rare, but Possible...the "Happily Ever After" Relationship

It goes against the odds, but it still happens. There are couples in this world who have stayed together for years. Happily at times. Not so happily at other times. They might be legally married or they might be married in spirit. For the most part, they've been faithful to their partners...not necessarily physically faithful, but faithful nonetheless.

They have weathered the inevitable ups and downs that life throws at everyone. They've battled financial problems, health issues, problems at work, emotional upsets, battles with their children...you name it. And after all of it, they can still look at each other with love and affection in their eyes. They can look beyond each other's battle scars and honor the person who has traveled life's trails with them.

Yes, they love each other, but they can also act lovingly toward each other even when they don't really feel like it. They have written a "lifescript" and have built a firm foundation for their lives together. They understand each other's needs and motivations, and they are respectful of them. And when things get tough, they pull together, not apart. They stand united as a couple, willing to face whatever adversity confronts them as a team.

Perhaps most important is the realization that relationships don't just happen; they take a lot of effort, both when they start and to keep them going. As Yale University psychologist Robert Sternberg put it, "You have to work constantly at rejuvenating a relationship. You can't just count on its being O.K. or it will tend toward a hollow commitment, devoid of passion and intimacy."

Couples in happy long-lasting relationships make their time together a priority. They commit time, energy and skill to inventing and reinventing their partnership. They look out for each other, searching to find agreement even during the most disagreeable times.

Successful relationships have another distinguishing characteristic. These couples put their relationships first, ahead of their work, their friendships, even their children. They consider their relationship the foundation of their lives and their family's life. As Jesse describes his attitude, "If Bess and I don't take care of each other, what's left?"

Affair Speak

Faithful means keeping faith; being worthy of trust, honest, loyal, reliable, and dependable.

Recognizing One When You See It

It's easy to identify examples of relationships that don't work. Just turn on any afternoon talk show. You'll be amazed at how skillfully these shows can make a whole hour out of a very specific relational malfunction.

What you'll rarely see, if ever, are shows that focus on folks in relationships that *do* work. Why? The simple fact is that most of us won't watch such shows. Most people would much rather see a couple duke it out on the *Jerry Springer Show* or read about how a star couple's marriage broke up. Bob and Doris Hope have one of the longest marriages in Hollywood, yet it's Bruce and Demi's very visible breakup that grabs our attention.

Best Friends

One of the ingredients that seems to be present in happy and long-lasting relationships is being one another's best friend. Simply put, the partners like each other.

Henry says, "No one said Etta and I had to spend time together and do things together; we wanted to. There just wasn't anybody I would rather spend my time with. Other guys wanted to go off hunting and fishing with each other, but not me. Etta liked fishing but not hunting, so we fished. We had fun. Yeah, we had bad times, but we laughed a lot, too. She was a fiery little thing, still is, but when the dust settled, we laughed."

The Successful Relationship Quiz

The indicators of a successful relationship are often very subtle. And we tend to misread them more often than not. Take a few minutes for this quiz—to see how keen your observations are.

1. You've just closed a big deal at work, and you go out with some friends in your department to celebrate. After one drink, your coworker Judy excuses herself and says she has to go home to her husband, even though it's clear that she'd rather stay and enjoy herself. You:

    a. Tell her you'll see her tomorrow.

    b. Think she's being too subservient. She's always running home to him!

2. You and your partner are out to dinner with another couple. During the course of a lively conversation, you happen to notice the other wife subtly replacing her husband's empty water glass with her own untouched one after the waiter has failed to refill his more than once. You:

    a. Smile inside at her small display of caring.

    b. Flinch a little at how she mothers him.

3. Your best friend shows up at the office Christmas party solo, telling you that her husband decided to go to a basketball game instead. You:

    a. Wonder why you have never met her husband.

    b. Give her a big hug and tell her you're glad she's there.

What Your Answers Mean

Each of the situations illustrate successful relationship techniques that are detailed later in this chapter and in other sections of this book. If you've circled mostly *a* answers, you're pretty good at spotting them. If you've selected mostly *b* answers, you're misreading the subtle indicators. You also might be missing them in your own relationship.

Elements of a Successful Relationship

O.K., so successful relationships don't just happen. They take work. But that sounds depressing, you might be thinking. If two people love each other, why do they have to work at their relationship. Shouldn't success just happen?

Maybe it should, but it doesn't. Relationships that are allowed to motor along on their own power will eventually run out of fuel. They need to be fed, watered, nurtured. If you're a gardener, you know what happens to your flower beds when you just set your plants out and let them fend for themselves. If they don't all die, they'll end up riddled with bugs and choked with weeds. And some of them will grow wild, far beyond their borders if they're not contained in some fashion. Growing wild can also happen to relationships that go too long without attention.

Working at a relationship means caring enough about your partner to stay actively involved, rather than sitting passively by. It means setting some mutually agreed-upon goals. It means taking the time to nurture one another, both physically and emotionally. It means honoring your partner enough to allow him or her the freedom to maintain a separate identity within the relationship. And it means keeping a certain sense of humor about life's inevitable ups and downs.

Dr. Lana's Secrets

It is easy to confuse a comfortable relationship with a happy relationship. Comfort is not a bad thing, but it's also not engaging, dynamic, or intimate. So if your relationship is more comfortable than enticing, consider making it more lively. There has to be growth, or a sense of expansion, within the individuals and between them for a lasting connection to be maintained. Without a connection, couples don't stay together. Often one or the other connects with someone else.

Pay Attention to Me!

On the face of it, Gretchen and Karl are one of the most mismatched couples you'd ever care to meet. Gretchen, a flamboyant former interior designer turned local talk show host, has the mannerisms of Bette Midler—with the looks to match. Karl, a recently retired pro football player, is stoic and conservative, more given to letting his wife carry the conversation than contributing much himself. Gretchen and Karl spend a lot of time in the public eye, where, as you might imagine, she grabs more of the spotlight than he does. But Karl always takes center stage in Gretchen's mind.

"I'm constantly aware of what Karl's doing, of what his needs are, when we're out and about," Gretchen says. "It may seem like I'm not paying much attention to him, but believe me, I know to the second when he's had enough and it's time to go. And the same is true in reverse. Karl knows when it's time to rescue me from a situation that's gone on long enough. We're kind of like a tag team, and with our diverse personalities, it works really well."

Dr. Lana's Secrets

Listen and *silent* are anagrams. They have the same letters, but that is not all they have in common. They are also quintessential components for developing a sense of connection to one another. Be silent in your thinking and in your voice when you are listening to your partner. Be fully present in your willingness to hear and understand one another.

The two literally debrief each other, not only after special events but also on a daily basis. "We set aside time every night to talk about everything," Gretchen says. "If there are any issues or concerns, we get them out right then. If there's anything either of us feel we need to follow up on, we sit down and make a to-do list."

Early on in their marriage, Gretchen and Karl knew they'd have a busy life together and that they'd have to develop a way to ensure that they'd devote enough time to their relationship. Their system may sound a little extreme, but it's a good example of a relationship based on active involvement.

"We saw what happened to couples that had a kind of laissez-faire attitude toward their relationships," Karl says. "Sooner or later, they'd just drift apart. They'd end up looking at each other from the opposite ends of the playing field and wonder how they got there. We didn't want that to happen to us, so we decided to do a very simple thing. We decided to pay attention to each other everyday."

Talk, Talk, Talk

Gretchen and Karl's system also illustrates a vital ingredient in all successful relationships. They have found a way to effectively communicate with each other. It's no secret that partners have to talk for their relationship to work. Couples who are the most successful at creating successful relationships talk to each other as best friends. They confide their thoughts, their fantasies, and their behavior, both good and bad. But they also have to develop a common ground, or communication style, that works for both people.

Couples whose individual interests and styles are different have to find a way to bridge the distance between them. They have to spend more time communicating and have to be more disciplined about putting in the time and energy to understand one another.

Make Communication Work

In Gretchen and Karl's situation, there was a strong potential for miscommunication. Gretchen is much more open and vocal than Karl ever will be and has to consciously slow herself down so she doesn't miss what Karl tells her. Karl's natural tendency to reticence could have led him to just digest Gretchen's comments instead of giving her immediate feedback. Their debriefing sessions take place at a small table in their kitchen, which puts them face to face so they can also watch each other's body language. "It levels the playing field," Karl says. "I can tell instantly by Gretchen's body language when I'm not giving her as much feedback as she'd like."

Tune In to Each Other's Limits

Knowing one another's limits is a way of understanding each other. A behavior that is upsetting to one person may be perfectly acceptable to another.

Boundaries do not have to be identical. A limit that may apply to one partner may not apply to the other. For instance, Justin had no concerns about Lila meeting with clients after work, but Lila was upset when Justin went out after hours. Initially, Justin argued, "What's good for the goose is good for the gander," but then he realized he really didn't care about going out after work anyway. He didn't drink alcohol, and that was the reason his friends went out.

Lila's Dad had a drinking problem and Friday nights were often the beginning of a weekend binge that caused brutal fights between her parents. So while Lila trusted Justin, his going out for drinks always created anxiety in her. She acknowledged that her feelings were irrational but Justin reassured her, saying, "I don't need to go out to prove that I can go out, and if it eases your mind for me not to go, it is a gift I am glad to give you."

It is normal and healthy for couples to have different boundaries between them. Understanding and supporting one another's boundaries adds a sense of intimacy and respect.

Knowing Where "No" Is

Many years ago, a wealthy young couple asked a leading financial consultant for advice on how they should determine their annual philanthropic efforts. "First, you must learn how to say no," he told them. "Then, you'll know when to say yes."

Quite simply, their trusted consultant was telling them that they needed to set some boundaries for their giving. Knowing which charities they *weren't* going to support gave them the freedom to say yes to those that *did* interest them.

Successful couples know where their no's are. Either by trial and error or through planned conversations, they've established boundaries for their behavior, both apart and together. Until their boundaries are in place, they tend to function like puppies that haven't been housebroken. They're constantly pushing the edges of our newspapers to see how far they can go and having little accidents when they've gone too far.

Setting Boundaries You Both Can Live With

Boundaries are real and understood limits. Rather than being confining, however, they can be quite liberating.

For Janelle, discovering Pete's boundaries when it came to her relationships at work gave her new freedom with her coworkers. "My partner prior to Pete frowned on my having to do anything with anyone I worked with," she says. "That was O.K. when I worked in a more sterile office environment, but the place I'm at now really puts a high value on socializing. It's almost like *Ally McBeal*—they're always going out after work to a club down the street just to relax and let off steam. I was assuming that Pete would feel the same way as my old boyfriend did, so I went home to him more often than not without thinking about whether I wanted to join the group.

"At my six-month review, my supervisor mentioned that my coworkers had commented that I almost never joined them at anything. She wondered if I liked them. That night, I went home and talked to Pete about it. Was I surprised! He said he was getting ready to talk to me about the same thing. We even talked about what was acceptable behavior and what wasn't. I realized that Pete had a good understanding of the kind of office environment I was now in, and he trusted me enough to encourage me to become a part of it."

It takes a shared belief in the value of boundaries in a relationship for a couple to want to set them. Because each partner is bound to have different ideas of where some limits should be placed, going through the process necessary to situate them calls for a willingness to cooperate rather than fight. Reaching an accord calls for compromise more often than not.

Be Willing to Compromise and Adapt

Boundaries should be adaptive. They can address legitimate concerns without being oppressive. The goal is to find a way to meet your needs, and there are always a variety of ways to do that.

"Rick is a guy's kind of guy," says Phoebe, "and I knew that when I married him, but every weekend our home is like a frat house." Phoebe complained, "Somebody is always here. I like your friends but no matter what we have planned one of the guys is always with us. I feel like I spend all weekend fixing meals and cleaning up after your friends." After much disagreement, Rick agreed that all day Sunday and Sunday night would be reserved for just him and Phoebe. They agreed that Phoebe didn't have to be home on Saturdays and Rick would clean up. He told his friends, "We have an open house Friday and Saturday but not on Sundays." He even bought a sign for the front door, "Do Not Disturb."

Being clear about what you do want rather than just what you don't want is important in finding the right solution. If Phoebe had focused on not wanting Rick's friends around, they would have found it difficult to find a solution that worked for both of them. Instead Phoebe made it clear that Rick's friends were not the problem, not having time for just the two of them was the issue.

Separate but Equal

Phoebe and Rick's agreement also illustrates another important element in successful relationships. There has to be a little breathing room—both physically and emotionally—between the partners, or they'll end up smothering each other. As a very wise woman named Marnie Reed Crowel once wrote, "To keep the fire burning brightly there's one easy rule: Keep the two logs together, near enough to keep each other warm and far enough apart—about a finger's breadth—for breathing room. Good fire, good marriage, same rule."

Couples and individuals have different tolerances for being together. Some couples want a lot of time together, and other couples spend more time apart. The amount of time they spend together does not say anything about the strength of their marriage, as long as both are satisfied with the level of emotional connection they have with each other.

Dr. Lana's Secrets

Across economic and educational boundaries, some of the qualities that set successful relationships apart are mutually satisfying communication, clear boundaries, and a strong physical and emotional connection.

Close, but Not Too Close

The "falling in love" period is a wonderful time in a relationship. It's the time when love is giddy and exciting, and you're soaring high on your PEA rush. Eventually, however, it comes to an end. Does that mean the relationship's over?

For some couples, it does. These are the relationship junkies who bounce from one relationship to another in search of the next hormone high. Others cling to each other and their togetherness as they attempt to regain the feelings they lost. Instead of regaining them, they snuff out any fire that may be left between them.

Donnie and Kendall always seemed in perfect harmony, so everyone was shocked when they split up. They were the two who went everywhere together. Kendall was so supportive that many of Donnie's friends joked with their wives that they wished they had a wife like Kendall. She took care of everything. She was a great cook, she furnished their home beautifully, bought his clothes, made all their social plans, plus she crafted and managed their budget. She did everything, which was exactly why Donnie left.

He explains, "One day I looked around the house and thought, there is nothing of me here. I felt that way about our whole life: Where was I? Kendall took care of everything, and I didn't make any choices or decisions. I just went along until I no longer knew who I was or what I cared about."

Delight in Each Other's Uniqueness

"Happily ever after" couples honor the bond between them as well as the uniqueness and separateness of each partner. These couples function as individuals within the broader concept of the relationship. They share a mutual respect.

They're more likely to encourage their spouses to make their own contributions to a conversation instead of finishing sentences for them. These couples don't just love each other, they extend their love to each other, helping the other reach the goals they have set for themselves in life. In doing so, they reach their own goals as well.

Their mutual respect is obvious in how they talk *to* one another and how they talk *about* the other. They eagerly tell you about their partner's experiences and successes. They take pride in one another's successes and share each other's sorrows. They view their individuality as adding richness to each of their lives. They hold each other in high esteem.

Michael's relationship with Randi is a good example of the importance of both partners being successful separately. Randi explains, "Michael and I met at work. I was a sales trainer and Michael was in charge of customer service for a software company. After we had children I decided to stay home. While I loved being with our children, I also felt restless and started feeling resentful of Michael's success. Michael repeatedly argued, "You should be thankful that we have enough money for you to stay home. This is what you said you wanted." Michael felt unappreciated and Randi felt guilty for being unhappy.

Michael and Randi were arguing constantly and decided to take a week away and talk about how to change their lives. Michael made it a point to listen to Randi without taking responsibility for her unhappiness. It was the first time he understood that her complaint was about herself not about him or their lifestyle. Once he was able to separate himself from the problem they were able to find a solution.

Randi went to a career counselor and decided that since she had always loved reading and editing, she would do some freelance editing at the University. In a short time, Randi developed an excellent reputation and soon had a thriving business.

40

Michael admits he was nervous at first because he wanted her to stay home with their children but now he says, "Seeing Randi happy and excited has made our relationship with each other and our kids the best it has ever been. Randi is very talented and knowing she is using her talents is important to her and to me."

Dr. Lana's Secrets

A successful relationship doesn't mean that you're joined at the hip. Being separate is as important as being together. Cultivating interests and relationships apart from one another adds freshness and vitality to a primary relationship.

Connecting Physically and Emotionally

"Keep in touch" is more than just a throwaway line in successful relationships. Long-term couples know the importance of maintaining physical and emotional connections. Without daily doses of affection and intimacy, it's easy to drift apart. A sentiment often heard in marital counseling is that one partner, or both, feel like they're sharing their home with a stranger. That's what happens when the effort to connect isn't made on a regular basis.

Some couples literally schedule their physical and emotional time, making dates with one another, planning rendezvous for sex, or taking time out to call their spouse on a regular basis. While this may sound artificial and contrived, it works very well, especially for busy people with full lives who want to ensure a continuity of effort.

It also works well for couples who spend a significant amount of time apart. "Knowing that I'll get a call from Darren every day at the same time is a big part of what keeps me going in our relationship," says Bobbi, who keeps their busy family and home together while Darren travels overseas for months at a time. "I know it's not always convenient for him to call, but his making the effort underlines how important this relationship is to him. We also schedule some time each week for evening calls…and those can get pretty steamy."

Bumps Ahead

Falling asleep on the couch too often can put your relationship on the fast track to disaster. Get your butt up and into bed, no matter how tired you are!

Isn't It Rich? Aren't We a Pair?

Life can be funny. Life can be tough. But it can also be enjoyable, even when it gets tough. Some people are born with the ability to approach life with a positive attitude, no matter what happens. But for many of us that ability has to be learned, and once learned, practiced. Long-term couples, especially those who have endured some tough situations, have learned that it's just as easy to roll with life's punches than not. Worrying has never been shown to yield anything beyond wrinkles, gray hair, depression, and other emotions that don't do anything positive for us or anyone around us. So why not look on the bright side? And even laugh at things when they seem especially silly?

Stephanie and Frank are a good example of two people who have learned how to find the positives in a negative situation. Frank was a bank president when he met Stephanie. Prior to knowing her, he approved a loan for a friend who was starting a new business. When the friend's business failed, the federal government took a look at all the transactions related to it and uncovered some inaccurate statements Frank's friend had made on his loan application. Although Frank maintained that he had no idea that the application was fraudulent, he was indicted and sentenced for loan fraud.

Bumps Ahead

Negative thinking leads directly to negative behavior, which inevitably creates negative outcomes.

"I was with Frank almost a year when we learned he was under investigation," Stephanie says. "He lost his job and all of his money in a very short time after everything came to light. My initial reaction was to run in the opposite direction when he first told me everything. I felt like the life we had built together had crumbled.

Dr. Lana's Secrets

Anticipating the worst does not ease the pain, it only makes the worst more likely to happen. Look at what you're doing and what you are thinking about. We usually find what we are looking for. Look for what's right and you will find it. Let the trivia slide and put your energy into what really matters.

Happiness comes from our ability to set and achieve our goals. It is solving day-to-day problems and enjoying day-to-day pleasures in life that builds self-esteem and creates individual and mutual happiness.

"What I realized after I got over the initial shock was that the only thing that had crumbled was the veneer. What Frank and I still had together was very real and true. Since then, we've been able to approach what could have been a horrible situation with a great sense of acceptance. Every so often, we'll both look around the place where Frank's incarcerated and just start laughing, the contrast between what our life was then and what it is now is really pretty funny. But what we have now is also better than ever before."

Frank and Stephanie learned—the hard way—what was really important in their lives: each other. They also learned to appreciate what they have and to live in the moment. Instead of worrying about what Frank will do for a living when he gets out of prison or bemoaning the fact that life as they once knew it is over, they now spend time enjoying each other's company in ways they never had before. Their conversations are deep and long. They sit and hold hands more than they've ever done. They watch squirrels play in the prison courtyard and delight in the vivid sunsets. "It seems so strange," Stephanie says, "but we've never been happier in our lives."

It's the Little Things That Count

"God is in the details," architect I. M. Pei said a number of years ago. So are good relationships. Successful couples learn to do, recognize, and appreciate the little things. Things like enjoying a walk with each other instead of needing to be entertained on an ocean cruise. Things like making the bed a certain way because you know your partner likes it that way. Things like not taking the last piece of cherry cheesecake because you know it's his favorite. Little things, but they add up in a big way.

The Least You Need to Know

➤ Successful relationships take attention, caring, and work.

➤ Couples must agree on the importance of setting boundaries in order for their relationship to be successful.

➤ Togetherness is important, but a balance between time together and time apart can enrich a relationship and make it grow.

➤ Paying attention to the little pleasures in day-to-day life reaps big results.

Chapter 4

An Affair Is the End... or Is It?

In This Chapter

➤ Can relationships survive affairs?

➤ The message affairs send

➤ The difference between surviving and thriving

➤ The importance of a positive attitude

In my end is my beginning.

—Thomas Stearns (T.S.) Eliot

It's one of the primary rules of the universe, so intrinsically part of our existence that we generally don't pay close attention to it. But T. S. Eliot is just one of many who have given voice to this very basic fact of life: Our day-to-day existence is full of tiny little deaths and rebirths from the moment we arrive on the face of this earth until the day we depart it. Our world is always in a state of change, and it's meant to be that way.

In the grand scheme of things, an affair is also nothing more than a death and rebirth experience. Yes, it's unfortunate. It causes pain, and it can cause destruction. But that's just one side of the affair equation.

Death and Destruction—or the Start to Something New?

Relationships are chock full of endings and beginnings. They have to be to maintain the elements that attract us to them in the first place. Remove the flow and friction from a relationship for any reason, and it starts a slow, inevitable slide toward death. As Woody Allen wrote some years ago, "A relationship is like a shark. It has to keep moving or it will die."

While it can be difficult to think about an affair being anything other than a negative experience, the message it sends and the lessons it teaches can also have a positive impact on a relationship. Spouses in relationships that have weathered an affair won't necessarily recommend the experience, but many will say that what they experienced was an integral part of the maturing process they needed to go through for the long-term success of their relationship.

Dr. Lana's Secrets

Stunned, shocked, jolted, jilted, floored, and flattened are all words people I've counseled have used to describe how they felt when their partner uttered those life-altering words, "Honey, I've been seeing someone." Believe it or not, every single one of these people lived through it and grew from it.

Affair Facts

A study from the University of Washington found most spouses who know about an affair find out from their partner—more than 66 percent of them, according to one study. About 25 percent uncover some evidence and confront their spouse; another 7 percent learn about the affair from someone else.

Affairs Aren't Just Bad News

Emotions tend to clump together like a nest of snakes when an affair first rears its head in a relationship. As long as they stay so tightly balled up, it's almost impossible for those involved to consider anything beyond the fact that there's an affair here. Even if all that happened was a one-night stand, it's something that wasn't present before. It's a betrayal, a breach of contract, a stepping-out-of-bounds. For now, and maybe for a long time, life will be measured in preaffair and postaffair terms. Just the thought of it takes on mythic proportions. It's not just an affair. It's an AFFAIR.

But when emotions finally return to a somewhat normal state it's possible for most couples to see that what may seem like an end can actually be a beginning to something that can be pretty wonderful ...eventually.

Avoiding Doomsday Thinking

As with almost everything that challenges us in this world, the way spouses decide to react to and handle an affair largely determines how it will turn out. If the non-affairee tends to react negatively to bad news, the discovery of an affair may spell the end for her. If she believes that it can be the straw that breaks her relationship's back, there's a very good chance it will be.

Affair Facts

The odds that a spouse will leave a marriage for an affairee are low. The odds for a successful marriage should the affairees get together are lower still.

At the time an affair is exposed, it's more common than not to take a somewhat negative approach to the whole matter, even when the couple decides to stay together and work things out. "Sure," couples might think, "we could get through this, but what will life be like when we do? Will we miss how things used to be between us too much to even try? Or, heaven forbid, how will we feel if we get through this and it happens all over again?"

This is doomsday thinking—basically putting the cart way before the horse and trying to predict how things will come out. Couples who persist in doing it, regardless of the situation, set themselves up for failure before they even start. When this kind of thinking is employed in an affair situation, relationships rarely survive.

Leaps and Bounds

An affair can cause a relationship to make a quantum leap instead of just a few measured paces. It can be a long jump worthy of an Olympic medal...or a giant step backward. The direction in which a relationship travels once an affair affects it is largely determined by several factors, including

➤ How the non-affairee responds to the knowledge of an affair

➤ The strength of the relationship prior to the affair

➤ The desire of both spouses to repair their relationship

Dr. Lana's Secrets

One of the real losses during this period for most injured spouses is the loss of self-confidence. Before now, they thought they knew what to expect from their partners, and they thought they would know whether their partners were lying. Now they feel like fools, because they realize they were wrong.

But hiding an affair doesn't mean that everything was wrong with the relationship. Chances are that lies were told on a few occasions, but everything was not a lie. We're all deceived some of the time. And it's better to allow ourselves to be hoodwinked now and then, rather than question everything we're told.

Time to Wake Up!

An affair is often a strong indication of the need to make some significant changes in a relationship. It is one of the most powerful calls to action a couple can ever receive. Couples whose relationships have survived almost categorically state that the affair served as a very necessary wake-up call.

As Catherine describes it, "It took my literally running into my husband and his girlfriend at a home and garden show to realize how far apart we had drifted. We loved going to these shows together when we were first married, but I had lost interest over the years for some reason or another—in fact, I only came to the show that day because a friend had dragged me to this one so I could look at something she was thinking of buying.

"When he came home, I told him I had seen them and how horrible I felt. I didn't want a divorce, and he said he didn't want a divorce either. He admitted that he had felt very much alone. That evening, we talked about the many different things we used to enjoy doing, and we decided it was time to make the time to do them again."

When Inertia Sets In

There's nothing like a big dose of harsh reality to make us realize that we've let something that was once quite wondrous and precious to become somewhat staid and ordinary. It's a very common problem, and there are lots of reasons why it can happen. But here's one you may not have considered: Often, we let important relationships die because we're too lazy to keep them going.

As good as our intentions often are on the front end of any relationship, and as much as we might swear that we won't let it happen, it's still more natural for us to let our relationships—with our spouses, our families, even our friends—slide backwards as time goes on than it is to actively work to move them ahead. Psychologist M. Scott Peck calls this backward or downhill flow of energy the force of entropy. If left unchecked, it returns us to our lowest common denominators, and it reduces what we're capable of giving and getting from our relationships to such a low level that we wind up expecting very little from them.

Once we're aware of this downhill force working against our relationships—and the discovery of an affair is a great way to bring it to light—it's easier to marshal the forces necessary to fight it. And make no mistake; it is a battle. As one former affairee said, "Any time I think I can afford to take a breather, I know it's actually time to rekindle my efforts."

Dr. Lana's Secrets

You are so busy; there is so much to do. How much of what you did last week do you remember? Probably not a lot. We get caught up in so many things to do, places to be, and people to know that we forget or postpone the relationships most dear to us. If your partner isn't complaining, or at least there aren't any new complaints, it's easy to forget how tenuous love really is.

Affairs can also indicate other parts of our lives that need attention. The behavior that leads people into affairs is often the very same behavior that causes problems at work and with other members of their families.

Most Relationships Can Make It

No matter how devastating an affair can be, it's important to keep in mind one very basic fact: Most relationships survive. An affair, in and of itself, doesn't have to spell the end.

If there is genuine love between two people, it is possible to resurrect a relationship. The level to which the relationship is restored depends on how strong things were to start with and how hard the spouses want to work at it. For some couples, the level that approximates where the relationship was before the affair took place is as far as they can go, at least in the beginning.

But time, as we all know, really does heal us. As the time lengthens from when the affair occurred, these relationships can move beyond merely existing to becoming stronger, as long as both spouses desire to reconnect and to actively work at making things better.

...Or Even Thrive

The ideal for a postaffair relationship is that it not only survives—it thrives. It won't come right away, it could even take years, but the goal should be to end up with a relationship that is stronger and better than it was before the affair. If you've ever broken a bone, you'll see striking similarities between mending a relationship and recovering from such an injury. First, you pick up the pieces and put them back into place. If you've been living apart or sleeping apart, you go back to sharing the same residence and the same bed. Then you support your relationship while it mends. For some couples, this means going into marital counseling or individual therapy. Some seek help and support from their priests, ministers, or rabbis. Some turn to books or even videos for assistance.

Eventually, the relationship emerges with its core elements stronger than ever before. It takes time, just like it does to get bones to knit back together. It hurts, sometimes more than you'd like. There are uncomfortable moments. You may have to make changes that you really don't want to make. But the result can and often is a better quality product than what you started with.

Worth All the Effort

After several months of escalating arguments and increasing distance in a relationship that had been fairly steady, Annette told her husband Jim about her year-long affair with her business partner. Jim's immediate reaction was to end their marriage, but he reined in his emotions and waited a few days before doing much of anything. "I had to let what Annette said sink in," he says. "I felt really betrayed—both by Annette and by Dave, who I thought was a pretty good friend—and sad that Annette was so unhappy with our relationship. Letting it sit for a few days helped me gain some perspective and realize what I had done to contribute to the problem."

Annette and Jim decided to try to work things out. "We both had a sense that our relationship was worth the effort," Jim says. "Also, we always wanted to have a family. We had gotten off that track, but when we sat down to start sorting our lives out, Annette told me how much she still wanted to. That really touched me and made me feel like I was still important to her."

Bumps Ahead

Both spouses must want to save their relationship for reconciliation efforts to work. Although one might be more enthusiastic about the process than the other, both need to keep a positive attitude. Start believing that efforts are fruitless, and they will be.

Meeting Halfway

Several weeks into their reconciliation, Jim made a request that Annette really didn't like. "I told Annette I would feel better about going forward if she and Dave no longer worked together. I couldn't handle the thought of them being together at work after they had been intimate. Maybe it was irrational, but it was something I really needed."

Annette resisted Jim's request for several weeks, and it looked as though their efforts at reconciliation had come to an end. "Then Annette came home one afternoon and said, 'I realized I was asking you to do a lot for me, and I wasn't really willing to commit to you. That is not the kind of person I want to be or the kind of partner I want to be.'"

Annette decided to honor Jim's request and sold her part of the business to Dave. "With the money Annette got, we could have gone away to somewhere fun—Annette said she wanted to—but it was too early for me," Jim says. "I told her to keep her money and invest it in something else. We needed to spend day-to-day time together, not divert our time and energy on a vacation."

Annette used her funds to support some time away from work while she and Jim began seeing a counselor. "It was the best investment I've ever made," Annette says. "Not only did it allow me to get a fresh perspective on what I wanted to do for a living, it also gave me the time to really work on my relationship with Jim. After a few months, I could see the patterns in my behavior that led to my affair. I also realized that I liked my work, but I had been unhappy with how and where I worked. Not surprisingly, both issues were intertwined."

After six months, Annette and Jim were still moving forward and both felt that their relationship would survive. "We've had some setbacks—a real tough one was getting back together physically—but we got through it," Jim says. "Annette decided to start a business in our home, and it's going really well. I can't believe how much happier and relaxed she is. Her frustration over her work and my reaction to it—I would try to force things out of her when she really wasn't ready to talk—were major contributors to our problems. Now she's happier with what she's doing, and I've learned to back off and let her come to me when she's ready."

The Work of Restoration

Resurrecting a relationship following an affair takes a lot of work. Beyond restoring basic issues like trust and respect, other areas must also be addressed, such as restoring intimacy if it has fallen by the wayside. Sometimes, it is necessary for one spouse to make a significant change to ease the fears of the other. Getting through these issues and making these changes, while difficult, is much easier when both partners agree that their relationship is worth saving. But this isn't always the case.

Dr. Lana's Secrets

A rule of thumb for deciding how much to invest in your relationship is to ask yourself if you're behaving like the person—the partner—you want to be. If you're being your best and are proud of the way you are behaving as a partner, then your relationship is probably moving forward. But if it isn't, step back and take a good look. Are you listening to yourself and to your partner? Are you doing your best to be a good friend to yourself and to your mate? As much as you may want the relationship to continue, if you're doing all the work, it is time to talk to your partner and ask these same questions of him or her.

Some spouses rise to the challenge. Sadly, many others aren't willing to reopen old wounds, and they resist any changes to the status quo. These are the marriages that don't heed the messages that an affair sends. They're the ones that end up being only hollow shells of what they once were.

These partners may stay together for the rest of their lives, but it's probably because of a sense of duty and obligation than anything else. There may be children involved, a position in the community or in a business could be threatened, or an inheritance might be at stake. For whatever reason, these couples stay together but often in name only. The spouse who had the affair is very likely to have another. And subsequent affairs are conducted much more clandestinely and are almost never revealed.

When the End Is the End

There are times, no doubt about it, that an affair does mean the end. Infidelity can be used as a tool to accelerate the death of a relationship. A spouse can deliberately enter into one affair, or many, to force the other spouse to declare the relationship over. The adulterous partner may even go so far as to have a child with his lover to really end his marriage.

Affair Facts

When asked what strategy they would use if they wanted to break up their marriage, the vast majority of men responded with the words, "Have an affair."

Sometimes in these situations, the wayward partner makes only a halfhearted attempt to keep his affair under wraps, especially if there is already a great deal of acrimony in the primary relationship. He's asking to be caught so that his spouse can be the one to instigate whatever needs to happen to end their relationship. Some affairs can go undisclosed until the bitter end or even after, but the spouse usually gets fed up with the affairee's lack of attention and forces the issue.

If there's a confrontation, errant spouses in these situations usually lack remorse and may actually seem glad that they've been caught. In their minds, they left the relationship long ago—they just didn't know how to end it or lacked the desire to do so.

Chances are, you'll never find yourself in a relationship like this, but if you do, think long and hard about devoting any additional effort or resources to it. Remember that most relationships can survive an affair, but not all should. If you have a straying partner who clearly seems to be itching to get away, your best move may be to let her go and focus your efforts on the next chapter of your life.

The Least You Need to Know

➤ Most relationships can survive an affair.

➤ An affair can actually revitalize a relationship.

➤ Relationships must move forward to thrive.

➤ Your attitude about an affair will determine your success in rebuilding your relationship.

➤ But…sometimes the end really means the end.

Chapter 5

Affair Anatomy 101

In This Chapter

➤ The different types of affairs

➤ Affair or addiction?

➤ The role emotions play

➤ Affair risks and pitfalls

Why do fools fall in lust?

—Bonnie Eaker Weil, *Adultery: The Forgivable Sin*

An affair is an affair is an affair…or is it?

At first glance, it may seem so. But when you go below the surface, there are just about as many different kinds of affairs as there are people to have them. There are love affairs, in-love affairs, sex affairs, revenge affairs, even hate affairs that masquerade as love affairs. There are affairs between total strangers, affairs between best friends, and affairs between total strangers who end up being best friends.

For some people, affairs are addictions. These people crave the hormonal rush that happens at the beginning of a new relationship, and they go from one to the next in search of the next big hit. However, addictions are not affairs. Sure, it's possible to spend way too much time away from your partner, maybe at the health club or at the neighborhood garage tinkering with your vintage car. But unless it's a cute weight-room attendant or the garage owner's girlfriend who's drawing your attention, these behaviors do not constitute affairs.

On the other hand, they can very definitely contribute to the possibility of an affair happening in a relationship. Plenty of husbands look outside their marriages for companionship because their wives are addicted to spending hours at the spa or the gym in the pursuit of physical "excellence." And there's a whole host of women who would rather spend their weekends in the arms of a lover than sitting on cold football bleachers.

Because we've defined an affair as an illicit relationship between two people, we'll focus this discussion on the many different types of affairs that people are capable of having and their main characteristics.

The Elements of an Affair

All affairs revolve around two very basic things:

➤ Two people (sometimes more, in very complicated affairs)

➤ A desire to fulfill physical and/or emotional needs

Beyond this, affairs fall into two main categories: love affairs, which always involve an emotional component, and sexual affairs, where physical needs always come first.

Dr. Lana's Secrets

When I speak with people who had affairs, I have found that most affairees were not out looking for an affair, at least not consciously. Many affairs began with people just talking. Some affairees worked on projects together, or their children were involved in the same sports. And a surprisingly large number were close friends of one of the affairee's spouses.

Love Affairs

There are many different types of love affairs, and they all share one common characteristic: They have as their primary element an emotional bond between two people. The depth of that bond can vary greatly, which is what distinguishes one type of love affair from another. There's also a sexual component to almost all love affairs, but it takes second place to emotions. These relationships are almost always driven by self-esteem issues, not physical need.

Oh God, I Love You!

The most intense love affairs are so highly emotionally charged that they defy reason. Some people describe their feelings in such relationships as similar to being struck by a lightning bolt. Others say that the intensity of their feelings for each other literally hurt, whether they're together or apart.

What causes these intensely emotional and often highly dramatic relationships is a high level of PEA and the amphetamine rush that accompanies it. They are a strong reflection of our most basic biological needs, and as such, can border on obsession.

Affair Facts

A 1977 study by Travis and Sadd showed that 47 percent of women who worked out of the house full-time and 27 percent of full-time homemakers admitted to an affair.

These affairs can be some of the most damaging to a marriage, as the euphoria that drives them can blind the participants and block out the world around them. These are also some of the most enjoyable affairs that two people can have, thanks to their intensity…and they're some of the most devastating when they end.

Can't Get Enough Love

Love junkies—those people addicted to love—have an unusual craving for the PEA high. Most people don't like the tension and anxiety that accompanies this high…but love junkies get hooked. The reason? Those who crave excitement carry a longer version of one gene in their DNA. This little gene gives them an extra hit of pleasure and euphoria when they experience excitement or risk.

Although the "high" may be terrific for them in the short term, their addictions are devastating to those around them. Ultimately the addiction dominates their lives, destroying them both personally and professionally as it becomes more and more powerful and ubiquitous. These people really are addicted to love and need professional treatment.

Addictions have a physiologic basis and a lot of psychological consequences. People with addictions can succeed at controlling them, and medications are available—but they are very difficult things to live with.

Comfort Food

At the other end of the scale when it comes to love affairs are the relationships that are as comfortable as an old shoe. These loving affairs are primarily emotional and may not have a strong sexual component. Often, there's no sex at all. Instead of lovers, these affairees see each other as best friends. They have loving feelings toward each other, but it's more the love between two very good friends.

Affair Facts

Sociologist Pepper Schwartz disclosed that the longer people are married, the more likely they are to have affairs that meet emotional needs rather than satisfy sexual urges.

Affair Facts

Love affairs often subsidize marriages that are basically healthy but have a missing element that's important to one of the spouses. Sometimes it's sexual, but usually it's emotional. These affairees are looking for someone to talk to, share their feelings with, and have fun with. The nature of these affairs is affirming, comforting, and nurturing, and they often fill in for what's lacking at home.

Affair Speak

Transitional, or bridge, affairs often happen when primary relationships are going through times of change.

These affairs, because they lack intensity, are some of the safest to have. Even when discovered by or confessed to a spouse, they're often tolerated, and it's common for affairs of this nature to last for a very long time, if not a lifetime. These affairs can often revitalize lagging marriages and boost sagging egos. Indeed, it's not unusual for the spouse not involved in the relationship to be thankful for its existence.

The relationship that existed for many years between Franklin Delano Roosevelt and Lucy Mercer is a good example of a loving affair. A more current example is the recently revealed relationship between the former governor of Colorado, Roy Romer, and B. J. Thornberry, a former staff member. When Governor Romer held a press conference to explain the relationship, Bea Romer was right by his side, and even told the press that her husband's relationship with Ms. Thornberry had helped him tremendously over the years.

Bridging the Gap

Somewhat in the middle of the love affair spectrum are transitional or bridge affairs. These often occur when primary relationships are going through periods of change—such as when relocating for a new job or when a spouse goes back to school. They're sometimes seen as a reward for a major accomplishment, such as passing the bar or a big promotion at work. Or they can happen when a primary relationship is going through a period of stress, maybe caused by outside forces such as the death of a parent or a lingering illness of the spouse.

Cynthia, married to Thomas for four years, found herself in the unaccustomed role of caretaker when Thomas suddenly became seriously ill. Following major abdominal surgery, Thomas was bedridden for several months while he regained his strength. Cynthia nursed him and continued to run their home-based business. She not only was exhausted by her increased responsibilities but also missed her husband, both emotionally and physically.

Late one afternoon, Cynthia felt the overwhelming need to cut loose from her obligations for a few hours. While Thomas was asleep, she walked to a neighborhood bar, where she sipped a martini and talked with Mikal, an artist who had a studio in the area. "I never thought I'd be the type to have an affair," Cynthia says, "but it started that afternoon and continued for several months. I didn't realize until I met Mikal that I was as lonely as I was. It wasn't just about sex, although we certainly enjoyed ourselves where that was concerned."

Cynthia still sees Mikal occasionally, and sex still rarely takes center stage. More importantly, she believes that her relationship with Mikal continues to benefit her marriage. "Thomas was sick for a long time and he has a lot of catching up to do," she says. "Spending some of my time with Mikal helps me to be more accepting and respectful of Thomas as he goes through this period in his life."

Dr. Lana's Secrets

Transitional affairs happen in times of change. The affairee is experiencing herself in a different way, sometimes good and sometimes not. Transitional affairs often last between a few weeks and a few months. They are generally either celebratory or sympathetic. These affairs are not revealed to the spouse.

Sex Affairs

Quite simply, sex affairs are about sex. The physical relationship is the focus of the affair, and there's typically little or no emotional involvement.

Dr. Lana's Secrets

Sexual experimentation is one of the top three reasons both men and women give for having an affair. This type of sex affair is based on sexual adventure and trying a few new tricks. They tend to be borderline kinky, but not violent or pain causing. Women report that they feel freer to experiment sexually with a lover than with their long-term partner. They say they feel less vulnerable with a lover.

Sex affairs range from torrid one-night stands to ongoing trysts between adventuresome partners. They can focus on sensual pleasures or revolve around highly charged sex play. Some of these affairs are conquests—one affairee conquers the other. Some are driven by spouses retaliating against wayward partners by having affairs of their own. Sometimes, the partners themselves even encourage it.

Evening the Score

"When Roger finally told me about all the little flings he had had during the course of our marriage, my immediate reaction was, 'If he can do it, why shouldn't I have some

Affair Speak

Love affairs are extramarital relationships based primarily on emotions. In sexual affairs, physical needs come first.

fun too?'" says Michaela. "Roger was the only person I had ever had sex with, so I had always assumed that he had the same belief in marital fidelity, but that obviously wasn't true.

"When I mentioned this to him, he not only encouraged me to try it, he even offered to set me up with someone. That wasn't necessary—I was more than capable of finding a partner on my own. The best thing I can say about it was that I felt I had leveled the playing field between us when I had my affair. I couldn't just point my finger at Roger any longer—I had done it, too. It became a 'so what?'—not that big of a deal."

Other Reasons Why They Happen

Other reasons for sex affairs include:

➤ The desire to try something sexually that a spouse might not endorse
➤ A mismatch between the sex drives of the spouses
➤ The belief that it can improve the quality of sex in the primary relationship
➤ The need to satisfy desire if one's spouse is incapacitated or disabled

Dr. Lana's Secrets

People who indulge in sex affairs tend to be more self-centered than most, putting their own needs before anyone else's. If they're not getting what they need at home, they're very capable of finding it elsewhere and feel they have the right to do so. Some, especially habitual philanderers who derive more pleasure from the conquest than from the sexual act itself, will still pursue outside sexual encounters even if they have a satisfactory sex life with their partner.

It Doesn't Mean Anything...or Does It?

Sexual affairs are often not directed at the partner or the relationship. People who have sex affairs are usually protective of their committed relationship. These affairs are more about a search for self or a desire to experiment. Affairees often view these affairs as helping their committed relationship.

As Delora explains, "I like sex, but mostly I like affection, being touched sensually. Reid, my partner, is twelve years older than I and just doesn't have much sex drive anymore. He either isn't interested or isn't able most of the time. I'm not willing to end my sex life before I reach forty. I am discreet and committed to one lover; I am not promiscuous."

Because the emotional involvement in sex affairs is generally low, the people who have them often argue that they really aren't that significant and that they pose little if any threat to a primary relationship. In some respects they have a point, but sex affairs, like all others, may indicate unresolved issues between a couple. You may not be giving your heart to your affairee, but you're still betraying a marital trust if your relationship doesn't provide for sex with other people. And sex affairs do pose a threat in the form of increased risk for sexually transmitted diseases, especially if the affairs encompass a string of one-night stands.

Love on the Line

An affair doesn't always have to be up close and personal to be an affair. Telephones have linked affairees for years and provided the stuff for town scandals when party lines were more common than not. Today, relationships ranging from mere companionship to space-age sex are just a keyboard stroke away via the Internet...and a lot of people are pushing that particular button.

Dr. Lana's Secrets

In the last few years, several couples have come to see me after the discovery of a cyberaffair. These affairs are not harmless. The feelings between the affairees are real and powerful, and when a partner discovers one, they are just as devastated as they would be if it had been any other type of affair.

There is a strong sense of irony to these affairs because they wouldn't exist if the technology wasn't available. Remove the online access, and most cyberaffairs

Affair Facts

An estimated one million Americans access the Internet daily.

Affair Facts

It's estimated that between 30 and 45 percent of all digitized images on the Internet contain explicit sexual elements or are pornographic.

end abruptly. But not all do. Although Internet affairs are popular for many people because of their anonymity and distance, some do move offline and into the bedroom—sometimes to the great disappointment of the affairees. There are also documented cases of divorces being filed because a spouse spent too much time with an online lover—even if there was no actual physical contact between them.

Email Love Letters

Cybil found Jon's email messages really by accident. When she read the letters she couldn't believe Jon had written them. Jon was so quiet and so...good. He didn't swear, tell sexy jokes, or say anything bad about anyone. Now, as she read the letters, Cybil saw a side of Jon that she didn't even know existed.

He was describing sex and masturbation in lewd terms. Many of his words were ones she'd never heard before. As she read on, the messages became more and more graphic and also more and more loving. He said he loved that woman, Julia. How could he? Cybil thought to herself.

When she confronted Jon, he was embarrassed but insisted his feelings were real. He said he felt more alive with Julia than he ever had with Cybil. He said he was glad it was out in the open because he wanted to meet Julia. He insisted he could open up to Julia and talk to her in ways Cybil would never accept. He reminded Cybil how she always made all the decisions and how critical she was when she didn't get her way. Cybil felt like she was in the middle of a nightmare.

Jon and Cybil split up. Jon met Julia, and they corresponded for a while, but the relationship didn't last. Jon says the experience changed him for the better. It allowed him to communicate more openly and to make his own decisions, rather than allowing someone to mother him. Cybil remained angry and dejected for several years.

Fantasies in Cyberspace

An online affair is no less an affair than a face-to-face affair. It breaks the bond of the relationship, and it takes away resources that belong to the couple and invests them in someone else.

But things are almost never as they seem in cyberspace, thanks to the technology that allows communication between human and machine. Translating emotions into digital communication renders even the steamiest sexual fantasies a bit hollow. There hasn't been a computer built yet that can transmit sex's more sensual elements. Words and pictures still look better in books and magazines.

But technology also lets people live out their fantasies in cyberspace in ways they never could in the real world. Don't like that bald spot? No reason to divulge it. Think you're too heavy? Unless there's a video camera hooked up to your system, no one will ever know.

Most cybersex denizens protect themselves with a veil of anonymity. Code names are used instead of screen names, and accurate identifying information is rarely revealed. More often than not, the people who have dropped the veil of anonymity have soon regretted it. What started as casual sex play can turn into something much worse when phone numbers or screen names are disclosed.

Risks and Pitfalls

No affair, regardless of its type or duration, comes with a risk-free guarantee. Some of the problems are obvious: A tryst can be discovered. We can fall in love when we don't mean to. Other risks aren't as apparent, or maybe we just don't think about them. But they can be just as troublesome, if not more so.

Sexually Transmitted Diseases

No one can afford to be lulled into a false sense of security about disease. You may think your age, your socioeconomic level, even your sexual orientation or preferences may protect you, but nothing could be farther from the truth. An STD doesn't take the time to consider who it should infect; everyone is at risk. Nor does limiting your encounters to specific types of sex protect you. AIDS, gonorrhea, and syphilis can be transmitted by both oral and anal sex.

Older STDs, like gonorrhea and syphilis, are now treatable with antibiotics. Others, including genital herpes, AIDS, and nonspecific urethritis (NSU) caused by chlamydia infections are on the rise. According to estimates from the Surgeon General's office, some thirty million people have genital herpes—an extremely contagious disease that can cause painful sex and even spread into the bloodstream and infect other organs. Once contracted, genital herpes never goes away; it only goes into remission.

Bumps Ahead

Most people take the "it can't happen to me" approach when it comes to thinking about sexually transmitted diseases (STDs). This attitude is the main reason why they're so prevalent—The Center for Disease Control estimates that forty million people worldwide (twelve million of them Americans) have at least one STD.

Bumps Ahead

Chlamydia, a bacterium and a parasite, lives inside the cells of another organism. Sexually active women should insist on being checked for chlamydia each year at their annual physical exam, since it often exhibits no symptoms. If diagnosed, chlamydia can be readily treated with antibiotics. Left untreated, it leads to infertility and can be life-threatening.

Affair Facts

According to figures from the Centers for Disease Control, the state with the highest rate of syphilis is Mississippi, with a reported seventy cases per one hundred thousand residents. Next highest on the list: Louisiana, with thirty-eight cases per one hundred thousand residents reported.

AIDS is probably the STD that has received the most press in the last decade or so. Thankfully, new medications do a better job of delaying the onset and managing the problems related to this disease, but there's still no cure for it. Sadly, the old myth that AIDS is a disease that only homosexuals or habitual intravenous drug users can get has led many heterosexuals to be much less cautious about their sexual partners than they should be. AIDS infection rates are on the rise in increasingly younger age groups and among people in all parts of the United States, not just in coastal population centers. Having an affair definitely increases one's risk of contracting the AIDS virus.

As much as you don't want to think about it, your partner has probably had other partners and so have you, and those other partners have had other partners, and that puts both of you at risk.

Hepatitis B

Although not always classified as an STD, hepatitis B can also be transmitted through sexual contact. This disease is gaining the public's attention now that studies have shown that it's much more prevalent than it was once believed to be. Because it can cause chronic liver disease and damage, it's a more serious disease than its cousin, hepatitis A, although the symptoms—jaundice, weakness, loss of appetite, and so on—are similar. In hepatitis B, these symptoms last longer and are more severe. But it's also possible to be infected with hepatitis B and remain symptom-free, which means that the disease can be passed to other people without anyone being aware that there's a problem.

Protect Yourself

If you believe your partner is sexually involved with someone else, actively protect yourself from STDs and hepatitis. Use a barrier contraceptive every time. In other words, use a condom.

Obsessions

What may have started as a fairly rational, even-keeled relationship can change when an affairee either develops or begins to exhibit hidden feelings that the other affairee doesn't have. Maybe one affairee wants to spend more time together than the other does. Jealously over a lover's primary relationship can also develop. A desire to be more than just a lover can turn into a quest for attention that can destroy both the affair and the affairee's primary relationships. Remember Glenn Close in *Fatal Attraction*? Affairees may not stalk their victims with fine-honed knives, but often what they do can be just as dangerous.

Much Too Much

Fiction is often not much different than fact. Take Robert and Angie. Their lives were wrecked by Robert's obsession with Tasha.

Robert and Tasha felt an awesome attraction between them the moment they met in the store he managed. Although Robert was in a committed relationship, Tasha wasn't, and she pursued him by becoming a regular shopper. "Every time I looked at him, I felt like I was blinded by an intense ray of light," Tasha says. "Just touching his arm made my head spin." Several weeks after they first met, Tasha managed to be in Robert's store at closing time. He offered to drive her home, and they could barely contain themselves long enough to get inside her front door.

Tasha came to the store every day, enticing him to slip away so that she could make love to him. She called several times each day and introduced him to phone sex. On weekends she would call him at home, begging for a brief encounter. At the beginning of the affair, Robert made it clear to Tasha that he wasn't interested in leaving his other relationship, but he started feeling that he couldn't live without Tasha. He was mesmerized by her intense sexual desire. He was preoccupied and obsessed, even his kids started asking, "What's wrong with Dad?"

Finally he told his wife, Angie, about the affair and that he had to leave her. She was blindsided and devastated. When Robert told Tasha he was leaving Angie to be with her, she was ecstatic. But within a few weeks, Tasha started missing dates. She didn't call every day anymore. Three months after Robert had left Angie, Robert discovered Tasha was seeing someone else, who was also married.

When Robert confronted Tasha she complained, "Look, you aren't fun anymore, and I'm not in love with you now." And that was the last time Robert saw Tasha. But it was definitely not the last time he thought about her. He was obsessed with her and reveled in his memories for more than a year. By the end of that year, his wife had filed for divorce, his kids didn't want to see him, and he had gotten so distracted with thoughts of Tasha that he couldn't function properly; he was passed over for a promotion at work.

Obsessions and addictions are different. *Obsessions* are singular fixations or preoccupations, whereas *addictions* are ongoing compulsions. Although they are different, both are often destructive.

The sheer intensity that drives these affairs can also lead to poor decision making by the affairees. These are the affairs that can very quickly lead to divorce, and, sadly, the ensuing relationships are often doomed when the affairees finally come to their senses, which they will, and realize they may have left their other relationship for someone they don't even know that well.

When Casual Becomes More

Jennifer was away on a business trip when she met Keith, who worked for one of her company's competitors. She had just changed jobs and was feeling insecure about her new position. Over drinks at an industry event, Keith lent an understanding ear, and they spent a delicious, giddy night flirting with one another. That encounter led to a casual long-distance relationship over the phone. Then it led to something else.

"Keith began calling me more frequently. We had never talked more than once or twice a month. Then he started calling me weekly, and that progressed to daily. At first I was flattered by his attention. But when the daily calls began to feel like he was checking up on me, I wasn't very happy about it," explains Jennifer.

Although Jennifer had limited her contact with Keith to her office, he somehow obtained her home address and phone number. That's when the real trouble began. "I began getting cards and letters from him at home. At first they were friendly and cute. Then they became sexually explicit and graphic, almost threatening. And he started calling the house, but I think it was more to check up on me than to talk to me, because he'd hang up, no matter who answered the phone."

Jennifer realized that what had been a casual relationship to her had somehow become an obsession to Keith. She was able to end it by enlisting a number of diversionary tactics—using voice mail extensively at work, changing her home phone to an unlisted number, and returning all mail that looked like it came from him.

Not all obsessions end this easily. Some can drag on for years and years, making life miserable for all involved. While most obsessions don't progress along the lines of a "fatal attraction," they can still cause harm. Obsessed people are determined and persuasive, and their goal is to control the target of their affection.

Dr. Lana's Secrets

Affairs that start off being more free than the primary relationship often end up actually being more confining and restrictive. Adjusting schedules, a limited number of rendezvous locations, and avoiding being seen in public can seem romantic and clandestine at first. Later, it just becomes a hassle.

And Baby Makes—a Mess

There is more than one guy running around out there who was convinced that his woman friend had no intention of having children with him. Never. Ever. No way. Then—voilà! The phone call comes, and life changes forever.

As unsavory as it may seem, getting pregnant is actually a fairly common tactic among women who want to maintain contact with their affairees or who are out to get their guys by wrecking havoc in their marriages. It can happen in the reverse as well, when claims of infertility or of having a vasectomy throw caution to the wind.

Rarely do these situations come to a happy conclusion for anyone involved, for the obvious reasons. Of all the reasons not to have an affair, this might be one of the most compelling.

Affair Facts

The Janus Report says 56 percent of married men and 49 percent of married women believe it is important to be open to sexual experimentation within their marriage.

The Least You Need to Know

➤ Love affairs are emotional; sex affairs rarely go there.

➤ While you can be addicted to affairs, addictions aren't affairs (no matter how much you love that chocolate!).

➤ Affairs in cyberspace can be just as damaging to a marriage as face-to-face trysts.

➤ Affair risks go way beyond just being discovered.

Part 2
Secrets to Affair-Proof Love

There's an old Scandinavian joke that goes something like this: Sven and Ole are enjoying a day of ice fishing in a little shack on a frozen lake deep in Minnesota. As the hours go by, they catch some fish and do a little talking. Eventually, the conversation turns to Camilla, Ole's wife of many years.

"Dat Camilla, she's a fine one," Sven tells Ole. "Pretty she is, and a good cook too. And what a good mother to all your little ones. You have a good wife with her, Ole."

"Yah, sure, she's a keeper," Ole replies. "I should tell her that one of these days soon."

You've probably seen people like Ole and Camilla, or you may even know people like them: older, fairly set in their ways, pretty non-demonstrative but clearly in love and utterly devoted to each other. They generally don't say much about how they feel, but you can see it in the way they act and look at each other.

Without knowing too much about how to do it, Ole and Camilla somehow fashioned a life together that works, and there's a good chance that what they have will last as long as they do. If you were to ask them how they did it, they'd probably blush and stammer and tell you there's really no secret. They could be right, but the number of relationships that fail points to the fact that there must be some secrets to success that many people don't know about—or at least don't put into practice.

What does it take to build a love that lasts? You'll find the answers—and the secrets—in this section.

Chapter 6

The Custom-Made Relationship

In This Chapter

➤ Getting rid of all those other, unnecessary influences

➤ Why you should tailor your relationship

➤ Building the foundation

➤ The trust and respect quiz

➤ The importance of knowing and supporting each other's values

There has to be, between the male and the female who are going to stay together, some mysterious attraction. And it can't be just sexual. It has to be a respect, an admiration, as women, as men, as something.

—Katharine Hepburn

The next time you're in bed with your partner, take a good look around you. It's just the two of you there, right? Maybe there's a cat or a pooch parked at the foot of the bed, but just two humans, right?

Wrong! There are at least six people crowded together on top of that mattress. Sure, there's the two of you, but there's also your mother. His mother. His father and your father. Maybe even a sibling or two or a couple of stepparents. And guess what? There's a very good chance that the interactions you witnessed between these people as you were growing up have strongly influenced the relationship you're currently in.

Well, it's time to kick these folks right out of your bed. Even if any of them do have the kind of love relationship you'd like to emulate, there are a lot of reasons why you shouldn't. You are not your mother, even though you may have inherited her corn-flower blue eyes and witty personality. And he is not his dad, even if his hairline is starting to move in the same general direction.

Creating the Relationship of Your Dreams, Together

The type of relationship that your parents, or his parents, had or that your brother or sister have with their spouses may be similar to what you think is the ideal one for you. Or these models might be a far cry from your ideal. Chances are, however, that your relationship incorporates elements that are very similar to how the people who are closest to you pattern their lives.

Dr. Lana's Secrets

Couples who have happy, long-term marriages consistently rank these three qualities as the most important assets in their relationship: being best friends, having mutual respect, and sharing common goals and values.

We all bring beliefs and behaviors that were shaped by how we were raised into our relationships. But we're also unique unto ourselves. As we mature, we refine and augment our basic behaviors and beliefs to create the kind of people we want to be. Our relationships with other people are best when they're based on our own standards, which may be different from the ones we were raised with.

Affair Facts

A Time/CNN survey reported that 64 percent of those surveyed believe people should be required to take a marriage education course before they can get a marriage license.

The ideal is to establish the parameters for a relationship that's made just for you. Do the job right, and the relationship will fit just like a custom-tailored suit: The seams will be straight, the darts will fall where they should, and the shoulders will sit just right. And most important, there will be room for adjustment and change as you wind your way through life's challenges.

Establishing the Foundation

Successful relationships have at their foundation a set of core beliefs or values. They serve as an anchor for everything that happens between the two people who start the relationship and for the others (that is, kids) that get added to the mix later.

What do these core values and beliefs consist of? Couples in successful, long-term relationships cite these as the most important:

➤ A basic respect for and trust in each other

➤ Knowledge of each person's values and the desire to live by them

➤ A commitment to knowing and meeting each other's needs

➤ The willingness of each partner to take responsibility for his or her own happiness

➤ Each partner's desire to support the other's growth

O.K....so this is pretty no-brainer stuff, right? Doesn't everyone know you should respect and trust your spouse? What kind of a relationship would you have if you didn't meet each other's needs?

While we might understand why these beliefs are important, there's often a big gap between understanding them and knowing what it takes to shape a relationship based on them. You'd be amazed at how many couples enter therapy a few years into their marriages because they really don't know what their partners are all about and their attempts to find out have been stymied.

So, let's take a closer look at each item of that list.

Trust and Respect

From the moment you meet a likely life partner, you process information about that person that allows you to form an opinion about his basic character and qualities. You watch how he responds in various situations. You listen to what he has to say. Before too long, a pattern emerges that helps you determine whether this person is the one you'd like to spend a good portion of your life with.

Feelings of respect and trust evolve as you go through this process. If you note that your potential partner responds in ways that you honor and admire and believe are appropriate, your respect and trust for her grows.

Why do so many people end up with partners they don't trust and have little respect for? The simple answer is that these individuals also don't trust or respect themselves very much, and they're attracted to people who either have similar problems or who will prey on their weaknesses. If your self-esteem is low, if your upbringing didn't instill feelings of trust in you, or if you're feeling insecure thanks to some recent life blows, it may be very difficult to establish a relationship with someone you respect and trust.

Affair Speak

Trust is confidence in a person because of the qualities one perceives in him. *Respect* is the special esteem or consideration in which one holds another person.

Couples with trust and respect issues often try to control each other's behavior because it's easier than addressing their own concerns and fears. They'll call each other constantly if they're separated for any reason. Anything having to do with someone outside of the relationship calls for scrutiny and possibly attack. Although these couples often stay together, they often make each other's lives miserable.

Affair Speak

Rebounding means reversing direction after an impact—what we might do after we've been in a bad relationship, bouncing in a direction opposite of what we had before. If the previous relationship was volatile and complex, we may seek refuge in one that's simple and calm. Problems can arise when over time we realize that what we needed was less volatility, not an entirely different trajectory.

Affair Speak

Projection is a psychological term that means attributing qualities or behaviors that are within ourselves to others. We all have parts of ourselves that we are uncomfortable with or we believe are bad, and rather than admitting they are within us, we see these characteristics in others. When we believe these qualities are bad, we try to control the other person rather than ourselves.

Deadly Distrust

Trust was an issue between Bonnie and Bob almost from the moment they met. "I had just gone through a divorce and was feeling less than wonderful about myself," Bonnie says. "When I met Bob, I was flattered by his attention to me, which could only be described as intense. Although I told him I wasn't ready for a relationship, he was so sweet and kind that I couldn't resist him. I guess my insecurities overrode what I should have seen in him."

Bonnie's job required her to travel, and she grew to dread her trips because of how Bob acted while she was gone. "Constant phone calls, checking on me all the time—it was a nightmare," she says. "When I'd get home, the interrogation would begin. Where had I gone? With whom? What did we do? How late did my meetings last? If the answers didn't match what Bob thought was appropriate behavior, he'd badger and belittle me.

"Bob clearly didn't trust me, but he expected me to trust him. It was fine for him to go barhopping when I was away, but I sure couldn't do it. After a few months of this, a friend of mine called to tell me that she had met Bob at a bar and he had propositioned her. It then dawned on me that Bob didn't trust me because he knew what he'd do in the same situation. But instead of admitting his own failings, it was easier for him to undermine my confidence by making me feel like I was betraying *his* trust. I didn't feel he would ever be able to trust me or respect me enough to not feel like he had to monitor my every move, so I broke things off with him."

A few years later, Bonnie was out with some friends and ran into Bob. He offered to buy her a drink for old time's sake and the two chatted for a few minutes. "He must have ended up with a woman as insecure as he is," Bonnie says. "After the third call from her on his cell phone, he quickly paid the tab and left before he even finished his drink."

Distrust Can Lead to Control

Spouses who trust and respect each other are able to function as separate individuals within the context of their relationship. When they're apart, their thoughts focus more on missing each other than on hoping they're not doing what they shouldn't. They're not obsessed with trying to control behavior that's out of their control.

Usually, trying to control someone else simply makes them more devious and deceitful. The need for control is evidence of a lack of trust, and when people don't feel trusted, they don't feel respected either.

The lack of trust and respect leads to tension and anxiety in one or both partners. It undermines self-esteem, leading to the end of a positive sense of self or the end of the relationship.

Affair Speak

Control means to restrain or regulate. Self-control is a possibility but controlling anyone else is impractical and unrealistic. Obviously, you cannot be supervising another person day and night, observing and correcting their every move and every thought. At best, we can influence others.

Trust Leads to Honesty

Trust and respect also allow for complete honesty between spouses. You should be able to feel that you can tell your spouse everything, no matter what it is, and that he'll accept and honor your deepest thoughts and emotions, even if they're different from his. This level of disclosure can be a challenge for many people, especially if they're not in the habit of being completely honest with themselves. Many people don't even believe in complete honesty. They withhold bits and pieces of information, believing that "what you don't know can't hurt you." But it can and it will, and it just might destroy your trust in your spouse.

The Trust and Respect Quiz

Do you trust and respect your spouse? Take the following quiz—and ask your partner to answer it as well.

1. Your partner is two hours late and hasn't called to explain his absence. You are:

    a. Concerned but know he has a solid reason.

    b. Going to knock his block off when he comes home. That inconsiderate oaf!

    c. Pretty sure he's doing something he shouldn't be.

2. After eighteen years of working at the same job, your spouse suddenly announces she's going to quit and learn how to be a beekeeper. You:

   a. Tell her you never knew she had any interest in beekeeping, but will support her decision if it makes her happy.

   b. Can't understand why she'd make both of your retirements less financially comfortable by leaving her job before she's fully vested in her pension.

   c. Are wondering who the king bee is.

3. The two of you have taken a day off to ski. Halfway through, your husband says he's going to tackle a few runs separately. A few runs later, you spy your husband on the chair lift above you, convulsed in laughter with an attractive redhead. You:

   a. Are curious about the redhead, but you know your butt looks better in stretch pants than hers.

   b. Are pissed that he took off and left you on your own.

   c. Will make sure he has forgotten everything about that redhead by the time you get done with him.

4. Your partner comes home one night and announces that she's opened her own investment account. You:

   a. Think it's great that she wants to learn more about investing on her own.

   b. Are irritated that she'd open the account before talking to you about it.

   c. Are wondering who talked her into it.

Scoring: Calculate your score by giving yourself 5 points for every *a* answer, 3 points for every *b* answer, and 1 point for every *c* answer.

a _____ b _____ c _____

What Your Answers Mean

A perfect 20: Your level of trust and respect for your spouse is high and your self-confidence is strong. Your concern for your spouse's well-being is appropriate.

14–18: While you generally trust your spouse, you may not respect his decisions.

6–12: Your trust is shaky, and you find yourself thinking your spouse is a bonehead more often than not.

Below 6 points: You may have trusted and respected each other once, but you sure don't now. This relationship is headed for disaster.

Value Judgments

Do you remember that game about deciding which three things you'd most want to have if you were stranded on a desert island? If you ever played it in a big group, you might have been amazed at the things people said they couldn't live without.

Realizing what's important to us—whether they're tangible assets or the assurance of having good friends—is necessary for our own happiness as well as the health of our relationships. These things shape what we strive to accomplish during our lives. While it's not imperative for spouses' values to match, each needs to know what the other believes and finds important and be willing to honor these values and beliefs, if nothing else.

Check off all the statements below that you either agree with or believe that your spouse would agree with. Then cover your answers and have your spouse take the quiz.

Question	This Is Me	This Is My Partner
1. I'd rather have lots of friends than a few close companions.	❏	❏
2. I look forward to having enough money to do everything I want to do.	❏	❏
3. I put other people's needs before my own.	❏	❏
4. I would rather go out on the town than stay home.	❏	❏
5. I regularly give money to causes I believe are important.	❏	❏
6. I believe in God or a higher power.	❏	❏
7. Once I make up my mind to do something, I do it, regardless of what others may think.	❏	❏
8. I put aside some time every day for self-improvement and exercise.	❏	❏
9. I admire powerful, successful people.	❏	❏
10. Cuddling and snuggling with my partner is just as important as sex.	❏	❏
11. It is important to me to look good and feel good.	❏	❏
12. My checkbook has to balance down to the penny.	❏	❏
13. Having a close-knit family is important to me.	❏	❏

What Your Answers Mean

Ideally, there's some agreement between both of your answers. If you've checked off a statement that describes you, your spouse should have indicated it, too. If so, you have a pretty good idea of what makes each other tick. If not, you've probably already had some disagreements over things that you find important but that your spouse doesn't, or vice versa.

Dr. Lana's Secrets

There is no question about it, opposites attract. The trouble is they don't live together very well or for very long. The more similar your values, background, religious belief, and goals, the better chance you have of a happy long-term relationship.

Are You Willing to Compromise?

Having wildly disparate interests and values doesn't mean that you can't live happily ever after, but it does require higher levels of acceptance, tolerance, and flexibility than if you were more similar. Opposites attract just as easily as like marries like. The key to success is in understanding what the other believes, accepting it, and honoring it. You may have to agree to disagree on some things, and sometimes you may have to compromise.

Money issues were a major concern for Ellen and Roger. Ellen's parents had struggled financially all their lives, and she was intent on working as hard as she could so she wouldn't have to suffer like they did. At thirty-four, she had risen to the top, often at the expense of her relationship with Roger, who had a successful career of his own. Then Ellen was offered a new position with a big raise. The only catch: She would have to spend a majority of her time traveling to other cities. For Roger, it was the last straw. For him, having Ellen at home was much more important than the money.

"Money was important to me too, but it had nowhere near the significance for me as it did for Ellen," Roger says. "I realized we had never talked about how we felt about money and success in the years we were together. When we finally did discuss it, Ellen was astonished that I felt as I did. She had always assumed that I agreed with how she felt about work and financial success taking priority in her life. And I realized that I really resented Ellen for putting our relationship in second place."

Roger and Ellen decided it was time to draw up a financial plan. It forced them into setting both financial and personal goals. "I realized, once we started working on it, that I had no idea what my real goals were," Ellen says. "I was just working toward some magical place in the future where I felt I had made enough money to make me happy. I never thought that my goals were any different from Roger's."

Like Ellen and Roger, it's easy to assume that your partner believes what you believe, but this state is rarely true. While there are similarities, there are also subtle or not-so-subtle differences. Know your differences and appreciate that it is your differences that make you two distinct individuals and not a clone.

Dr. Lana's Secrets

There is a wonderful dialogue in Woody Allen's movie *Annie Hall* when he is asked during a therapy session how often he and his partner, played by Diane Keaton, have sex. Allen answers, "Hardly ever, probably three times a week." When the therapist asks Keaton the same question, she responds, "All the time, about three times a week."

While we may share an experience, our interpretation or the value we place on it is generally different. These differences are not a problem as long as we accept and honor one another's point of view.

Your Needs, Her Needs, Our Needs

Many serious disagreements between couples revolve around one of two issues: sex and money. Either there's not enough or there's too much. What these disagreements often indicate is a lack of understanding of what your and your partner's needs are, financially, emotionally, and physically. Needs that go unmet in any area can cause serious problems in a relationship.

What are your financial, emotional, and physical needs? Do you need lots of cuddling and an outward show of affection, or are you more the strong silent type? When you're having problems, is your spouse the first one you want to talk to, or do you work on them by yourself? Do you want to be a billionaire by age thirty, or are you comfortable with much less?

If you've never really thought about it, the quiz below will help you identify your needs in these three critical areas. Check the answer that best describes your behavior in each situation. Both you and your spouse should take this quiz. Then compare your answers.

My Emotional Needs Include	Important	Of Some Importance	Not Important at All
Having someone to turn to when I feel blue	❏	❏	❏
Knowing that my spouse understands me, even when I don't understand myself	❏	❏	❏
Having my accomplishments publicly acknowledged	❏	❏	❏
Being coddled and nursed when I'm sick	❏	❏	❏
Celebrating the good times	❏	❏	❏
Knowing that I have the complete support of my spouse	❏	❏	❏

My Physical Needs Include	Important	Of Some Importance	Not Important at All
Being able to show my affection in public	❏	❏	❏
Having a skilled lover who is willing to try new techniques	❏	❏	❏
Being well matched with my partner when it comes to sex drive	❏	❏	❏
Satisfying my lover as well as myself	❏	❏	❏
Lots of touching, intimate and not	❏	❏	❏
Having a partner who's more interested in satisfying me	❏	❏	❏

My Financial Needs Include	Important	Of Some Importance	Not Important at All
Knowing exactly where I stand with all of my accounts	❏	❏	❏
Having enough money so I can lead a comfortable lifestyle	❏	❏	❏
Having lots of credit so I can take that spur-of-the moment trip	❏	❏	❏
Having a solid financial plan	❏	❏	❏
Knowing that I can share financial responsibilities with my spouse	❏	❏	❏
Having enough money saved so I know I'll be O.K. even if the worst disaster strikes	❏	❏	❏

Everyone's Different

Some of us desire constant affection and confirmation. What one person finds nurturing, another would be smothered by. You might need a lot of cuddling when you make love, but your spouse may be very satisfied with significantly less.

Barbara, an effusive, outgoing type, found herself increasingly frustrated with what she felt was Michael's lack of responsiveness to her needs. In the privacy of their home, she couldn't be happier. But she bemoaned his unwillingness to display affection for her in public. As Michael describes it, "Barbara was raised in a very touchy-feely family. Everyone went around hugging each other. My family was more reserved; everything happened behind closed doors. It just doesn't feel right to me to be affectionate with Barbara in public. She tries to force it by grabbing my hand or rubbing my arm or back, and that makes me even more tense."

Because Barbara was looking for more overt shows of affection, she often missed Michael's more subtle displays, very specifically, the soulful way he could look into her eyes. "It was what attracted me to him in the first place," Barbara says. "He can turn my knees to jelly if he looks at me just right. I guess once we got married, I stopped looking for that look."

Barbara and Michael both decided to work on developing a better understanding of their emotional needs. Barbara learned to watch for Michael's more subtle displays and not to take his reluctance in touching her in public as a sign that something was wrong. Michael learned that Barbara needed him to be more demonstrative at times and to not feel like he was on display if he held his wife's hand in public.

Something Old, Something New

You or your partner may believe that you are the way you are and that's that. But, don't throw out the option of bettering yourself. Learning can occur as long as we live and what we learn affects our behavior. While personalities don't change, behaviors, attitudes and skills do.

Dr. Lana's Secrets

It shouldn't come as a big surprise that happy people have happy relationships. It's not the other way around. Relationships do not make anyone happy for very long. A healthy relationship adds to your happiness and fulfills certain needs, but don't look to a relationship or a partner to make you happy. That's up to you.

Learning to be a better partner actually increases your self-esteem and self-confidence. So, if your partner has a request, give it a try. Your personality won't be altered and your partner will appreciate your efforts.

Color Me Happy!

The best, most satisfying relationships are those built by individuals who have learned one of life's most important lessons: The key to happiness is being happy with yourself. Not giddy, ha-ha happy, but pleased and satisfied with who you are and what you're able to accomplish. Some people describe this happiness as feeling comfortable in their own skins.

Have you known people who are so pleased and content with who they are and their lot in life that nothing much ever seems to rattle them? Maybe you're one of them yourself. If so, you know exactly who bears the responsibility for the way you feel. You've been walking that walk for so many years that there's no doubt about it. It's no one else but you.

Being happy with yourself includes having a generally positive outlook on life. Some people, lucky ducks that they are, are born with an innate sense that they can rise above whatever life flings at them, that they can achieve success no matter what. They're like those round-bottomed inflatable toys that kids play with. It doesn't matter how many times or how hard you sock them; they just keep on bouncing back.

Affair Facts

Happiness researcher Mehaly Csikszentmihalyi found happy people have the same hassles and hazards in their lives as unhappy people. They face the same number of sorrows but experience normal life with more joy.

What often isn't apparent about these people is that they can have the same fears of self-doubt and self-confidence that the rest of us do. But they're also very capable of casting down those dancing demons and taking a broader view, of focusing on valid issues and concerns, and of pulling themselves through the tough times because they believe that they can and that it's worth it.

Spouses that accept responsibility for their own happiness are sheer joys to be around, even at times when things aren't going their way. They prefer to solve problems by being a part of the solution instead of casting blame and pointing fingers. They focus on what they can do to resolve things. They involve their spouses in the process, especially when the problem involves the two of them. But it's more in a spirit of joint problem solving than in blaming the other for what happened.

You were born together, and together you
shall be forevermore.
You shall be together when the white wings of death scatter
your days.
Ay, you shall be together even in the
silent memory of God.
But let there be spaces in your togetherness,
And let the winds of the heavens dance between you.

Love one another, but make not a bond of love:
Let it rather be a moving sea between the shores of your
souls.
Fill each other's cup but drink not from
one cup.
Give one another of your bread but eat not
from the same loaf.
Sing and dance together and be joyous,
but let each of one of you be alone,
Even as the strings of a lute are alone
though they quiver with the same music.

Give your hearts, but not into each
other's keeping.
For only the hand of Life can contain
your hearts.
And stand together yet not too near
together:
For the pillars of the temple stand apart,
And the oak tree and the cypress grow
not in each other's shadow.

—Kahlil Gibran, *The Prophet*

Supporting Your Partner's Growth

Of all the elements that make for a successful relationship, this building block is probably the most important. Maybe that's why it also requires the presence of the other elements to make it work. Supporting your partner's growth means being willing to put his needs before your own, and doing so when appropriate. You have to love someone a lot to be able to put his priorities before yours. It's tough to have your heart in it, or even want to do it, if you don't trust each other, don't know what the other values, or really care much about meeting each other's needs.

Affair Speak

Growth means developing new branches, deeper roots, and strong limbs. It means reaching, stretching, and yearning to touch the sun.

Being willing to support your spouse's growth is one of the most eloquent expressions of love that you can give. It requires a level of maturity that, quite frankly, most of us don't reach until we've lived a little and gone through some of life's bumps and wrong turns. It's a selfless act and a selfish one at the same time—selfless because it calls for submerging the ego to a certain extent and selfish because you're making an investment in something that should pay off very handsomely in the years to come.

The Least You Need to Know

➤ It's important to shape a relationship based on what you and your partner think is important, not what your parents or your siblings think is.

➤ Partners in successful relationships have a good idea of what they want and how to get there.

➤ If there are self-esteem issues in your life, you're more likely to attract someone with the same problems.

➤ You need to be able to trust your spouse with everything and believe that you can always find safe haven with this person.

➤ Know and respect your differences. Allow your individualities to be treasures in your togetherness.

➤ One of the surest ways of bringing happiness into a relationship is to be happy.

Chapter 7

Paying Attention to Your Love

In This Chapter

➤ Why paying attention is work

➤ Identifying time wasters

➤ Finding the time to pay attention

➤ Learning how to listen

The principal form that the work of love takes is attention.

—M. Scott Peck, *The Road Less Traveled*

Think back to how your current relationship started (hopefully, you can remember it!). After you first met, what moved things along between you? Chances are, you planned time to be together. You called each other. Maybe you sent cards and letters. You thought about each other and about the things you could do to win each other's hearts. In short, you created a spot in your lives by paying attention to what was happening between you.

Unfortunately, many people don't realize that the same effort they put forward in the beginning stages of a relationship must be continued for it to last. They shift their focus, sometimes intentionally, often not. They stop talking to each other and start spending more time away from one another. They stop sending the cards and the flowers. They spend little time planning ways to make their spouse's lives easier or more enjoyable. In short, they take things for granted and ultimately end up with a barren relationship.

The Work of Attention

Relationships never just happen. They have to be created. They take time and energy, and they take attention. Just like anything else, they flourish when you focus on them and flounder when you don't.

What does paying attention in a relationship really mean? Psychologist M. Scott Peck provided one of the most powerful explanations of what he calls "the work of attention" in his classic on love and relationships, *The Road Less Traveled*:

"When we love another we give him or her our attention; we attend to that person's growth. When we love ourselves, we attend to our own growth. When we attend to someone we are caring for that person. The act of attending requires that we make the effort to set aside our existing preoccupations...and actively shift our consciousness."

Dr. Lana's Secrets

Couples who are happy with the way they manage their time report that they spend between ten and eleven hours a week together. About half of this time goes to the business of living, which means planning time with friends or family, managing money, conferring about the kids or chatting about work.

They spend another five hours a week developing and maintaining intimacy in their relationship. This time is to pay attention to each other, and to learn about one another. It is not time spent on watching TV together, working out, reading the paper or talking about other people. It is time focused on knowing one another's deepest nature, or in a word, intimacy.

It seems like paying attention should be an easy thing to do, but it's actually very difficult, primarily because we're so easily distracted. Our priorities shift, our other responsibilities get in the way, and the time we spend actively involved in our relationships dwindles down.

Paying attention means giving one's mind to what is going on. It is being present in the moment with your mind fully engrossed in what your partner is saying, feeling, and doing. Paying attention—that is, eliminating all those tangential thoughts that intrude into the moment—is not a simple thing to do. Those little musings like, "Did I take the clothes out of the dryer?" "Has the dog been out?" "What time does the game start?" are all distractions. They are the opposite of paying attention.

Giving your partner your undivided attention is a big gift that requires discipline, energy, time, and devotion.

Dr. Lana's Secrets

If it seems like your parents had more time for recreation than you do, you're right. In 1973 the average person had 26.2 hours for leisure. By 1997 time away from work had dropped to 19.5 hours. That means they had about 7 hours more discretionary time a week than you do.

Because elective time is scarce, you have to be more deliberate in your choice of activities. You probably have several that are really not very significant but absorb chunks of your discretionary time, while meaningful connections are left to last and lost.

"I Don't Have Time"

Have you ever figured out how you spend your time? Most people have a loose idea of what they do and when, but it's usually a revelation to them when they actually put pen to paper and really account for all the hours in the day and how they fill them.

Identifying Your Time Gobblers

Want to see where your time goes? Then take a few minutes for the following quiz. It's based on one that originally appeared in *Walking* magazine and was designed to help people get past the claim of "I don't have time to exercise." You can use it to determine how much time you have to devote to your relationship.

1. Estimate the time you spend on household chores and errands. Estimate the average hours per week you spend on each item below, add them up, and circle the closest answer.

    Cooking: ___ hours/week

    Cleaning: ___ hours/week

    Laundry: ___ hours/week

    Yard work: ___ hours/week

    Home maintenance: ___ hours/week

    Other (such as washing/maintaining your car): ___ hours/week

Less than 4 hours/week . . . . 0 pts.

4–8 hours/week . . . . 1 pt.

9–12 hours/week . . . . 2 pts.

More than 12 hours/week . . . . 3 pts.

2. If you have children living at home, how old is the youngest?

No children under 18 years . . . . 0 pts.

12–17 years old . . . . 1 pt.

6–11 years old . . . . 2 pts.

0–5 years old . . . . 3 pts.

3. How many hours per week do you spend working? Include any formal employment, either in or out of the home, plus commuting time.

Not at all . . . . 0 pts.

Less than 15 hours/week . . . . 1 pt.

15–35 hours/week . . . . 2 pts.

36–50 hours/week . . . . 3 pts.

More than 50 hours/week . . . . 4 pts.

4. On average, how much time do you spend watching television, using the Internet (non-work related), or talking to friends on the phone each day?

Less than 30 minutes . . . . 0 pts.

About 1 hour . . . . 2 pts.

1–2 hours . . . . 3 pts.

More than 2 hours . . . . 4 pts.

5. How much time per week do you spend on other things that you consider necessary, such as doing volunteer work; participating in community events; exercising; attending your children's activities; or going to your house of worship, classes, or school?

Less than 2 hours/week . . . . 0 pts.

2–4 hours/week . . . . 1 pt.

5–7 hours/week . . . . 2 pts.

More than 7 hours/week . . . . 3 pts.

6. If you're formally employed, is your daily schedule flexible?

   Not formally employed . . . . 0 pts.

   Very flexible; I can come and go as I please . . . . 1 pt.

   Somewhat flexible with plenty of breaks . . . . 2 pts.

   Fairly rigid with fixed hours and some breaks . . . . 3 pts.

   Rigid hours with few breaks . . . . 4 pts.

7. How many children under age 12 or other dependent people (such as an aging or ill parent) are in your household who require your care?

   Give yourself 1 point for each.

8. Are other adults (spouse, family, friends, hired help) available to help with children, home care, cooking, and errands?

   Someone helps all the time . . . . 0 pts.

   I have help most days of the week . . . . 1 pt.

   I have occasional help . . . . 2 pts.

   I run the household alone . . . . 3 pts.

Your total: _____

What Your Answers Mean

The higher your point total, the greater the demands on your time. If you've scored 20 points or more, chances are that you shoulder a great deal of responsibility for keeping your household going. You might have small children or are taking care of an elderly parent. You may also have a demanding and inflexible job, whether you're working away from home or not. There generally doesn't seem to be enough time to get everything done.

If you scored in the 15 to 20 point range, your schedule is busy but probably not overwhelming. Your job may be flexible and reasonably demanding but not excessively so. You're involved in the community and/or in your kids' activities at a level that feels comfortable to you. Still, you often feel that your relationship with your spouse comes second to the rest of your responsibilities.

If your point total is in the 9 to 14 point range, your life is fairly low on the responsibility scale. People who score in this range are often young marrieds or recent graduates just starting their careers. They haven't shouldered a great deal of responsibility because there isn't much of it for them at this point. They generally have lots of time for leisure activities.

Scores of 13 or below usually indicate a lack of balance or a narrow focus on life. You might spend all your time working and leave all other responsibilities to your spouse. Or you really aren't aware of how you spend your time. If you're in this category and you still feel you don't have time to devote to your relationship, it's time for a wake-up call and your spouse will probably be the one to hand it to you.

Finding Time

Taking this quiz should have given you a better perspective on how you spend your time each day. If there really is more to do than you have time for, you may legitimately have only a few hours to spare when it comes to spending time with your partner.

Let's now look at what you can do to increase the amount of time you can spend paying attention to your relationship, based on where you scored.

Dr. Lana's Secrets

Having more takes more. Elevated expectations can lead to buying bigger homes, more gadgets, or new cars. Advertisers bombard us with an endless array of goods that we should want and can have for a price. The hidden cost is the amount of time and life's energy required to take care of them. It's easier to control wants than to satisfy them, since there is no end to what we are capable of wanting.

On the High End of Responsibility

If you always feel as if you're up to your eyeballs in work and commitments, your challenge is to off-load some of your responsibilities or eliminate some of your obligations.

People with point scores of 20 or above are fairly common in this day and age. And there may be good reasons why your life is so full. Maybe you've taken on a bigger load at work to get ahead or bought a big, new house that is far from your office and requires a long commute. Or you may be filling your life with activities just because they are the things you have always done.

Dr. Lana's Secrets

One of the modern dilemmas is having so many good opportunities that we want to seize them all. Do you want to go hear the Rolling Stones, would you like tickets to the football game, how about dinner with friends, or checking out that new movie? They all sound like fun. There are so many great experiences to be had that spending a quiet evening exchanging backrubs doesn't seem very exciting. Besides, you can always do that another time, right?

Interestingly, when people have love affairs, they pass up the concert tickets, the dinners with friends, or the game just to give their lover a backrub.

Buying Time

One of the first things you need to do is determine why you're as busy as you are. If your life is hectic because you took on too much without realizing it, decide where you can scale back or reassign some of what you do. Determine where your time is best spent and figure out ways to get the other things done. Try the following:

➤ Hiring someone to clean your house

➤ Eating out instead of in (with your spouse, of course!)

➤ Saying no to chairing the next volunteer event

➤ Getting a handyman to come by to take care of the "honey-do's"—the little things around the house that you need to get done but never find the time for

➤ Having your own kids, or the neighborhood kids, mow and rake your lawn

➤ Taking your car to the car wash instead of washing it yourself

➤ Having your laundry picked up and delivered

➤ Hiring a bookkeeper to pay bills and reconcile your bank statement

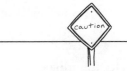

Bumps Ahead

If you're having problems at home, don't continue to use your busy schedule as an excuse for not addressing them.

Other Creative Solutions

People with lots of responsibilities often have to get creative when it comes to finding time with their spouses. Here's a few ways to do it:

➤ Call your spouse during the day. You don't have to spend a lot of time—just a two-minute phone call to say, "I'm thinking of you."

➤ Don't rely on home-cooked meals. Even if you're a health nut, you can find healthy take-out. Use the time that would have been spent on meal preparation for the two of you to talk and snuggle.

➤ If you travel for business, find ways to take your spouse with you. Plan your schedule so you can stay over a weekend together.

➤ Change your exercise routine if you generally exercise alone. Find an activity that you and your spouse can do together, even if it's not something you'd usually want to do.

Since your life is so full, don't leave things to chance. You will have to schedule time to be with your spouse, especially if your spouse's life is as hectic as yours.

Dr. Lana's Secrets

One of my favorite routines with my husband is our brisk twenty-minute morning walk. It is good exercise and a good time to connect with one another at the beginning of the day. It is just the two of us, listening, talking, and walking.

It's nice to spring a romantic weekend getaway as a surprise, or schedule it together. If you can't go overnight, then steal away for a day, just the two of you, and don't tell a soul. Your little secret adds excitement.

Too many couples who are very busy just don't seem to find the time to do anything nice for themselves. If this attitude describes the two of you, don't let it continue for much longer. Life can change in a heartbeat.

Busy but Not Crazy

If this describes you, then your challenge is to pay more attention to the distractions in your life and determine whether all of them are really worth your time.

People in this category generally have time to devote to their partners and may actually spend a great deal of time with them. The problem here is not so much finding the time to pay attention, but being aware of the things that distract you from connecting with your partner. For example, how many hours a week do you spend on the following:

➤ Watching television. More than two hours a day in front of the tube, even in the company of your spouse, is too much. Try limiting your viewing to an hour a day and spend that other hour looking into the eyes of the one you love. And don't turn on the TV for background noise the moment you get home. Television is one of the greatest distractions in our world today. When it's on, you cannot hear yourself think and conversation is diluted.

➤ Working on the computer at home. The computer is another wonderful diversion, and it's easy to spend hours searching for information. Search your partner for some new information, instead.

➤ Volunteering, taking classes, or participating in other activities away from home and spouse. Try cutting back on your volunteer time, or find things the two of you can do together. Giving of yourself is a noble endeavor, but be sure you aren't giving yourself to everyone but your mate. Maybe this year the two of you can work the Thanksgiving-dinner line together, instead of you chairing the committee that plans it.

➤ Cooking and housekeeping. If you bear the responsibility for your family's meals, streamline your meal-preparation time. Maybe you can prepare a weekly menu plan and stick to it. If you're a cook-from-scratch person, learn how to work some convenience items into your repertoire. If you're the primary housekeeper and want to keep it that way, try spreading out your duties, rather than saving everything for one day. Or take a tip from Heloise and focus on the things that are most important to you, rather than embarking on a complete cleaning every time.

On the Low End of Responsibility

If you have lots of leisure time, your challenge is to spend that time wisely.

Lucky you! Life isn't terribly overwhelming, is it? Take advantage of this period because you may very well get busier later. Now is the time to develop good relationship skills; you'll be glad you did when your responsibilities increase. Focus on these:

➤ Spending less time with your friends and more time with your partner. If the two of you regularly go out as a couple with a group of people, try leaving the group behind occasionally. Socializing with a large group splits your attention.

➤ Developing mutual interests. Try to find activities that allow you to engage each other while you're doing them. Save some energy just to be interested in him or her.

Bumps Ahead

Spending interactive time together is important, but don't spend so much time in one another's company that you have no time for yourself or your independent interests. Too much of a good thing is still too much.

➤ Managing your money together. This is a prime time for developing a budget and learning how to live with it. Money is a reflection of your values and your dreams. Learn how you think and feel about money. Talk about retirement even if it's many years away. What you do now is going to determine just how comfortable your retirement will be. Don't put the entire burden for planning it on your spouse. Even if you don't like to work with financial concepts or don't feel that you're very good with them, get involved and stay involved in this process to learn about yourself, your partner, and your future.

➤ Limiting the amount of time you spend watching television, working on the computer, and talking to friends on the phone. When you have a lot of free time in your life, it's easy to fritter it away.

Off Balance or Out of Focus

Your challenge is to equalize relationship responsibilities and develop an appropriate focus on life.

If you scored at the bottom of the responsibility grid, it doesn't necessarily mean that you don't have a lot things going on in your life. In fact, you may be exceptionally busy. But your life isn't in balance, or you have a bad case of tunnel vision. It's not healthy to spend sixty hours a week developing Web sites. Nor should you be a full-time caretaker, with no time to care for yourself. It's time to come up for air, expand your horizons, and balance your participation in your relationship. Your to-do list includes:

Affair Facts

When do couples talk the most to each other? Researchers pin it to the third date and the year before they divorce.

➤ Setting strict limits on the amount of time you spend at work. If you're consistently putting in ten-hour days or working seven days a week, you are a workaholic and it's time to decide if working round-the-clock is really the way you want to spend your life.

➤ Seeking assistance for taking care of children, parents, and other household responsibilities.

➤ Limiting the time you spend volunteering, taking classes, or exercising on your own. Again, these are all wonderful pursuits, but it's easy to let them become out of balance.

Dr. Lana's Secrets

Taking care of the kids, taking care of your boss, taking care of the house, taking care of the car, or taking care of the garden can take up all the caring you have. Don't get so immersed in taking care of everybody and everything else that you neglect yourself and your partner.

Every year shell-shocked women and men sit in my office, stunned by the discovery that someone else has been taking care of their spouse while they've been taking care of the kids, the house, the job, and whatever. Don't let this happen to you. The best thing you can do for your kids is to take care of your marriage.

Managing Change

Once you've identified what you want to change in your life, it may take some time to actually enact these changes. In fact, you're probably best off if you tackle them as an ongoing process, rather than making one clean sweep of things, especially if you're planning to make a lot of changes. Change occurs when you decide to change. Don't create a monster that's so huge that you wind up unwilling or incapable of taking it on. Break your goals into smaller objectives and tasks so you can get started today.

Dr. Lana's Secrets

Change is constant. Continually review how you're spending your time and keep making conscious choices about the value of the activities to which you're committing yourself. An activity or event that might have great value to you this year may drop to the bottom of the list next year, so keep rechecking.

Make a Game Plan

After completing the responsibilities quiz, Ken and Terri decided to map out the changes they wanted to make. Although both had some individual priorities, they shared their most important concern. They felt they needed a game plan to keep them on course with one another. One section of their plan looked like this:

Goal: Create more intimacy in our relationship

First objective: Spend five hours a week giving each other our undivided attention

Task: Record on each of our weekly calendars a two-hour weeknight date, a one-hour Saturday or Sunday morning date, and a two-hour weekend date.

Who's responsible: Both

Task: Mark each calendar a month ahead

Completion date: First of next month

Second objective: Create a place to spend quiet focused time at home

Task: Rearrange the living room so there is a place for private intimate talking

Who's responsible: Terri

Completion date: Two weeks from today

Goal: Establish privacy boundaries with the kids

Task: Post a calendar on the refrigerator with Mom and Dad's private time clearly marked

Task: Pick up a video for the kids to watch during date night times

Who's responsible: Ken

Ken and Terri knew they wanted to be closer and decided intimacy was a top priority. They agreed that five hours a week was a reasonable amount of time to be intimate with each other. They also knew that their busy schedules and their kids could absorb all their time. By determining what they wanted to accomplish and assigning responsibilities and completion dates, they were able to reach their goal quickly.

Focusing on one goal at a time and being specific gave Ken and Terri an immediate sense of accomplishment, which helped them stay focused. By planning their time together, they were able to tell other people when they already had a commitment and could truly put their relationship first.

Next Steps

While you're working on changing your schedules and rearranging your priorities, you might notice something else happening. Your feelings of not being connected to your partner may be dissipating. Chances are you're looking at each other more and thinking about each other with pleasure.

So here's the $64,000 question: Are you communicating effectively? And are you listening effectively? Do you feel connected?

Dr. Lana's Secrets

One item in your relationship that should take precedence over most others is time to fight. Don't laugh. Counselors know that couples who "fight" with each other to solve their differences are happier in their love lives than those who put off their conflicts or don't find mutually acceptable solutions.

We often believe that people who are happy with each other don't fight much, but the reverse is true. There is a 90 percent probability that if you don't argue and hash out solutions, you'll split up. Healthy fighting is not ugly, insulting, rude, violent, or hurtful.

Talk Isn't Cheap

There hasn't been a book written on relationships yet that doesn't stress the importance of communication, and you'd be living on the planet Neptune if you could honestly say that you didn't realize how important it was until now. Let's face it. We live in a world in which it's vital to communicate well, both professionally and personally. If you have problems expressing yourself, you know about it. If you're not good at saying what you mean, you're probably having difficulties at work and at home. Rarely do communication problems come as a great surprise to anyone.

If you've been with your partner for any length of time, you're aware of the differences between your communication styles. You might be an "outpourer" while your spouse is more reserved and restrained. This disparity explains part of the communication dilemma, but the issue goes deeper. What's perhaps more important than talking is listening. And that's where most couples fail in the communication arena.

Dr. Lana's Secrets

The more similar your communication styles, the better your chances of feeling emotionally satisfied. If your natural levels of expressiveness are vastly different, you will need to learn a combined style that bridges the gap. Generally, women tend to talk more and faster and men less and slower. So, slow down your talking and allow more time for listening if you are doing more than 60 percent of the talking.

Listen Up

Yes, it's important to convey your message clearly and directly. Yes, it's vital to tell your partner what's on your mind. You can't expect him or her to know what you're thinking about unless you do. But you're wasting your time and your breath if your partner doesn't know how to listen with understanding.

The most common mode of expressing attention is by listening, and this can be difficult to do well. Active listening requires focus, concentration, genuine interest, and caring. It means not only hearing what your partner is saying but also taking note of how it's being said. It requires your real involvement. You have to listen to compare her tone of voice to her words. Watch how she's gesturing, how she's sitting, whether she's at ease or tense. You're taking an active role in the conversation at this moment, not by talking, but by observing and paying attention to all the components of your partner's communications.

Dr. Lana's Secrets

Since both of you will continue to grow and change and have new experiences, you will have to keep listening to keep learning in order to know one another's deepest nature.

By listening intently to your partner, you're showing her how important she is and how much you care for her. In fact, it's one of the most loving things you can do. It requires you to put your own issues and ego on hold and train your entire being on your partner. You can't hold your own little conversations in your mind and listen attentively at the same time. Set aside your self and enter your partner's world. Share his world with him for a while. You become one with your partner, if only temporarily.

If you're successful at listening, you'll notice something almost immediately. It's tough! Listening well requires training your focus and keeping up with everything you hear and see. It can be quite a workout, both mentally and physically, especially if the conversation is long and intense. But what you gain from listening well is worth the effort.

The other thing you'll notice is that effective listening enables more effective communication. Just spending the time to really listen to your partner can help you gain a clearer understanding of what's on his mind, even if he's not a good communicator. Matching nonverbal communication with what's being said can help you gain a more complete picture from a reticent partner. The more you practice, the more comfortable both you and your partner will become in expressing your emotions and developing intimacy.

You might be wondering whether you'll always have to work this hard at your relationship. The answer is yes. You'll always have to pay attention to how things are going between you and your spouse and work at making changes and adjustments. The time does come when effective listening becomes second nature, but it never really gets easy. But you'll find that the things you do come easier the more you do them, and the payoffs are definitely worth the effort.

The Least You Need to Know

➤ Paying attention to your partner is one of the most important things you can do to keep your relationship healthy.

➤ "I don't have time" is not a valid excuse. We often spend way too much time on activities that are time wasters, not relationship savers. Take the time now to identify ways to free up more time for paying attention to your relationship and your partner.

➤ Communication is essential in a good relationship.

➤ Learning how to listen well is even more important.

Chapter 8

Knowing Where "No" Is

> ## In This Chapter
>
> ➤ Why boundaries are important
>
> ➤ How to determine where they should be
>
> ➤ Deciding when to compromise
>
> ➤ Putting your egos aside

Oh, give me land, lots of land,
Under starry skies above,
Don't fence me in.

—Cole Porter (from the 1944 film *Hollywood Canteen*)

Ah, the image of the American cowboy. Booted feet planted firmly on dusty Western ground, trail-worn eyes surveying the vast sweep of prairie land before him. Not a fence line or territorial marker in sight. It's an image that evokes the American dream of life, liberty, and the pursuit of happiness.

But here's the kicker on that dream: As much as we may revere or fantasize over the idea of unbounded liberty, most of us are actually much more comfortable when our lives are governed by some rules and regulations, legally imposed or not. Men and women, as they say, are creatures of habit, and our habits are largely based on our sense of what's right and wrong and on what might happen to us if we step over the line.

Drawing the Line

So the same theory should apply to our relationships, right? It should, but it often doesn't. Most couples don't address boundary issues until a partner steps out of bounds. Then all hell can and often does break loose. The wronged partner can't believe how callous and unfeeling her mate is for not knowing that having lunch with her girlfriend would upset her. The partner that got his toes burnt feels like he's getting a lot of grief for doing something that he didn't know was unacceptable.

One reason that partners don't discuss boundaries is they're not aware of the importance of doing so. The other reason is that many people don't have a clear sense of what they find objectionable until it actually happens.

Affair Facts

One boundary that is nearly universal is fidelity. Throughout the world, one omnipresent expectation is that partners will only have intercourse with one another and no one else. This boundary is discussed and steadfastly reaffirmed (but not necessarily adhered to) by most couples.

Affair Facts

Boundaries are often in place to protect resources we consider necessary for our sense of well-being, and that is why the most hotly contested boundaries are about things like money, time, energy, and sex.

What Makes Us Angry

We generally get cranked up over our partner's relationships with other people, especially if we're the jealous type. More often than not, it's over encounters with the opposite sex. But boundaries can get stretched any time you get jealous or upset over behavior that you think is less than acceptable or that doesn't meet your needs. More than one spouse has blown up over his partner's spending more time with her friends than with him. And who knows, you might resent the amount of time your partner spends with his dog.

Don't Fence Me In!

Setting boundaries in a relationship may seem restrictive and confining. If done correctly, however, quite the opposite is true. Couples who work together to decide what is and isn't acceptable behavior in a relationship often report that it gives them more freedom than they had before. They're aware of the rules that govern their behavior, and they know what the consequences could be if they break them.

For Glenn, it was a relief to find out that Carmel really didn't want to know all the money details that he'd been providing. "I always felt like I should give Carmel a lot of information about how I spend every penny," Glenn says. "I based my behavior on expectations from a prior relationship, and I just assumed that Carmel would want the same thing from me."

Dr. Lana's Secrets

Structure provides freedom. Healthy boundaries are those that provide guidelines about what works the best within a committed relationship. For instance, agreeing that you will pool your money and spend that money on living expenses and on tangible objects that create a home and not on clothing or playing golf, for instance, is an example of a typical boundary.

"When we decided to get married," Glenn continued, "she expected us to draw up an annual budget and live by it, and if we did it right, the only things we'd have to talk about were big expenditures or items not covered in the budget, not everyday stuff."

Defining Boundaries

Boundaries have to be consensual to work. If one partner dictates a boundary and the other feels that it calls for too much accountability or a reining in of individuality, little will be gained. The free spirit will continue to do what he likes, to the dismay of the boundary-loving spouse.

Dr. Lana's Secrets

Successful partners understand that boundaries are necessary. When partners agree on boundaries, they are nearly invisible. But partners who don't know where the boundaries are usually find them the hard way. She may be hopping mad that he made plans to go golfing on Saturday without checking first, or he may go ballistic when he sees her Nordstrom's bill. Often couples have the same fight over and over because they have not negotiated mutually acceptable boundaries.

Boundaries have to be sincerely shared, and they have to be open to renegotiation or they do more harm than good. To define the boundaries that you'd like to have in your relationship, you have to first decide how you feel about a number of things. Does it bother you when your spouse stays out at night without calling you? Would you prefer her not to have drinks after work with her coworkers, especially if they're male? How about your money management styles? Does it drive you nuts when he doesn't balance the checkbook? Do you expect to have a say in significant purchases or investments?

Other areas that may need boundaries in your relationship include

➤ Time spent on leisure activities

➤ Involvement with family members

➤ Time with the kids

➤ Commitments to hobbies, clubs, and volunteer projects

The Boundaries Quiz

Although there are many areas of your relationship that you may want to consider when determining what your boundaries should be, the quiz below can get you started. The first set of questions gauges your response to your spouse's behavior. The second set reflects what you think is acceptable for your behavior. Take it yourself and then ask your spouse to do the same.

Your Reactions to Your Spouse's Behavior

1. An old girlfriend asks your husband out for drinks. Your reaction?

    a. No way! I don't care how good of friends they were.

    b. I might feel a little jealous, but their meeting for a couple of hours at a bar doesn't threaten me.

    c. Sure, no big deal.

2. Your partner's office decides to throw a big party to celebrate a large contract. It's going to be held at a nearby resort, and spouses aren't invited. You're against it. What would your response be?

    a. You really think she shouldn't go.

    b. In your opinion, the people at her office need some attitude adjustments, but you understand why she should go. After telling her that you'd prefer she not attend, you don't raise any resistance.

    c. Have a good time.

3. Your spouse has developed a friendship with a coworker of the opposite sex. You're getting ready to go out of town, and she asks you if it's O.K. for the two of them take in a movie that you have no interest in seeing. Your response?

    a. Nope, sorry. You really don't think men and women can just be friends, even as much as you trust her.

    b. Although you really don't like the idea, it's O.K. with you if they go during the day.

    c. Sure, go ahead.

4. Most spouses like to be informed if their partners are going to be late coming home. Where's your tolerance on this?

   a. I expect a call if he's going to be at all late.

   b. A few minutes late, no big deal.

   c. He should call only if he'll be a half-hour or more late.

5. You share a joint checking and savings account. What's your tolerance level concerning your spouse's check writing and withdrawals?

   a. He should ask me before he does anything.

   b. We should talk about anything over a certain amount.

   c. He can do whatever he wants as long as there are sufficient funds in our accounts and he records the transactions.

Your Behavior

6. An old boyfriend calls you and asks you out for drinks. Your response?

   a. I would feel uncomfortable and would turn him down.

   b. I'd ask my husband first to see if he's O.K. with it.

   c. I'm ready to go!

7. The guys decide to have an impromptu touch football game. It's on a Saturday morning, which is when you're usually doing household chores with your spouse. What do you tell your buddies?

   a. Can't do it in the a.m. Can we change it to the afternoon?

   b. Let me talk it over with my wife. I'll get back to you.

   c. What time and where?

8. You're working late and just about ready to wind things up when your supervisor (who's of the opposite sex) invites you out for dinner. Everyone else has gone home, and you know it's just the two of you. You:

   a. Decline politely. People might jump to the wrong conclusions.

   b. Call your spouse and ask whether she minds.

   c. Call your spouse to tell her you're grabbing a bite before you come home.

9. You're running late. How do you handle it?

   a. I'll call as soon as I know I'll be late, and I'll keep her updated every few minutes or so until I get home.

   b. I'll call and give her an idea of how late I think I'll be. If I go past that period, I'll call again.

   c. I'll call and give her an approximate idea of when I'll be home and tell her to go on with her plans.

10. You need to withdraw some cash from your joint savings account. What do you do?

    a. Ask my spouse if it's O.K. and tell him what it's for.

    b. Tell my spouse that I'm making a withdrawal and the amount so we can keep our account balanced.

    c. Withdraw now; ask later.

Scoring: Assign the following points to each answer: 3 points for each a answer, 2 points for each b answer, and 1 point for each c answer. Enter your totals here:

____my behavior   ____my partner's behavior

What Your Answers Mean

25–30 points: Your own boundaries are strict, and you expect your spouse to be very accountable as well.

20–24 points: You have well-defined boundaries with some flexibility, and you expect it in return from your spouse.

15–19 points: You may want stronger boundaries in some areas than others, but you're willing to be flexible about it.

Below 14 points: You aren't going to hold your spouse accountable for much, nor do you want to be.

If the score you gave yourself is higher or lower than the one you gave your partner, there are differences between how you expect your partner to behave and what you believe is appropriate behavior for yourself. Generally, one partner will expect higher accountability from the other partner. Rarely are our expectations higher for our own behavior. Not only isn't this terribly fair, it's bound to create problems if one spouse feels unfairly constrained while the other thinks he should be free to fly like a bird.

Take a look at how you answered the questions related to relationships with other people and at those that address issues such as accountability to the relationship and financial responsibility. Are they consistent? You may desire strict boundaries when it comes to seeing other people, but not expect your spouse to consult you when she writes a check. Knowing your differences is important when it comes to actually placing your relationship boundaries.

Mapping the Variables

Once you have a general idea of what your expectations are, it's time to consider all the little details. There may be issues you feel very strongly about regardless of the situation. Would it be a problem if your spouse socialized with an old boyfriend, or is it just the one she almost married before she met you? Are you a little more tolerant of his mixing it up with coworkers when you're out of town? Is the cat never welcome on the bed, or just when you're making love? (You might as well map everything out while you're at it.)

Think about the boundaries that you'd like to put in place. Be very specific, but leave room for flexibility. If you don't mind your spouse seeing an old flame for lunch at the local deli, say so. But if having lunch at the Ritz Carlton downtown would spin your top, say that, too. If an afternoon watching football with the guys isn't a big deal unless it continues into the evening, get it out in the open.

Affair Speak

A boundary is a real or understood limit. Boundaries are guidelines; they are based on agreement and mutual respect. They are not externally enforceable. They have to be open to interpretation, and they have to be negotiable.

There are thousands of situations and dynamics to be considered. Try to cover as many of the who, what, when, where, and whys as possible. The clearer you can be, the less room there will be for boundary disputes. But disputes are inevitable—and healthy. That said, as hard as you try, you'll never cover all the details when it comes to defining boundaries. Rather than dragging the process out until you're both exhausted, focus on the most important areas first.

Placing Your Markers

When's the best time to put boundaries in place? The sooner you begin the process of placing, moving, and removing boundaries, the better. Introduce this process in your relationship as early as possible. Go too long, and you'll end up feeling like you're navigating a minefield, never quite sure where it's safe and where it's not.

Boundaries Are Not Stagnant

Those that are important at one time in your relationship may be meaningless or constraining at another time.

Georgia and Miles had agreed early in their relationship to go out on weekend nights only as a couple. Over the years, several of their friends had divorced and were now solo. Georgia found it difficult to get together with two of her lifetime friends, Janice and Ellen, because of complex schedules. Miles heard her explaining on the telephone that she couldn't go to the ballet with Janice because it was on Friday night. After she got off the phone, Miles asked Georgia why she didn't go with Janice.

Georgia explained that she doesn't go out with single friends on a weekend night. Miles said he would have no objection if she wanted to go. Georgia and Miles changed their boundaries about weekend time. They realized the boundary they had set early on when they were establishing themselves as a couple was obsolete now.

Recheck your boundaries from time to time. Limits that were once important may now be unnecessary and confining.

Submerge Those Egos!

Most couples define their boundaries only after they've had a few (or many) blowups. When one of them finally suggests that it might be good to discuss some boundaries, the spouse who has erred resists the process because he feels like he's being punished for his behavior. Then his partner gets upset because he isn't willing to toe up to her behavior. Ego takes on ego, and the ensuing battle of wills goes nowhere fast.

Put your emotions on the back burner when you approach boundary setting. Your first goal is to get the issues between you out in the open, and that's always a good thing. Once you've heard what you both have to say about specific issues, you can decide what you can and can't do about them. Remember that this isn't a turf war. It's a sharing of beliefs about how you want your relationship to function.

The Art of the Compromise

Sometimes you have to give a little something to get a little something. When it comes to boundary setting, this is especially true. To be successful, you're going to have to relinquish some things that you were dead set on, or modify your position until it's acceptable to your spouse. Your spouse has to do so, too. That's where the compromise part comes in.

When setting boundaries, pick your battles. Focus on the areas that are most important to you and be ready to give in on areas that are less important. This is when your best negotiating skills will be the most challenged. Keep talking to your spouse. Make sure she or he understands why a particular issue is so important.

If you can't get an agreement, experiment a little. Try it his way, then talk about how you felt. Some things we think we feel strongly about are really not all that bothersome when we experience them.

Collette had been adamant about Jeffery being home for dinner at 6:00 even if it meant his going back to the office afterward. He felt frustrated and angry that he had to leave when another hour at the office would mean being able to stay home for the evening. She agreed to an experiment for one month. She would feed the kids first and wait to have dinner with Jeffrey so that he could finish up at work.

At the end of the month, she agreed it really had not been a problem. She realized that her father had been home for dinner at 5:30 every night, and so she just thought that was the way it should be. They negotiated a new boundary that was more flexible and a better fit for the reality of their lifestyle.

You may find yourself at loggerheads in certain areas. If you do, experiment with different options until you find something that you both can tolerate. Try not to let these disagreements bog you down or make you want to abandon your efforts completely.

Remember the purpose of negotiating your boundaries, which in this case is the comfort you can derive from a clearly defined relationship. It may take some time, and most likely more than one argument or disagreement over what the decision should be, to get there. There will be times when you'll find the process more exasperating than helpful, but in the long run, you'll be glad you went through it.

Adjusting the Lines

As you continue your relationship with your partner, it's inevitable that you will want to modify your boundaries, eliminate some, or establish new ones. For these reasons, it's a good idea to walk the lines from time to time. Keep communications open; don't just assume that once a boundary is placed, it's there for life. Few things are that permanent, and relationship boundaries shouldn't be.

The Least You Need to Know

➤ It's important to know what's acceptable and not acceptable in your relationship.

➤ Setting boundaries involves determining your own feelings in a number of areas.

➤ Spouses often disagree on appropriate behavior.

➤ Boundaries should be firm yet flexible. Don't treat the process as if you're Moses delivering the Ten Commandments.

Sex, Sex, and More Sex

When things don't work well in the bedroom, they don't work well in the living room either.

—William H. Masters

It's a pretty good bet that William H. Masters knew what he was talking about. After all, Masters and his wife, Virginia Johnson, once filmed and monitored some seventy-five hundred female orgasms and twenty-five hundred male orgasms for one of their studies on what makes us tick sexually. Among their conclusions was the idea that the more satisfied people are in the bedroom, the happier they are in general. (Masters and Johnson also found that the orgasms women achieved through masturbation were usually more satisfying than those reached through intercourse. This discovery had a lot to do with the sexual revolution of the 1960s and 1970s...but that's another story.)

Sex, more than anything else, is the fuel that fires our love and keeps our relationships going. It's the rare marriage that fails when the sex is good and plentiful. When sex is absent, it's almost always a sure indication that something is wrong or about to be wrong.

Such a logical conclusion. And we know it's true. When we're sexually satisfied, the world looks brighter. A good romp between the sheets soothes us, settles us down, and sweetens our dispositions. Our intimate moments make us forget—even if only temporarily—all the tugs and pulls on our relationship, all the little spats and disagreements we heap on each other because it's easy to do so. Sexual intimacy brings us closer together and helps to develop the deep bonds that allow us to face the world as a couple.

One of the most fundamental keys to a successful marriage is keeping the flames between you burning strongly and consistently. The desire you feel for one another will wax and wane over the years, but it needs to be maintained at some level for you to want to continue the commitment to your relationship.

Affair Facts

The all-important sense of connection comes primarily from intimate touching. Lovers hold a special place in one another's hearts, saving that special intimate union of making love together to affirm and reaffirm their physical and emotional attachment to one another.

Birds Do It, Bees Do It, and You'd Better Keep Doing It, Too!

Remember the early days when you first met? Remember the yearning and the burning desire you both felt? Chances are you couldn't get enough of each other, and you spent every possible minute exploring just how deep each other's wells were.

It's at the beginning of a relationship that sex is most frequent. Our bodies are pumped so full of the chemicals of arousal and desire that it almost can't be anything but. We feel electrically charged, so desirous of the other that there's little that we won't do to ensure our partner's availability.

Affair Facts

Is getting older an excuse for waning interest in sex? Not really. Frequency may diminish, but our desire for intimate encounters shouldn't. Experts encourage older men and women to keep on making love for both its psychological and physiological benefits. According to the Janus Report on Sexual Behavior, people in their seventies, eighties, and nineties who have a sexual relationship report that it's gratifying physically and emotionally and an important part of their relationship.

These are wonderful feelings, but they can't last forever. Most people can't function at such a high state of arousal for long. Eventually, our calming, sedative chemicals kick in, and we settle down—sometimes just a little, other times a lot.

This is the point when many people believe that true love actually begins, but it's also when sex can become boring. Without our chemical high, our once-passionate acts can seem ordinary, routine, and perfunctory. We stop trying so hard, and we begin to take things for granted. The sexy lingerie gets shelved in favor of the comfortable jammies. Romantic, candlelit dinners become twenty-minute stuff sessions with our eyes glued to the TV screen. Instead of making sure we end the evening on a high note, we're now too tired to get anything going. Gotta get up early. Better get our rest.

There's nothing wrong with a relationship settling into a routine, but that routine has to include a commitment to maintaining quality intimate contact. Maybe it's not intercourse every night. Maybe it's cuddling and snuggling. Maybe it's mutual masturbation. Maybe it's one partner giving the other a sensual massage. Whatever it is, make sure it happens.

Make Intimacy a Priority

Scheduling and planning are integral parts of contemporary life. Scheduling a time for sex is no different than reserving time for other activities that are important.

You may be wincing at the idea of scheduling sex, but try it. Couples who try scheduling time for sex seldom go back to relying on spontaneity. They reach a level of agreement about the importance of intimacy and decide to maintain their intimate contact at that level or something close to it. You will find the anticipation is part of the fun.

If it comes down to the date and time and you don't want to make love, then reschedule, but at least spend some time touching and talking.

Dr. Lana's Secrets

A variety of sexual interactions should be part of a couple's intimate repertoire. Sport sex; sensual sex; sexual fantasy role-playing; and long, slow intimate lovemaking are all part of a healthy sexual menu. A satisfying sex life is the best prevention for infidelity. If you're really serious about affair proofing your relationship, keep sex in the foreground of your daily life.

"Are You Free Next Friday at 2?"

For most couples there's no other way to ensure that they'll find the time for quality intimate encounters. Think of it like scheduling time for exercise. The only difference is that you're setting aside time for exercise of a more intimate nature.

Couples who plan their intimate time find that they enjoy the added element of anticipation in their relationships. They look forward to their time together. Knowing that time has been set aside for intimacy also builds feelings of value and worth in a relationship. It also allows for planning ahead and doing things for your spouse that you may not ordinarily find the time to do.

"When we first decided to schedule intimate time, I found my head just full ideas for the special moments I wanted to orchestrate for Mimi," says J. D. "Now that I knew when we'd be together, I could really plan for it. One time, I had a complete dinner catered for the two of us while we luxuriated in our hot tub. Another evening, she had a massage therapist visit us at home, table and everything. Neither of us felt the need to elevate every one of our encounters to these heights, but it sure gave us the time to make plans when we wanted to."

Other possible activities for couples on a schedule include

➤ Spending an evening at that bed and breakfast you always wanted to visit.

➤ Enjoying a quick tryst at the five-star hotel in the heart of the city, followed by room service.

➤ Picking him (or her) up at the office in a limousine. Even if you can't afford to hire a driver, meet your spouse halfway once in awhile and drive home together. Interesting things can happen in a car, chauffeured or not.

Bumps Ahead

One reason sex becomes boring is partners stop putting thought into making it interesting. In the beginning, there is a lot of exploring and experimenting; then after a while, routines set in and so does boredom.

Scheduling can be as informal as agreeing to spend a night a week at home together while someone takes care of the kids. Or you may find that you have to develop a rigid schedule, specifying exact dates and times. It doesn't much matter how formal or informal you make your schedule. What does matter is that you adhere to whatever schedule the two of you set.

Revising Our Expectations

If you've depended on one type of intimacy for most of time you've been together as a couple, it's probably time to expand your horizons. Too many couples get their noses bent out of joint when the amount of time they have to spend together doesn't match their expectations of what they'll be able to accomplish during that time. If all you have is twenty minutes, make the most of it. Don't get upset because you don't have time for a full menu of sex. Maybe there's only enough time for one spouse to reach orgasm. Giving can be as nice as getting, as long as things stay in balance between the two of you. Just don't let brief encounters become your only encounters.

Affair Facts

The 1994 report *The Social Organization of Sexuality* says of women who always experience orgasm, 65 percent report they are extremely happy; on the other hand, only 8 percent who do not have orgasms are extremely happy.

Dr. Lana's Secrets

Many women deny that having an orgasm is important, but women who regularly orgasm are happier with themselves and their partners than women who seldom orgasm, reports sex researcher E. Laumann.

It is important for both men and women to find ways to reach orgasm with one another. If you are not currently having orgasms during sex, get some books, watch some videos, or experiment with masturbation and discover how to achieve this pleasurable high.

Making the Best of the Situation

Another way to work toward a consistent level of intimacy in your relationship is to take advantage of every situation in which there's a potential for intimate contact. Remember, it isn't necessary to have intercourse to be intimate. Think back to your high school days. You may think you're too old for some hot action in a closet or some heavy groping in your car, but it's almost guaranteed to ignite the same fires now as it did when you were younger, especially if one partner initiates the contact when the other least expects it.

When Scott decided to fulfill a lifelong dream and accept an offer to be visiting professor at a nearby university, he knew his decision would eat into the amount of time he could spend with Kendra. "Being the new guy on the block, I was given less-than-choice teaching assignments, which kept me away from home most evenings during the week," Scott says. "But Kendra found a way to find some time with me. She showed up at my office one afternoon as I was eating a sandwich before class. I was thrilled to see her, but I had no idea she had something else on her mind.

Dr. Lana's Secrets

Be a little opportunistic. Necking in the elevator, running your hand up her leg under the dinner table, going to his office and showing him that new lingerie you're wearing or making sexual innuendoes over the phone are all things that pique desire and add a thrill to your love life.

"My office was little more than a closet, but it was mine alone and the door locked," Scott adds. "We had a pretty good time in that little place before class started, and it wasn't the only time we availed ourselves of it. It really touched me that Kendra went out of her way to find time to spend with me, and I have some very fond memories of that period in our lives."

Affair Facts

Marital sex is best. According to the 1994 Sex in America Survey, of those men who said they achieved extreme emotional satisfaction during sex, 49 percent were married. Only 32 percent of single men reported this maximum level of satisfaction.

Similarly, of the women who reported that they experienced extreme emotional satisfaction, 41 percent were married, whereas, only 31 percent of single woman ranked their satisfaction this high.

Affair Facts

The Sex in American Survey revealed only one area where respondents rated sex with multiple partners as better than sex with their mate. They said sex with multiple partners was more *thrilling* than sex with their mate but not more gratifying. So, keep your sex life varied, adventurous and a little daring and you will have the best of both worlds.

Be creative. Don't limit yourselves to the confines of your bedroom or to other familiar spots. You'll be surprised at the number of opportunities that exist once you start searching them out. You might really enjoy getting a little hot and bothered in a new locale.

Keeping the Sparks Flying

One of the biggest complaints from couples who have been together for awhile is that they're bored with their sex lives. They still desire each other and enjoy their intimate time, but they miss the excitement they once had. If allowed to continue, sexual boredom is one of the surest roads to extramarital affairs known to mankind.

The simplest solution is to maintain your interest in your partner by devoting time and energy to your relationship. Spicing things up by adding a little variety to your routines is always a good idea, too.

Treat Your Partner Like a Lover

Think back to all the special things you did that attracted you to each other in the first place. If you put them on the shelf once you settled into your relationship, pull them out again. Do your sexy little number in your garter belt and hose. If they don't fit anymore, buy ones that do. Book a reservation at the restaurant where you ate before the first time you made love. Reenact the evening in as much detail as you can. The point here is to not stop doing the things that attracted you to each other in the first place.

"One of the things that always touched my heart was the first vacation Jim and I ever took together," says Lorrie. "We saved up for months so we could go on a five-day trip along the Gulf Coast. It was during the spring, and the air was full of the scent of magnolia blossoms. We stayed at wonderful old bed and breakfasts and antebellum plantations. It was the most romantic thing anyone ever did for me.

"It was years before we could afford anything so nice again, but Jim always planned a little surprise during the same time of year that reminded me of that magical trip. I knew the time was near when the doorbell rang and the deliveryman left me a spring bouquet. That was my cue to assemble my wardrobe for whatever lay ahead. Sometimes it was just an overnight stay at a local hotel. Sometimes we'd go away for a few days. Where we went wasn't important. Keeping the memories alive of that first special trip was.

Make Time for Foreplay

Foreplay is a wonderful way to set the stage for sex, but it doesn't have to take place immediately before intercourse. Extended foreplay, involving both physical and emotional stroking, can really set a spouse on fire. It can go on for hours or even days.

"Karen once kept me going for three days while she was away on a business trip," Randy says. "She started by giving me a long, deep kiss before she left for the airport, followed by brushing her fingertips against the back of my neck. I never could resist that! When I dressed for work, I found a card she had left me, perfumed with her fragrance, telling me to keep the following Friday evening open. While she was away, she called and told me how she was fantasizing about seeing me in the new pair of silk boxers she had bought me and how much the new bra she bought enhanced her cleavage. Man, I could just see her! By the time Friday came, I decided I couldn't wait for her to get home. I met her plane at the gate and pulled her into the first secluded spot I could find."

Maybe you start with a gentle touch and the right look as you leave to go to work. Follow that up with a midday call where you tell her how really lovely she is. Instead of just coming through the door at the end of the day, ring the bell. Pull her outside for a romantic walk while the sun sets. Hold hands. Stop for a kiss under the streetlight. Whisper "I love you" in her ear. When you reach home, head for bed.

Dr. Lana's Secrets

The major reasons both men and women have affairs is sex, more sex, sexual variety, and sexual experimentation. So have an affair with your partner, have fun, don't be serious all the time. Think about creating more adventure, more variation, and more investigation of one another. If you can't come up with anything new, buy some books or watch some movies.

Spice Things Up

If your sex life is generally healthy but uninspired, add some new elements to the mix. Depending on how inhibited your feelings are about your body or about sex, you may find this a little difficult at first. But there are lots of fun, nonthreatening things you can do that can really put the spark back in your sexual life, and trying them can pave the way for more daring activities. Try a few of the following:

Flavored Lotions and Body Powders

These not only feel good when they go on, they can taste pretty good, too. You can paint or dust your way to some very erotic encounters if you so choose. There's one body powder made with honey that comes with a special feather duster. It looks great when dusted in a cleavage (you can choose which cleavage you want to accentuate), and it smells and tastes great. Some lotions even have cooling or heating properties that can heighten physical response. Check the resource list in Appendix B if you're interested but don't know where to shop for such items.

Sexy Dressing

It's such a classic turn-on that we often overlook it in search of something new, but sexy lingerie still ranks at the top of the erotica list. If your lover keeps on buying you flimsy little nothings or has a fondness for the Victoria's Secret catalog, heed those signals and fasten on those garter belts. If sexy bras and panties aren't your style, find something that is—maybe a filmy negligee or a camisole and tap pants are more to your liking. You don't have to be obvious to get your point across. Just the suggestion of some lace at the top of an open shirt can be enough to invoke an erotic response.

Lots of couples ditch the sexy set dressing when they get a little older and things start to jiggle where they didn't before. But if your weight gain isn't a source of acrimony between you, don't cover it up. Flaunt it! You may have to shop for your own lingerie and other sexy garments to get ones that fit, because people often underestimate their spouse's size when buying these items as gifts. Big can be beautiful if you let it be. Don't cling to memories of how you looked when you were a size six if those days are long past and you aren't terribly motivated to be that slim again.

Erotica

Sexually arousing books, magazines, and videos can not only heighten our sexual responses, but also expand our knowledge of sexual techniques and activities. Contrary to what you may believe, women often enjoy erotica as much as men do. However, they're generally less aroused by material of strongly pornographic nature, especially if it presents sex primarily from the male point of view.

Try to consider both partners' taste for such material when you decide to search it out. Don't overlook mainstream movies and books in your search for erotica. Some of the most highly erotic movies are created for mass audiences. If you haven't seen such a classic as *9 1/2 Weeks* (starring Mickey Rourke and Kim Basinger), you're missing a great treat.

Sexual Fantasies

Act out your fantasies instead of keeping them to yourself. Most people have sexual fantasies, whether we admit them or not. You may not be able to enact some of them, and there are some that may not be appropriate to act upon—like having sex with someone other than your partner if it's not accepted in your relationship. But there are other ways to put your dreams in motion. If you're fantasizing about making love on a tropical beach, you can create the setting by using scented candles and environmental music. Make sure the room is warm and stir the air a little with a small fan. It's the next best thing to being there, and you don't have to worry about removing sand or seaweed from certain body parts.

Toys

Some people think that there's no room in a satisfactory sex life for devices and toys. If you're in this group, you're depriving yourself of some potential fun. While the more overtly erotic items may be too much for you, using a vibrator or a clitoral stimulator usually isn't too off-putting. Sex toys can be very innocent—think of the erotic response you can create by using a soft feather duster to apply some body powder or the way your partner's hair stands on end when you drape a soft silk scarf across his chest.

Remember, almost nothing is out-of-bounds when you love each other. If you've always fantasized about a particular sexual situation that necessitates some props to carry it off, maybe it's time to divulge that fantasy to your spouse. Who knows what it might lead to?

Affair Facts

When men and women were asked to rate their overall sexual satisfaction, both rated their emotional connection as more important than physical attractiveness.

Be Comfortable with Your Body

Nothing is sexier than a healthy sense of self-esteem, especially in the bedroom. If you are constantly finding something wrong with your physical self, you will hold back sexually, robbing the two of you of the real joy of sex.

Survey after survey reports the same thing: We are much more critical of our own bodies than our partners are, so lighten up and throw off that baggy shirt and tell him how dearly you love him and how much you appreciate him.

The greatest sexual satisfaction comes from feeling loved and appreciated, not from touching a perfect body. Most people want to be with someone who is emotionally warm and loving, not picture perfect and untouchable.

P.S. Most men think models are too thin, and prefer women who are more rounded and softer.

Managing the Monkey Wrenches

Ideally, partners should be able to maintain a consistent level of intimate contact with each other. The reality is that doing so is difficult. Even if you're blessed with extremely compatible sex drives, such things as changes in emotional and physical health can throw your intimacy level off-kilter. Intimate urges can fluctuate a great deal without any diminishment of the love we feel for our spouse.

And sometimes we're physically unable to have sex for one reason or another. These can be difficult times for couples, especially if an illness or separation causes the disruption. The key to getting through these times is in taking the long view. If you love each other, a break in your sex life doesn't mean the end of your relationship.

How can you manage difficult times when they happen?

➤ If the problem is caused by illness, find alternative ways to keep close. Continue to show your love by staying close. You may have to spend more time than you'd like sitting by your spouse's bedside and keeping him company. If sex is an impossibility, do what you can do. Hold hands. Kiss. Give her a sponge bath or a rubdown. Brush his hair. If the ailing partner is up to it, try masturbation, either manually or with a vibrator, as an alternative to intercourse.

➤ If the disruption is caused by a separation, the goal again is to find ways to maintain as much intimacy in your life as you can. If you're able to have phone contact, spend some time whispering sweet nothings to each other. Try to plan your calls so you can talk to each other without distraction. Share a fantasy or two. If you have a cordless phone, answer the call while you're in the tub. Even if talking about being naked in a bubble bath makes you blush, just telling your spouse where you are may be enough to fuel some nice fantasies. If you're limited to written communication, now's the time to send the steamiest love letters you can imagine.

➤ Certain medications, such as those used to treat high blood pressure, can reduce sexual desire or cause erection problems in men and orgasmic problems in women. Even over-the-counter antihistamines can cause problems. They dry up nasal secretions, and they dry up other secretions, too. If you begin experiencing sexual problems after you start taking a new drug, check with your physician to see whether the dosage can be reduced. In some cases, alternative drug therapies are also available. Very often, a drug that doesn't affect your sex life can be found to treat an illness or disease. It is not usually the bad things that happen that unravel an intimate relationship; the real damage occurs when you withdraw emotionally from your partner. Stay involved with one another, physically and emotionally. As long as you stay connected, you will survive the crisis.

➤ Illness, stress, and emotional upsets can cause significant diminishment in sexual drive and ability. It's not uncommon for men to suffer from impotency during times of severe pressure or stress. Women can lose the desire to have any physical contact at all when they're depressed, working too hard, or going through hormonal changes, such as those caused by childbirth and menopause.

If any of these factors are causing problems for either of you, try not to overreact or take things personally. Doing so will only make the situation worse. Instead, follow your spouse's lead on what you should do. If your partner is having trouble maintaining an erection but wants to give you pleasure in other ways, go for it. If your wife says she just wants to be held, do that and nothing else.

Don't push things until or unless it becomes obvious that you're dealing with more than a temporary problem. In this case, don't let too much time pass before you seek professional guidance. Sexual dysfunction can indicate more severe issues. The New York Times reported around 40 percent of men and 30 percent of women have some sexual dysfunction, so you are not alone, and effective treatment is available.

The Least You Need to Know

➤ A satisfying sex life is an essential ingredient in a successful relationship.

➤ Keep intimacy a priority in your life together, even if it means scheduling your private time.

➤ Always try to maximize your opportunities for intimate encounters, and don't feel that you have to limit your sexual activities to the bedroom.

➤ Always treat your partner like a lover. Don't get into the habit of taking your life together for granted.

➤ If you're bored with each other, spice things up between the two of you. Reawakening your feelings of desire is preferable to searching for excitement outside of your relationship.

Chapter 10

Making Magic in Your Relationship

In This Chapter

➤ Why sex is not enough

➤ Being an everyday romantic

➤ The importance of dating

➤ Keeping romance alive when you're apart

There is magic to love.

—Helen E. Fisher, *Anatomy of Love*

When you think about all the variables that can bring two people together or keep them apart, finding the special someone you want to spend your life with really does seem like the work of a master alchemist. How many people are there on the face of this earth, living in how many countries? The mathematical odds of meeting someone who's right for you is staggeringly small. Yet, you managed to do it.

The hand of the master is at work at the beginning of a relationship as well. Think back to when you first met your partner. Didn't it seem like magic? How about the indescribable way you felt about each other when you touched or kissed. Didn't you wish you could just keep on feeling that way forever? Here's the good news...you can!

Dr. Lana's Secrets

The in-love feelings present at the beginning of a relationship do not last more than a few years. The in-love sensation is transient. That does not mean that being in love is temporary.

Love...The Renewable Resource

One of the surest ways to keep a relationship strong and healthy is to maintain or strengthen the emotions you felt when you first met each other. They're just as important now as they were when you were young lovers. The only difference is that then the magic you felt was created easily and effortlessly. Now you're older. Your relationship has grown and matured. You have to conjure up that magic now, rather than standing in awe of it when it appears.

It is possible to sprinkle a little fairy dust over a marriage at any time. You can re-create the romance that made your relationship so very special when it started. Work hard enough at it, and you'll find that your feelings for your spouse are truly a renewable resource. It is possible to fall in love, over and over and over again...and with the same person to whom you pledged your undying love and affection.

Dr. Lana's Secrets

I recently appeared on a daytime talk show and listened while partners professed their love despite the fact they had been repeatedly unfaithful, nonsupportive, and unreliable. As I listened I could see these people were sincere about their feelings, but feelings are not enough. Loving someone is about more than how you feel; it is about how you treat your partner and whether you honor your relationship. In other words, it is about what you do, not just what you feel.

Love is a verb, not a noun.

Keeping Those Loving Feelings Alive

While sex (and hopefully, good sex) is important for any healthy relationship, it's only a part of the equation. We must also show our love for our partners through what we say and do, by putting ourselves in their shoes and determining how we can expend our energy to make their lives fuller and more enjoyable.

Thoughtful gestures are among the greatest acts of attention, as they call for knowing your partner well enough to determine what he or she likes or needs. Bringing home a bouquet of long-stemmed roses is an extremely romantic gesture. Stopping by the sporting-goods store to buy a selection of flies for your fisherman husband to use on his upcoming trip is thoughtful and appreciated. But going out of your way to find a florist who carries her favorite kind of rose or a supplier that carries the special flies your spouse will be most likely to use reflects an extra dose of thoughtfulness and caring that can really put a romantic gesture over the top.

Keeping romance alive in a relationship requires an investment by both partners. While some money is often involved, the greater investment is of time and effort. You don't have to rely on grand and opulent gestures to express how you feel about your partner. In many situations, it's the little things you say and do that will really touch your spouse's heart.

Affair Facts

Research by John Gottman, author of *Why Marriages Succeed or Fail,* shows there must be at least five positive interactions for every negative one between partners for a relationship to last.

Dr. Lana's Secrets

It is not the size of the gift that matters; it is the thought behind it. If your gift reflects your understanding of your partner it will be appreciated. If it is a reflection of your taste or if it is something you think your partner *should* want, it won't be cherished.

Make Romance a Priority

At the beginning of your relationship, you made it a priority to express your feelings to your newfound love. Over time, your efforts to do so may have diminished. The stresses of life take over. You get more familiar with each other, and you start taking things a little—or very much—for granted. Your best intentions, when they come to showing your spouse how much you love her, get pushed aside to be revisited when you have the time. The problem is, you never quite find the time.

And even if you do make some time, doing the same things over and over is boring. Just because he loved the sweater you bought him last year doesn't mean he wants another sweater this year…and next. Going out to dinner may have been a dating favorite, but having all your dates center around eating suggests that you are getting lazy and don't seem to have learned anything new about your partner. It is important to create new experiences with each other.

Daily Doses

Of the 1,440 minutes in a day, how many do you spend in active appreciation of your spouse? Not just thinking about him, but actually showing or telling him how much he really means to you? Even if you subtract the time you spend working and sleeping—roughly 960 minutes a day for the average person—that still leaves you with 480 minutes to do anything else you choose. Telling your partner you love him takes one second. But it's one second of effort that too few couples regularly bestow upon each other.

While it can be tempting to put off paying attention to our spouses for when we're less busy, greater success is achieved when we minister to our partners frequently and consistently. It's like taking vitamin supplements. They won't do you much good if you only take them when you're feeling a little run-down. You have to use them regularly to achieve the fullest benefit. Daily attention to a relationship will keep it from getting run-down as well.

Here are some ways to pay attention to your relationship every day:

➤ Say "I love you" at least three times every day.

➤ Turn that quick goodbye kiss in the morning into something deeper and more meaningful.

➤ Tuck an "I love you" note into a pocket of his suit.

➤ Do an unexpected chore. If it's your spouse's responsibility to empty the trash, do it yourself once in awhile.

➤ Leave a voice message for your spouse that just says, "I'm thinking of you."

➤ Spend an extra few minutes in bed with your partner in the morning, or go to bed together a few minutes earlier than usual.

➤ Don't just welcome her home after a busy day. Pretend that she's been away for a month and really show her how much you missed her.

➤ If you wind down in the evenings by watching television, don't sit on opposite ends of the sofa or in separate chairs. Use the time to show some physical affection. Almost everyone enjoys a neck and shoulder rub or having their feet massaged.

➤ Polish her shoes. You may think this rates as one of the least romantic things in the world, but it's actually quite the opposite. Why this particular gesture is so magical isn't clear. Maybe it's because the condition of our shoes can tell so much about us. You'd be surprised at the number of spouses who mention this act when they're asked to recall the romantic things their partners have done for them.

Stay in the Dating Mode

When you first started seeing each other, you didn't leave your encounters to chance. You planned time to be together. You dated. You used your time together to impress each other, to find out what made you both tick. You asked questions. You explored the intrigue that attracted you. So...when was the last time you and your spouse went out on a real date?

Most couples get out of the habit of dating sometime after they make a firm commitment to be together. It's easy to understand why this happens. Dating takes time and effort. You have to decide what you want to do and make plans for it. Even if you're not getting dressed up, you still have to spend some time making yourself desirable and attractive. It's a lot easier (and definitely more comfortable) to hang out together in your sweats and catch a movie on the spur of the moment, no doubt about it.

There's nothing wrong with maintaining a relationship based on casualness and ease. In fact, it's preferable to one that's too regimented and formal. But there's room in every relationship for adding some variety to your normal routine. Treating each

Bumps Ahead

It is the day-to-day intimacies, the sharing of small discoveries, the expression of appreciation, or words of love that create strong bonds between partners. If these gestures are not part of your everyday life, then you are putting your relationship at risk.

Bumps Ahead

Don't stop doing what works. Couples in trouble nearly always agree on what worked to bring them closer to one another earlier in their relationship, and they nearly always agree that they have stopped doing those things.

other with all the fascination you felt when you first met is one of the best ways to keep your relationship fresh.

Dating is something that should be maintained at some level throughout the life of a relationship. There's no denying the feeling of pleasure and expectation you can get when your spouse calls and asks if you're free for an evening out at your special restaurant. If it's been a few years since your partner wore that slinky black cocktail dress, maybe it's time to give her the opportunity. Ask her out for an evening of dining and dancing.

How often you decide to go out on a date with your spouse is entirely up to you. There's really no magic formula, just the desire to spend time together in a more formal or structured way than you usually do. Some couples like to plan a weekly date. They may choose a particular night, such as Fridays, as their date night, with each spouse taking turns planning their evening out. One date night at home and one date night out works for many couples as long as you are spending at least five hours a week attending to one another. Here are some more dating tips:

➤ **Keep it interesting and fun.** Making a date to eat at the same restaurant every week can be as boring as staying home. Find some new places to go that you think your spouse might enjoy.

➤ **Expand your horizons.** Planning an overnight stay at a bed and breakfast in town can be very romantic, but how about planning one in a city where you've never been?

➤ **Limit your dates to the two of you.** The key idea here is romance, right? Leave the double-dating to the teenagers.

➤ **Stay flexible.** While it's always a good idea to make plans with your partner, adhering to too strict a schedule can eliminate your chances for spontaneity. Be spontaneous anytime you can.

➤ **Reschedule your date right away if you have to cancel or postpone it for any reason.** Don't just vow to make it up to your spouse someday. Get that broken date back on your calendars.

Dating doesn't have to be fancy, but it's often very enjoyable when it is. We spend a lot of time in a casual mode when we settle into a relationship. Why not get gussied up once in awhile? On the other hand, maybe your favorite place for a romantic evening out was the pizza joint at college. Put on your investigative cap and find one like it where you now live.

Don't be surprised if you find yourself looking forward to the dates with your spouse as much as you did when you were starting out. Dating is a big part of the human courting ritual, and everyone likes to be courted. Keep on dating, and you can keep on courting—and falling in love—with each other.

Dr. Lana's Secrets

What makes us feel love? Feeling I am special, knowing she is thinking of me, feeling appreciated, and feeling understood are the responses I hear most often from my clients. Men frequently mention feeling trusted, which means believing that you have confidence in him. The latter response is one of those male/female differences. I seldom hear this answer from women.

Romance Across the Miles

Business demands may necessitate long periods of separation. Maybe you planned to consolidate your lives in the same city, and it hasn't happened yet. Or your spouse was transferred, and it will be some time before you can join her. Other occurrences can cause prolonged separations. But being apart doesn't have to spell the end of the romance in your relationship.

Dr. Lana's Secrets

Whether your love is about yourself or about your partner is made clear by the choices you make. If what you chose to do is what you would like to have done for you, then it is a reflection of you. If the things you do in the name of love are a demonstration of how completely you know and understand your partner, then it's about loving him. Feeling known and understood are essential elements of feeling loved.

Distance can make the heart grow fonder, or at least keep things on as even a keel as possible, but both partners must be committed to working at it. Out of sight, out of mind can become a reality if you don't devote a significant effort to keeping in close touch with each other as much as possible. Here are some ideas for keeping your loving feelings intact across the miles:

➤ **Call each other every day unless it is not practical.** Be sure you hear each other's voice on a regular basis. If you can, call and say goodnight to each other at the end of the day. Faxes and emails work, too, although there is no substitute for the sound of her voice.

➤ **Send romantic cards.** Do it even if you're not usually the type to send anything gushy. When you're separated from someone you love, it's almost impossible to paint with too broad a brushstroke. Go to the card shop and buy an assortment so you have a good supply on hand. Don't let a hectic schedule or the excuse of too little time get in the way.

➤ **Plan some time for reunions.** You may not get the chance to see each other as often as you'd like, but it's better than not at all. If time, convenience, or expense is an issue, maybe you can meet halfway.

➤ **Make sure you express your emotions.** Don't assume that your partner knows how much you love him. Tell him. Reassure him that what you have is real and true and will withstand the test of time and distance.

Being separated from a partner for even a short time can be very difficult to handle, but it's bound to happen at some point in almost every relationship. If you've been good at keeping the romance alive in your life, your efforts will serve as a cushion to help you get through the times when you're sad and lonely and wondering if you'll ever be together again.

The memories of all the special things you did together can take you through even the toughest times in your life. Take the time for creating magic in your relationship. Just a little bit can go a very long way.

The Least You Need to Know

➤ The magic that brought you together never has to disappear.

➤ Keeping your romantic side alive helps recreate the feelings you had when you first met.

➤ Maintaining a romantic relationship takes work and an investment of time and effort.

➤ Be sure to make romance a priority in your life together. Make a commitment to do something romantic every day.

Chapter 11

Live, Love, Laugh and Be Happy

In This Chapter

➤ The definition of why happiness is hard work

➤ The self-love quiz

➤ The power of positive thoughts and actions

It's good to be just plain happy; it's a little better to know that you're happy; but to understand that you're happy and to know why and how...and still be happy, be happy in the being and the knowing, well that is beyond happiness, that is bliss.

—Henry Miller

Happiness. Bliss. Even the words sound positive. There isn't much that the world can do to you if you're feeling happy. But there's a lot it can do if you're not. The same is true of relationships. It's nearly impossible to have a good relationship if you're less than happy with yourself, your spouse, your job, the world around you...you name it. The simple truth is this: It takes happy people to build happy relationships.

Me Happy, You Happy, We Happy!

A happy relationship is a successful relationship. Ask anyone who has successfully lived with the same person for a number of years how they managed to stay together, and you'll hear one statement almost immediately: We're happy with each other.

Some couples begin, continue, and end their lives together being happy together. They can bank on each other's optimism, and they simply don't have very many bad things happen to them. They know themselves and seem to get what they expect. For others—probably most—reaching a state of happiness with themselves and their marriage is a challenging journey. The road is full of twists and turns, potholes and craters. Sometimes the only way those partners can negotiate their marriage is by sheer determination and will. Yet they do so because they know how important it is. And they know that it's better than the alternative.

Happiness in a marriage comes about when both partners are working toward similar goals. And here's the good news: Both partners don't have to be blessed with the sunniest of dispositions to do it right. While happiness comes much more easily when both spouses are operating on an even optimistic keel, it also is possible for one spouse to set the course for the other. You can learn how to be happy. One of the best ways to do it is by paying attention to how a happy person approaches life.

Dr. Lana's Secrets

Happiness comes from embracing the positive experiences that surround us every day. It's not the big events that bring lasting happiness; it's the combination of a lot of little good things in our lives and the absence of a lot of negatives.

What Happiness Is

What does it really mean to be happy? If you've always assumed that you knew what the word meant but never looked it up in the dictionary, the definition might surprise you. There are many aspects to being happy; *Webster's New World Dictionary* defines *happy* as "favored by circumstances; lucky; fortunate; or having, showing, or causing a feeling of great pleasure, contentment, joy, etc." *Happiness,* the noun, is defined as "good fortune; luck; pleasure; joy; contentment." And bliss? It ranks even higher on the scale than happiness; it's defined as "a state of great joy or happiness, spiritual joy or heavenly rapture."

Being happy means being comfortable with who you are (the contentment part) and where you are in life (the circumstances part). It means that, for the most part, you take an optimist's rather than a pessimist's view. The glass for you is half full, rather than half empty. It means looking at the little things and treasuring them. It means, quite simply, that you are able to derive contentment and joy out of life's simple pleasures.

Having Good Relationships

One unwavering fact surfaces in all the studies on happiness, and that is people who have good interpersonal relationships are the happiest. If you are looking for happiness, loving those around you is the fastest track there. People who see themselves as interdependent are happier than those who consider themselves either dependent or independent. It is important to feel connected to others and to feel that the responsibility for the relationship is shared. Neither partner should be solely responsible for the quality of the relationship.

Having Good Self-Esteem

The second most-important factor in happiness is self-esteem. The happiest people are also capable people. They are successful at making good things happen in their lives. Winning the lottery only makes people happy for a short time because the element that is essential to good self-esteem and happiness—control—is lacking. The feeling that good things are happening to you because you caused them to happen is a crucial piece of the happiness puzzle.

Affair Facts

A 1994 *Psychology Today* article reports married people are happier than single people are. Here is how they rank people on the happiness scale, from the most to the least happy: married women, married men, unmarried women, and unmarried men.

Dr. Lana's Secrets

The prerequisite for couples to be happy with their relationship is for each person to be happy with him- or herself. This means having enough successes in your day-to-day life to give you a sense of self-satisfaction. Realistic expectations play a major role in your happiness. When you create an array of positive events and feel successful at many of them, you're most likely to feel happy. And if you allow yourself to savor them, your happiness will last.

Getting to Happy

By now, you've heard the basic party line of life so often that this next statement shouldn't surprise you. Happiness is work. It doesn't just happen. Psychiatrist Frank Pittman put it well in his book *Private Lies* when he stated, "Happiness, like sweat, is the by-product of hard work."

Work is effort, and effort must be headed in the appropriate direction for it to have much effect. When it comes to creating happiness in a relationship, the work begins inside each partner, and most of the effort expended is on the individual. Simply put, you and you alone are responsible for your happiness. No one else can make you happy or unhappy. Whether you are happy or not is entirely within your control and largely depends on how you react to life's challenges and pressures.

Finding Happiness with Yourself

April, married for eight years to Lance, is probably one of the happiest people you could ever meet. Everything about her exudes warmth and confidence. It would be easy to draw the conclusion that she has always been this way, but April would tell you it isn't so.

As the daughter of parents with a less-than-positive outlook on life, April picked up the same pessimistic view. "I'll never forget my father telling me I could never trust anyone," she says. "Both my parents felt that everyone was out to get them. Soon I felt the same way."

By the time she reached high school, there was little about April's life that gave her any pleasure. "I had few friends and the ones I was able to attract usually didn't last long," she says. "They enjoyed things like ice skating or going to football games. I didn't see the fun in any of it. I'd rather spend my time with a book."

April's attitude moderated some when she left home to attend college. "Being away at school helped me see things differently. Most importantly, I was now among people who didn't know me and weren't aware of my sour disposition. I had the chance to start over, and I tried hard to do so. But those old tapes were really hard to get rid of. I still approached things negatively more often than not. If someone thought something was possible, I'd find ten things that could go wrong. And I'd worry about all of them."

Affair Facts

A 1993 study from the University of Illinois found even-tempered people are happier than people who experience a greater range of feelings.

It took two failed marriages, several years of therapy and some intensive soul-searching for April to see that she could make her life better. "I married both of my husbands thinking they could make me happy. That's probably the worst thing you can do. After my second divorce, I was through. If this was what life was all about, I wasn't that interested in continuing. Fortunately, I was also in therapy when I made that decision. My therapist was the first person who ever told me that I had the power and ability to do anything I wanted, and that included changing my outlook on life."

Today, April's attitude is significantly more positive, and there are times when she even feels happy. "I finally realized that being angry and negative all the time hadn't done much for me, and I was fed up enough to explore the flip side of those emotions," she says. "Instead of looking for the downside in everything, I learned to focus on the positive. Instead of beating myself up over my weight, for example, which is something I had done all my life, I've learned to accept my body for what it is—strong, curvy, and pretty sexy, according to my husband.

"If there's anything that I still get angry about, it's that I wasted as much time as I did being angry and negative," April adds. "But those feelings are fleeting. There's a lot of people in this world, including my parents, who never get the chance to experience all the wonderful things life has to offer. I'm very thankful that I now can."

April spent years using her negative attitude to talk herself out of the things that she should enjoy in life. She didn't feel she deserved them, and she resisted them when they came to her. It wasn't until she decided that she was deserving of life's pleasures that she was able to turn her attitude around. April had to learn to love herself.

Dr. Lana's Secrets

Can you make yourself happy? Yes. Here are some specific things you can do: Act happy. Talk and behave as though you are happy. Find things to do that you are good at. The best choice is to select things that are challenging but that you can do well. Exercise; it is a powerful force in the physiology of happiness. Get involved with other people with whom you can give and receive support. Self-disclosure and mutual appreciation go a long way to building self-esteem, and good self-esteem is an essential element of happiness.

Exploring Self-Love

Pick up any book on relationships, and you'll see it right away. You have to be able to love yourself before you can successfully love anyone else. You need to have generally healthy attitudes about all parts of the person that is you: your looks, your emotions, your intellect. So how do you feel about yourself? The quiz below might help you identify some areas where you could use a self-esteem boost. Both you and your partner should take it; then compare answers.

The Self-Love Quiz

1. When I look in the mirror, I see:

   a. A healthy body, one that I'm pleased with.

   b. An O.K. body. It could be better but I can live with it.

   c. A failure to adhere to every diet and exercise program I ever tried.

2. When I think about my intelligence, I believe that I'm:

   a. Able to match wits with the best and the brightest.

   b. Not the brightest bulb out there but certainly able to use what I do know to its fullest.

   c. Less than competent when faced with anything complicated or new.

3. You have to replace a castor on your office chair. You've never done it before, but the replacement piece came with instructions. What's your response?

   a. Give me the tools. I'll be finished in a few minutes.

   b. I'm sure I can figure it out. It might take me a little time.

   c. Tools? Instructions? Too much for me!

4. Your partner challenges you to a game of Scrabble. Your response:

   a. Break out the board. I'm always ready for a challenge.

   b. Find a different game—his vocabulary is better than mine. I'll have a better time playing something at which we're more equally matched.

   c. No way. I hate how my partner lords her intellectual prowess over me whenever we play.

5. Your just-completed project at work receives great accolades. What's your response:

   a. Pride over an accomplishment well done.

   b. Thankful that you were able to complete a project to a satisfactory level.

   c. What are they missing?

6. You're walking down the street, and you hear a wolf whistle, obviously directed toward you. You feel:

   a. Flattered.

   b. Embarrassed, but pleased.

   c. Skeptical. Who'd whistle at this body?

7. You've just lost a key client. How do you feel?

   a. Confident that I can get another one in his place.

   b. Concerned that whatever I did that made me lose this client might affect my ability to attract another one.

   c. Like a complete loser. Who'd want to do business with me anyway?

8. You and your partner decide to run in a 10k race. She crosses the finish line minutes ahead of you. You:

   a. Are thrilled for her. She worked really hard to improve her time.

   b. Are disappointed in yourself because you know you're capable of running a better race. Next time, you will!

   c. Are ready to hang up the running shoes.

Scoring: Count the number of *a*, *b*, and *c* answers and enter them on the blanks below:

____ a ____ b ____ c

What Your Answers Mean

Mostly *a* answers: You are confident about your looks and abilities and approach life with a positive attitude. Your self-esteem is high. You like yourself, and you feel comfortable about what you're able to do.

Mostly *b* answers: You're generally self-confident and capable of accepting the things you either can't change or don't feel like spending the time on. You tend toward being a little self-critical at times, and you don't always give yourself enough credit for your abilities.

Mostly *c* answers: Don't like yourself much, do you? Your general attitude about yourself is one of defeat and disbelief. Either you really believe that you're not worth very much, or you've allowed yourself to become convinced of it.

Affair Facts

The American Psychological Association reports that the rate of depression among women is double the rate of depression among men.

Increasing Your Self-Love Quotient

If you racked up a number of b and c answers to the self-love quiz, it's time for some serious attitude adjustment. Your displeasure with yourself and your current situation might be motivation for you to make some changes. If you feel daunted by the challenge or less than certain that you're up to it, take heart in the knowledge that you're not alone. The biggest reason that people drop out of therapy before they're really through is that they're not willing to take on life's challenges.

One of the biggest challenges you'll ever face in life stares at you every time you look in a mirror. If you've read this far, you've already shown more courage about changing your life than most. So gear up. Gird your loins. Remember that you don't have to work on everything all at once. How do you eat an elephant? Bite by bite.

Dr. Lana's Secrets

If you almost never feel happy, you may be depressed. Many people function with a low-grade depression. They can go through life, do their jobs and maintain relationships, but never really feel cheerful or joyful.

If that is you, don't accept depression as normal. You may be able to work your way out of it, but if not talk to your doctor about antidepressant medication. In the meantime, here are a few things you can do: start exercising 20 minutes a day; write out some positive statements about yourself and repeat ten times morning noon and night; set one goal a day to do something nice for someone else; and choose a happy friend to tell about your successes.

Look Good to Feel Good

If you're down on yourself in general, it's time to focus on your appearance and what you can do to make it better. Take a good look at yourself in the mirror. When was the last time you changed your hairstyle or bought some new clothes? One of your biggest problems might be that you're living in a time warp. Go out and update your look. Get a makeover if you're still wearing the same eye shadow you wore in college. Update your wardrobe, especially if what you currently have doesn't fit well. People change. Our bodies and our faces change. How you dress and style yourself should change as well.

Dr. Lana's Secrets

Great wealth does not make people happy, nor does great beauty or great intelligence. Learning to focus on daily triumphs does lead to feeling happier. Minimize the negatives in your day-to-day life and take pleasure in your success, and you will find yourself both happier and healthier.

Beautiful people are not happier people. The key to happiness is to accept and enjoy yourself as you are. Self-esteem is built by reaching for goals that are attainable and complimenting yourself for all your successes.

Accentuate the Positive

Maybe you feel intellectually inferior to your spouse. Instead of putting yourself into situations that continue to underscore your intellectual mismatch, focus on ways to exhibit your strengths. Rocket scientists often don't have much in the way of street smarts. Your ability to negotiate the twists and turns of life might be exactly what attracted that Einstein to you.

Let Einy butt heads over a chessboard with someone else. Apply your superior negotiating skills in another area, say, the acquisition of that rare book that your spouse wanted but was unable to find.

Dr. Lana's Secrets

Happiness comes when you have many more positive experiences than negative ones. Create as many positive events as you can by setting goals you can reach. Adjust your expectations to eliminate or reduce failures. Negative experiences interfere with happiness, and it doesn't work to try to ignore them—those pesky negative memories will lower your level of happiness.

Level the Playing Field

Spouses are rarely well matched when it comes to athletic prowess. Don't create endless frustration for yourself by feeling like your only shot at participating in sports with your spouse involves things you really don't like or aren't very good at.

If possible, find a sport at which you're equally matched. If that's not possible, include an activity in your sports menu that you enjoy. Maybe you'll never be able to keep up with your spouse on the tennis court, but you might be a killer at table tennis or an ace at billiards.

Love the Shape You're in (or at Least Accept It)

Maybe you're no longer the size eight you were when you got married. If the fact that you've gained some weight isn't an issue in your marriage, don't make it one. Just gaining weight rarely causes problems in a relationship. What does cause difficulties is when a partner's behavior changes significantly because of it. If you're now self-conscious about being naked in front of your spouse, that's going to be an issue sooner or later.

Affair Facts

Researchers from the University of Illinois found women in Western cultures express more intense feelings—both positive and negative—than men do.

Being obsessed with diet or exercise can make the time you used to spend enjoying your spouse anything but enjoyable. Don't let your feelings about your body get in the way of loving your partner. What's more important to most people is how you look on the inside, not on the outside.

If you're critiquing yourself daily, fretting about your wrinkles or the extra flab, get your mind on to something more important because this kind of thinking is a dead end. Here is the profile of what happy people are like. They:

➤ Are physically healthy

➤ Are realistic about their abilities

➤ Have a good self-image

➤ Have a sense of control over their lives

➤ Are supportive of others

➤ Are involved in challenging work or leisure activities

➤ Get enough rest (more than eight hours)

Steer Clear of Negative Forces

Who is your worst critic? If you're like most people, you are. But, sad to say, there might be some others out there. Surprisingly, they're often the people you're closest to and you love the most.

These people are rarely aware of their behavior, but there are some who just feel compelled to go out of their way to be mean. Sometimes they're jealous of who you are and what you've accomplished. Maybe your sister never got over the fact that you beat her to the altar. Maybe your father has a hard time accepting the fact that you earn more than he ever did. For whatever reason, they're not happy with themselves, and they project their negative feelings right at you.

One of the best things you can do to develop a positive attitude is to surround yourself with positive people. This doesn't mean severing your relationships with those who aren't, unless you realize that you'd feel better emotionally if you do. What it does mean is limiting your exposure to the folks that bring you down, at least until you're strong enough to pit your positive attitude against their negative ones.

If all you hear around the Thanksgiving table every year are put-downs and digs, maybe it's time to skip that particular celebration and do something that you find more uplifting. If a shopping trip with your mother turns into a litany on how much better your sister would look in everything you try on, leave mom at home and take a good friend instead.

A Sense of Connection

If your family is a negative force in your life, surround yourself with a new community. Actively religious people are happier, but not because of any one belief system; it's because of their community involvement.

When you are part of a community that accepts you and affirms you, when you share a sense of life's meaning and have a focus beyond yourself, you can build a happy family-like environment outside of your biological family. This sense of connection with others is the number one predictor of happiness. So if you aren't respected, complimented, and appreciated in your original family, then create a new family. Believe me, a sense of connection to others is not something you can go without and be happy.

Replace No with Yes

Would you believe that it's just as easy to have a positive thought as it is to have a negative one? All it takes is learning how.

Focusing on the positive doesn't mean that you totally ignore the negative. What it does mean is being realistic about things that are less than positive. It's always a good idea to have a balanced perspective on life, and that requires you to be aware of booby traps and wrong turns. Work to minimize the negatives and accentuate the positives.

Bumps Ahead

Some family members or a few friends may criticize you when you make positive changes in your life. They may feel left behind or disconnected from you and react by trying to pull you back into old negative patterns.

Affair Facts

Recent studies from both Harvard and Yale show negative thinkers report poorer overall health, more stress and greater anxiety than people who have positive attitudes.

By focusing on the positive, you can actually minimize the negative forces in your life. Norman Vincent Peale explored this concept in great detail in his book *The Power of Positive Thinking*, which became a classic on the subject. Today hundreds of books address this concept from a variety of angles, but Peale's basic theory hasn't changed: Positive thinking is powerful thinking. It can create changes in your life that you never would have dreamed were possible.

If your mind is full of positive thoughts, it's hard to entertain the negative ones. So fill your mind with the good things. You might find it helpful to read Peale's book, or any of the others on this subject. You'll find some listed in Appendix B. Listening to motivational or inspirational tapes also can support your efforts. Before long, you'll find yourself automatically correcting your thinking every time a negative thought crosses your mind.

Dr. Lana's Secrets

Humor is a prerequisite to happiness. Those who take life too seriously rob themselves of the benefits of humor and laughter. There are physical benefits to laughter, such as lower blood pressure, and slower heart rate as well as emotional benefits to improved mood from the release of endorphins.

Plus, people who share laughter share an intimate connection. If you aren't having at least one good laugh a day start watching yourself to see what type of humor you do respond to, then start building your own humor collection. Whether you respond to slapstick or stand up comedy doesn't matter as long as whatever you like is part of your daily life.

Don't Worry, Be Happy

If part of your negative thinking also involves excessive worry, adopting a more positive attitude will eliminate a great deal of the mental gymnastics you put yourself through. Chronic worriers spend so much time thinking about "what if" that they rarely are able to just relax and enjoy the pleasures in life. If left unchecked, worry will create fear, and fear is an emotion we weren't meant to live with on a full-time basis.

It's a well-known fact that worry never makes anything better. How many times have you heard someone say that they're worried about someone or something? Did their worrying change anything about the situation? No. And it won't unless their feelings motivate them to actually do something about it.

There's a big difference between being worried and being concerned. Concern means that we've identified something that we need to take a closer look at and possibly act on. Your concern over your dog's painful paw will generally result in a call to the vet. Spend enough time worrying about it, and you'll convince yourself that your pet is dying from bone cancer.

If you do find yourself worrying about something, try to determine if your fears are valid and if you have any control over whatever is upsetting you. Too many people spend too much time worrying about things they can do nothing about. If you're worried about getting older, for example, direct your energy to something that you can control, like your physical and emotional health. You'll find yourself looking younger and younger.

Dr. Lana's Secrets

Those who are happiest care not only about people close to them, but also about strangers in faraway places. Happy people are concerned with the well-being of humanity and social responsibility. And instead of just thinking or worrying about others, they do something. It may be raising money, volunteering, writing letters to world leaders, or performing acts of kindness to those around them. They go out of their way for others without expecting to be rewarded for their efforts.

Living, Loving and Laughing

What happens when you eliminate the negatives in your life and focus on the positives? You get to live a life that's full and enjoyable. Instead of missing out on what the world has to offer because you're too worried to see it, you're able to take pleasure in even the smallest things.

Rather than seeming oppressive and cold, your universe abounds with joy and wonder. When fear crosses your mind, you replace that feeling with the knowledge that you have the power to conquer any obstacle that comes your way. You can give love because you feel love for yourself. You're contented, comfortable, and joyful. In short, you're happy. And most likely, your marriage is happy, too.

When there's happiness in a relationship, the relationship itself takes much less work. You still have to focus on your responsibilities and work to keep things on track. That job never goes away, but it's a lot easier to do when you don't have the added burden of trying to support a spouse with a negative approach to life.

Having a happy relationship doesn't mean that problems won't erupt between you. You'll always have challenges to face. But when you can face them together, with the belief that you have what it takes to be successful, there's very little in life that's insurmountable.

Take Responsibility for Your Happiness

Happy people are actively involved people. They are vigorously caring for their partner and doing thoughtful things every day.

Maintaining a happy relationship involves expressing your love in ways that have meaning to your partner—doing what you can to make his or her day a little easier; for example, making breakfast so he can sleep a few minutes longer or stopping for Chinese take-out so she can get in a tennis game after work.

The little things really count when it comes to personal and interpersonal happiness. It is the sense of connection—that feeling that you are looking out for someone else and that they are looking out for you—that makes the difference.

Know what has meaning to your partner and do all you can to fulfill those needs. When you individually and collectively close the gap between what you want and what you are experiencing, you find happiness.

Perhaps one of the loveliest things about a happy relationship is that it doesn't take much to please its participants. Millions, perhaps billions, of dollars are spent annually by couples who are searching for happiness in things such as cruises, new homes, plastic surgery, new cars, fancy stereo equipment—the list goes on. They're looking for happiness in all the wrong places, either because they don't know where they should look or they're unwilling to do what it takes to get there on their own.

Affair Facts

Wealth is equated with happiness, but only slightly. It is a factor in happiness only when it allows people to do things they would not otherwise be able to do.

Owning a new car can be very enjoyable, but in itself won't make you happy. If you aren't content with a simple walk, arm-in-arm with your loving spouse, the fanciest cruise won't make you happy either. You, and only you, can create your own happiness. Once you do, what you can do with it is limitless.

The Least You Need to Know

➤ A successful relationship is a happy relationship.

➤ It takes work to learn how to be happy.

➤ You must be able to love yourself before you can truly love anyone else.

➤ Self-acceptance is a big part of self-love.

➤ Changing negative thoughts into positive ones can also erase fear and worry.

Part 3
Danger: Affair Ahead!

As winter approaches in the North, rescue personnel prepare for the inevitable. They know that at least once during the season, they're going to have to drive to some spot of water and rescue a new—and almost always involuntary—member of the Polar Bear Club. It doesn't matter how many warning signs are posted. Somehow, somewhere, someone is going to venture out on ice that's too thin and fall right through.

Reading the warning signs. It's something that many of us fail to do, even when they stare us right in the face. We're too busy, too preoccupied, or we just don't get it. We ignore the signals that something might be amiss, and when problems erupt, we're not fully equipped to handle them. We fall through the ice.

This part of the book is about recognizing the warning signs of an affair and what to do should you see them. In Chapters 12 and 14 you'll learn when affairs are likely to happen and how to spot the developing signs of one. And in Chapter 13 you'll learn about things you might be doing that could possibly cause your partner to begin an affair.

Chapter 12

Affair on the Horizon?

In This Chapter

➤ Preparing for battle

➤ Identifying vulnerable times

➤ Is there a seven-year itch?

➤ When "ho, ho, ho" turns into who, who, who

Nothing in the world can one imagine beforehand, not the least thing. Everything is made up of so many unique particulars that cannot be foreseen.

—Rainer Maria Rilke

Have you ever wanted to gaze into a crystal ball to find out about the future? It's probably a good thing that we can't really predict what will happen in the years ahead. Think about it for a second. If you were given the chance to see your future unfold, what kind of a future would it really be? All the surprises, both good and bad, would be gone. You'd know where you'd end up, but not how you got there. What fun would be left?

We may not know the specifics, but we do have a good idea of what the stages of life are all about. For the most part, we can count on being a child for a certain period of time and taking on an adult role when that part of our life is over. We know we'll work, make friends, and have a family. We'll succeed at some things and fail at others. We'll get older, and hopefully wiser, as we wind our way through the amazingly complex passages that make up our lives.

We also have a pretty good idea of how we'll react to the experiences that we'll encounter along the way. However, there are certain times in our lives when something that usually wouldn't bother us sends us over the edge. As well as we know ourselves and as steady as we might be most of the time, some events can still completely disrupt our usual behavior and orient us in the opposite direction.

The loss of a job, the onset of a severe illness, the death of a loved one—these are all things that can come out of nowhere and turn our lives upside down for a time. As strong as human beings generally are, these events can make us fragile and vulnerable. They can also open the door to an affair.

Bumps Ahead

If you have become too busy, too tired, or too lazy to be lovers, your relationship is in jeopardy. Sexless marriages are twice as likely to break up as marriages that are full of sex. If you're one of the 14 percent of men and 22 percent of women who are married but haven't had sexual relationships in the past year, you're headed for trouble (*Seattle Times*).

Bumps Ahead

As the speed of life has increased and men and women have more freedom, there really isn't any "safe time" in committed relationships. Both affairs and divorce occur earlier than ever before.

Stomping Through the Tulips

There are two basic ways to approach the challenges that life throws our way. Some people tiptoe their way through, living in fear of what might happen. Others gear up, put on their body armor, and storm through those battlefields.

Being aware of the times when relationships can be vulnerable is like putting on the armor. Knowing where the traps lie can help you face them when they do open. If you're paying attention to your relationship as you should be, a part of you already monitors the situations that affect your relationship and the dynamics of these situations when they do develop.

Pair your knowledge of your relationship with the guide that follows, and you should be able to survive even the toughest challenges without having to wear full combat regalia. Although you may not stop the situation from developing, you might be able to launch a preemptive strike to keep it from escalating.

Many of life's challenges exacerbate whatever underlying issues and concerns we already have. Matters we thought we had resolved years ago can crop up and cause major problems. Being aware of this can help solve many of the situations that follow. Sometimes, just a big dose of understanding and some forthright communication is enough to get things back on track. When solutions lie beyond the basics, you'll find additional ideas for ways to get things turned around.

The Seven-Year Itch

The seven-year itch. We've all heard about it. But does it really exist? Is there a point in a marriage when an affair is more likely to happen than others?

Gear up, everyone. There's not just one point… there are many. Ironically, the thing we're most interested in keeping on an even keel is itself capable of causing some of the biggest challenges to our success.

Affairs can happen at any time; however, there are certain, very predictable times in a marriage when they're more likely to occur. Some are pretty obvious. Others are less so. Here are several crucial periods to keep an eye out for.

Bumps Ahead

Despite the popular notion that the first years of marriage are romantic, the fact is most couples find these years very difficult. It often seems like all the little things that were easy before are hard now.

The Honeymoon's Over

A couple will make more adjustments and changes in their behavior during their first two years of marriage than at almost any other time. The honeymoon phase is either winding down or completely over. Now it's time to learn how to live with what's left. The fact that we come face to face with this harsh reality when we've finally shaken the stardust out of our eyes can make the early phase of a marriage highly affair-prone.

Dr. Lana's Secrets

Early in my marriage, my mother-in-law advised, "Have your crisis early, don't put things off that bother you. Talk about it and figure it out now. If you can't find a compromise, then let it go and accept what you cannot change. If you really cannot find an acceptable solution for both of you and you can't let it go, then get help and get it solved. Don't just let it simmer on the back burner, because one of these days it will boil over."

I have come to appreciate the depth of her wisdom. If you really can find neither compromise nor acceptance, have your crisis now.

It is also during the early years of a relationship when basic issues about being married generally crop up. If one partner is immensely dissatisfied with the situation, this is when you'll hear about it. Some people just don't believe in fidelity with marriage, even though they feel they should make a commitment. Those who had affairs before they were married will likely continue having them. The bad news is that if affairs occur early in a marriage, a divorce is highly probable.

If you're with someone who really seems unhappy about being married, pay close attention to what that person says and does. There's a big difference between someone who doesn't want to be married and a spouse going through a difficult period of adjustment. If your mate is expressing dissatisfaction with almost everything, doesn't want to spend time with you, or puts you down at every turn, you might be dealing with a problem that goes far beyond your marriage. Get professional help so you know whether it is an individual problem or a marital problem. Some problems cannot be solved and as tough as it might be, you're probably better off cutting your losses early.

The "Itchy" Years

There *is* such a thing as a seven-year itch. Problem is, it usually sets in a few years earlier. By the time year four rolls around, spouses can get anxious. Not only do they know they're approaching a stage that has been associated with marital problems, they might be dealing with some very real ones that have cropped up.

Many couples at this stage are new parents and are having to adjust to the loss of intimacy with their spouses (see "The Wonders of Birth" later in this chapter). Others are just dealing with the realization that their marriages aren't living up to their expectations or aren't at all what they thought they would be. Professional and financial concerns also gear up during this period, especially if a two-wage-earner family is now living on one salary.

Affair Facts

Evolutionary psychologists believe humans are designed to pair-bond for long enough to produce an offspring and allow the child to reach an age of independent mobility, about five years of age, before the parents move on to new partners. In modern times, the age of independence is much later, but the pattern of leaving one family to start another at this time is still very much in existence.

Adjusting to marriage can take time, and sometimes it takes much longer than we'd like. It's very frustrating when nothing seems to work. Affairs at this stage are often seen as ways to keep a marriage going, to spice up a dull marriage, or even ways to blow off some steam. Again, they can lead to the end of a marriage, but they're less likely to than earlier in the relationship.

The key to getting through this period is to take a deep breath, step back, and give it time. If your relationship is solid, it can remain intact during periods when you're ill at ease or exasperated with your spouse. If you're bored, it's time to focus your energies on livening things up.

When the Nest Empties

Another prime time for affairs in a marriage is when the family's raised and gone and you're left to yourselves for the first time in many years. Couples who have maintained a good level of commitment to each other over the years often look forward to this stage. They'll finally be able to spend time with each other without too many distractions. However, it also hits at a time when death seems a little nearer than birth and that realization can ruin what should be an enjoyable time in our lives.

Some people at this stage are really beginning to feel the effects of aging and might not be as confident in themselves as they once were. Others look back at years gone by and start to wonder what they might have been missing. This behavior can be the beginning of the so-called midlife crisis.

During the middle years, 40 to 60, is also a time when the roles we play in our marriage can undergo significant changes. Husbands work less and wives decide it's time to take a job, or a more demanding one. Sometimes we end up taking care of a spouse or parents who have suffered a catastrophic illness. Even the most contented couples can be faced with situations that leave them vulnerable to seeking emotional or physical support outside of their marriages.

Bumps Ahead

Ten years into marriage men are more likely to have love affairs then sex affairs. Many say they feel disconnected from their wife. The classic refrain, "She doesn't appreciate me," is still the complaint most men voice when they explain why they became involved in an affair. These love affairs are often a symptom that something is lacking in the marriage.

Age or Illness Can Create a Barrier

After Ben suffered a moderate heart attack, his relationship with Phyllis crumbled. Although his recovery was uneventful, the fact that he was ill at all seemed to drive a wedge between them. "Phyllis seemed reluctant to even kiss me after I had the attack," Ben says. "I think she saw a new side of me when I was sick, and she had problems with it." What had been a good sexual relationship for both became virtually nonexistent. "I was afraid, and Phyllis was even worse," Ben says. "We couldn't get beyond that fear, so not having sex seemed easier than pushing it."

Both partners ended up in affairs, and they found that the affairs were pushing them further apart. "Ben finally confronted me and told me what he was doing and how much it hurt him since he really wanted to be with me," Phyllis says. "That's when we decided it was time to quit blaming Ben's heart attack for what had happened between us. It had been an excuse for us to stop working on our relationship. But we both realized that what we had together meant too much to us to let it go."

Ben and Phyllis do credit their improved love life to their affairs. "We both learned a few things while we were out there," Ben says. "More importantly,

Affair Facts

The common assumption that affairees search out younger lovers to build their egos is not always true. Finding someone to meet our particular needs often wins out over age and looks. A deserted wife may find that her husband's new lover is far less attractive than imagined and not any younger.

we realized that we have everything we need to keep this marriage intact, as long as we're willing to treat it like it's going forward instead of being dead in its tracks."

Career Failures

We live in an era where the things we once thought were sure bets no longer are. Mergers and restructuring have become a fact of corporate life. The stock market may swing up and down so fast at times that it makes us dizzy, but one thing is constant: change.

Losing a job through corporate restructuring or downsizing may seem less traumatic than being fired, but the same emotions usually come into play. We tend to equate our self-worth with our success on the job. Losing a job means we've failed. We're no longer successful. Depending on how the company handles the leave-taking, we may also feel some bruises to our pride and dignity. Such feelings can be very difficult to shake.

A New Sense of Self

Both spouses can become candidates for affairs when one of them loses a job. If finances are a concern, a stay-at-home wife will often go to work to help support the family. Not only will she be put into a new situation at a vulnerable time, she also will face more temptation than she may have had in the past.

A woman entering the workforce may be pleasantly surprised to find that she is appreciated by her male coworkers or her boss. And she may feel that her efforts at the office are more rewarding than her work at home. Feelings of excitement and challenge on the job lead to developing new skills and talents.

And both men and women often admit the shared bond of working together creates intimacy that neither was expecting and both were missing in their day-to-day lives.

Seeking Refuge Elsewhere

Men often seek out women who don't know about their failures. Even if they do have understanding wives at home, they're often too ashamed to bear their souls to their mates. Finding an impartial ear outside of home is much less threatening.

Brad, a successful entrepreneur, had sailed through most of his adult life on the crest of a wave. Everything he touched turned to gold, or at least it did until he embarked on one too many ventures at the same time. His highly leveraged position left him vulnerable to the slightest downturn in the market. When it came, he lost a great deal of his personal wealth. Perhaps worse, he was forced to leave his position as president of the company that he had founded.

"I was devastated, absolutely devastated," Brad recalls. "The members of the board of directors were all friends of mine. Never once did I think they were capable of doing what they did. Not only did I feel betrayed by them, I no longer had anyone I could talk to about what I was going through. I certainly couldn't go to *them*. I had never involved my wife in any of this, and I sure wasn't going to start now. All it would do is upset her."

Brad was so ashamed of what had happened that he kept up the appearance of going to his office for a short time. "Adele, my wife, almost never called me there, so it wasn't a problem. I just told her I would be spending a lot of time away from the office because I was putting together a new deal, and she should call me on my cell phone. I even suggested she take the kids on a trip, since I was going to be so busy, so she went to visit her family in Arizona for a few weeks."

Over the next few days, Brad spent hours driving around the city where he lived, piecing together what had happened and getting his mind back on track. One afternoon he stopped to put gas in his car and ran into his former executive assistant. "Beth was so understanding and so sorry about what happened," Brad says. "She offered to fix me dinner—I guess I looked like I needed a meal. When we got to her townhouse, she gave me a big hug, and I just started to cry. We ended up in bed soon after."

Brad and Beth's affair lasted the entire time his family was gone and continued for several months after. "I felt more able to discuss my needs and my problems with Beth," Brad says. "She was a very good sounding board and played a big role in helping me recover from the shock of losing my company. But, I am committed to my family and felt too guilty to continue seeing Beth.

"By the time it did end, I had a better idea of what I needed to do with my business. But more importantly, I felt strong enough to work on some things with Adele. Beth encouraged me to take a chance on Adele's being able to handle more than I had given her in the past, and she was right. When we finally talked about it, Adele told me she had always felt I excluded her from the things that were most important to me. I never told her about my affair with Beth—because I thought it would only hurt her and not solve anything—but I do tell her about everything else now."

Dr. Lana's Secrets

Times of change are by definition times of stress. We readily recognize that bad changes are stressful, but so are good changes. While someone who has lost their job may need extra support or an opportunity just to escape from his or her problems, so does someone who just got that hard-won partnership in the law firm or that contract that means a big bonus.

Too Much Success, Too Fast

Climbing the corporate ladder is always a challenge. For some people, it takes many years. Others seem to skip right up it. The fast track can be wonderful because it can give you an edge that will always put you out ahead, but it can also cause a lot of problems.

Success can come too quickly, and the way it can make us feel can overshadow other important parts of our lives. There are thousands of examples of couples who struggled mightily in their early years, only to have their marriages fall apart when the big break comes before they're ready for it.

Affair Facts

Although successful men may be more likely than others to have extramarital affairs, they rarely leave their wives and marry the other woman. They have fun with their lovers, but they return to their marriages when the affair is over. According to one study, only 3% of more than four thousand successful men surveyed ended up marrying their lovers.

In many cases, one spouse may have sacrificed his or her ambitions to support the other's goal. When the goal is reached, the roles aren't immediately reversed, nor should they be. But the sacrificing spouse may continue to play the support role long after the need to do so is over. Unless there's a change in personal goals, one spouse can start to resent the success of the other. And that resentment can lead to an affair, especially if the successful spouse is paying little attention to the home front.

In other cases, the successful spouse is so enraptured with what she's been able to accomplish that her achievements cloud her judgment in other areas. Affairs can be seen as prizes or rewards for outstanding achievement. They also can be seen as something we've earned or are entitled to for working so hard.

Dr. Lana's Secrets

Sex and money are linked in many complicated ways; both give people a sense of power. A man may find himself more desirable to women once it is obvious he has wealth. A woman may find her success makes her feel more influential, more independent, and more sexual. Either sex or money can be used as a commodity to acquire resources previously unavailable. Power is a potent aphrodisiac.

Financial Problems

Money is the number two issue that marriage partners argue about (emotional issues are number one and sex is number three). Surprisingly, having too much can be as much of a problem as constantly being in the hole, especially if spouses have different money management styles. Not being able to agree on how to spend their money is a significant point of contention for many couples. Even when money isn't a concern, one partner can become highly aggrieved over the other's spendthrift ways and might search for someone who has a little more respect for the big green.

There's a very easy solution to this problem, and it's called a budget. Most people think you only need one if money is tight, but budgets are just as important when there's plenty of it. Living with a budget puts boundaries on what you spend and why. It's as important as establishing other relationship boundaries (see Chapter 8, "Knowing Where 'No' Is") and should be addressed at the same time they are. If all you can do is fight over money, find a financial counselor to work with and resolve your disagreements.

The Wonders of Birth

Bringing a baby into a relationship, whether by pregnancy or adoption, changes it forever. What was once two is now three…or more, especially now that women are having babies later and multiple births are increasingly more common. Intimacy becomes a rare commodity when you're tending to the needs of a newborn. And the sheer lack of sleep is enough to push many couples to the edge.

Having a baby is one of the most highly anticipated events for most couples, but it can open up a hotbed of problems, especially if there is disagreement in the relationship over when a family should be started or if there should be one at all.

Being less than delighted over the news of an impending arrival is not unusual. Even couples who are generally thrilled over the prospect have times when they're not that convinced that it's a good idea. It's when a lack of excitement or interest continues beyond a few days, or a week or so at the most, that the problem is serious.

Trying to handle emotional issues while you're anticipating the arrival of a baby is difficult because the situation is already emotionally charged. But it's important to talk to each other and make joint decisions during this time. The immense hormonal changes that the woman goes through can significantly alter a couple's conflict resolution processes, even if they are firmly in place.

Bumps Ahead

A new baby in the house is often the time when many men stray. Some are anxious about the responsibility of a new baby and don't know how to discuss this concern with their wife. They feel they are losing their freedom and that their carefree days are over. For some men, becoming a father is the first time they have truly put someone else ahead of themselves, and they resist accepting this change in their responsibilities.

Happy Birthdays?

It's as inevitable as death and taxes and, to some people, about as loathsome. What we're talking about here is the effect that being alive has on our bodies. Unless you've

Affair Facts

Getting older is not a good reason to stop having a sexual relationship. Many couples continue enjoying their sexual relationship into their 70s, 80s, or beyond.

Bumps Ahead

Helping a loved one get back on his or her feet requires incredible patience. Even more is needed should the problem become chronic. Some spouses resent their new role, especially if their partner's problem has a long-term effect on their relationship. Resentment can also turn into guilt. Either emotion can propel either spouse into an affair.

really figured out a way to make a deal with the devil or you've discovered the magic fountain of youth, expect to wrinkle, sag, get gray and grow older—just like the rest of us.

There are two basic ways to handle growing older. You can do it gracefully. Or you can get dragged into it, kicking and screaming all the way. Guess which approach causes less wear and tear on a relationship?

The old saying "You're as young as you feel" is a good one to keep in mind when those wrinkles and gray hairs start popping up.

Losing Our Health

Illnesses can test a marriage to its limits. Caring for an ill spouse, especially one suffering from ongoing problems like heart disease, diabetes, or memory loss, can be a real test of patience and faith. However, it's when your beloved is suffering that you really come to understand the marriage vows, "…in sickness and in health."

The physical changes caused by some illnesses or diseases can put distance in a relationship even when both partners are working hard against it, as it did for Paula and Nick. When Paula discovered a lump in her breast, her physician recommended immediate surgery. Fortunately, all she needed was a lumpectomy. Still, her recovery was slower and more painful than she expected, and she was embarrassed about the discrepancy in the size of her breasts. "The last thing I wanted to do was alienate my husband, but I found it difficult to have anything to do with sex after the surgery," Paula says. "In fact, I encouraged Nick to find someone else as long as I didn't know about it."

Paula never knew if Nick followed up on her recommendation, but after several months of feeling blue, she decided to take her physician's advice and join a breast cancer support group. "The cancer came at a time when I was feeling a little down in life in general," she says. "Joining the support group gave me a new perspective on what I was going through and helped me feel more positive about the future.

"The best thing I got from the group was the assurance that my feelings were very common," Paula added, "and that I needed to work them out in the context of my marriage, rather than shoving Nick away until I was feeling better again. Nick was very supportive and very patient, which surprised me in a way as I'm not sure I would have been if the situation had been reversed. He even came with me to the meetings that were open to spouses. Between what I learned from the group individually and the work Nick and I did together, I was able to get past my concern about the appearance of my breast and not let it interfere with our relationship."

Finding a support group can help ease the burden and put you in touch with people who know what you're going through. Even if you think your thoughts are too evil to bare, you might be surprised at what the others have to say.

Facing the Final Curtain

The death of a family member or someone else close to us not only reminds us that the grim reaper eventually comes calling on everyone but also often highlights unresolved issues and concerns in our lives, especially as they relate to the person we've just lost.

Robert Redford's movie *Ordinary People*, based on Judith Guest's novel of the same name, is a poignant portrayal of how deeply death—in this case, the drowning death of a son—can affect a family. The surviving son felt that he had caused his brother's death and was suffering immense guilt. His mother also blamed him for the death of her favorite child. Although son and father sought help from a therapist and were willing to discuss their feelings about the loss, the mother preferred to deal with her pain by distancing herself from it and anything else that reminded her of her dead son.

Although an extramarital affair wasn't part of the movie's plot, in real life this is when an affair often begins. In *Ordinary People* it was easy to see how the husband could have gone that direction when his attempts to repair his family and air the issues between them were repeatedly rebuffed by his wife. As it was, the movie ended with the wife moving out after her husband confessed that he doubted the future of their marriage because of her inability to face the tough issues.

Dr. Lana's Secrets

Death of someone you aren't emotionally close with, like a neighbor or a co-worker, can trigger feelings that life is passing you by. Fear of missing out on excitement or dying without exploring a fantasy can lead you to taking risks you would otherwise not consider. Give yourself at least six months to grieve before leaping into uncharted territory just for the thrill of it.

Grief is difficult for everyone to handle. Time is a necessity for working through all its stages. However, some people grieve so deeply and for such a long time that surviving loved ones feel alienated. If what you're feeling goes so deep that your spouse or friends feel they can't reach you, it's time for professional counseling.

Danger: Holidays Ahead!

The carolers are caroling, street-corner Santas are out in force. It's almost time to light that first Hanukkah candle, and your kids are so excited that they can barely contain themselves. And you...well, there you are at your neighbor's holiday party, and you're having a hard time containing yourself, too. But it's that cute thing who lives down the street who's calling to you, not the food-laden holiday table.

It shouldn't come as any surprise that the end of the calendar year is a prime time for affairs to commence. Maybe it's the mistletoe over the doorway. But more likely it's the spirits in the punch or the eggnog that help to release any pent-up spirits party-goers might have.

Sadly, the same emotions that can make some people feel like life is no longer worth living are also often behind holiday-time affairs. The holidays are supposed to be a fun and joyous time of the year. Oftentimes, however, they aren't. The toxic memories of Christmases past can rear up their ugly heads years after you thought you had forgotten your disappointment over not getting that shiny new bike or that fancy dollhouse.

Bumps Ahead

More suicides are committed during the holidays than at any other time of the year.

Some people, knowing that their resistance is already down during this time of year, avoid holiday parties entirely. For others, staying away from alcoholic beverages is the answer. There are lots of things you can do to celebrate the season, and many of them are great ways to stay away from trouble. Sing in a choir. Take the kids on a ride to see the holiday lights. Go be a Santa. Volunteer at a homeless shelter.

It's a great time of year to get your mind off yourself— and away from any temptations that might be calling your name.

The Least You Need to Know

➤ Preparing in advance for life's challenges can help you head them off at the pass.

➤ The seven-year itch may miss the mark by a few years, but it does happen in most marriages.

➤ Keeping the lines of communication open is essential to working through sore spots in a relationship.

➤ Tough times don't last forever, but it takes a lot of personal fortitude and work to get through them.

Honey, can we talk for a-

Chapter 13

Five Bad Habits That Lead to Affairs

In This Chapter

➤ Identifying emotional sparring

➤ The difference between humor and hostility

➤ The pitfalls of living in the future

➤ Speak to me; listen to me!

Where do you think you're going?
From the looks of things, back to Cuba.

—Lucille Ball to Desi Arnaz, *I Love Lucy*

Remember the television show *I Love Lucy*? How many times did Ricky come home to their apartment to a clearly upset Lucy? How many times did he then ask her what was wrong? And how many times did she answer him by saying "Nothing"? No wonder he let fly with a string of Spanish epithets more often than not!

The on-screen marriage created by Lucille Ball and Desi Arnaz was brilliantly funny, in part because they so aptly portrayed some of the silly things that couples are so capable of doing to each other. Who hasn't indulged in a little emotional hide-and-seek when they're looking for attention? Who hasn't been less than forthcoming with their spouse, only to have their cover-up exposed?

What is funny on-screen, however, becomes less amusing when we have to deal with it in real life. Concoct too many cat-and-mouse games with your spouse, and you run the risk of having legitimate requests for emotional support unheeded. Let too many outside activities occupy your free time, and you may find yourself flying solo when you thought you had a copilot.

While many habits can lead a spouse to seek an extramarital affair, the ones discussed in this chapter are key.

Bad Habit #1: Playing Emotional Hide-and-Seek

No matter how well we think we know each other, or how intuitive we may think we are when it comes to discerning how our spouses feel, we can't read their minds. Unfortunately, this is what we force each other to do when, for whatever reason, we choose to hide our emotions instead of bringing them out into the open. Turning this behavior into a steady habit is a surefire way of thwarting whatever attempts your spouse may make to try to understand what's troubling you.

The behavior patterns that men and women use to relate (and not relate!) to each other are so universal that a host of books on male-female communication line bookstore shelves. Although women are often accused of using evasiveness to manipulate their relationships, men are just as guilty.

Dr. Lana's Secrets

Playing emotional hide-and-seek can be a prelude to a fight that needs to happen. Instead of using this game, be courageous. Speak your mind, even if it means setting off a fight. There's just not enough time in today's world to let problems fester. Settle your conflicts as they happen.

Women might try to make excuses for their evasive behavior by chalking it up to emotional swings, PMS, whatever. Men try to excuse it by pointing to their stoic natures and to the fact that they were taught to keep their emotions to themselves. But there's really no excuse for the behavior, which basically equates to a very subtle form of emotional blackmail. Telling someone often enough that you don't want to talk about something can indicate a basic lack of trust in that person, but it can also indicate your lack of interest in even trying to build that trust.

Trust Goes Both Ways

Trust issues lie behind a good deal of this emotional sparring. But they don't have to be issues related to how we feel about our partners. For Karen, a lack of trust in her own feelings made it very difficult for her to confide many of them in Jamie.

"I don't know why, but I came to believe that many of my emotions were inappropriate, which made it almost impossible for me to want to tell Jamie what I was feeling," she says. "It took several years of counseling, both individually and as a couple, for me to realize that whatever I was feeling was a valid emotion and that I was doing my relationship with Jamie more harm than good if I kept my feelings to myself."

Looking for Attention

Also known as "playing the martyr," attention seeking can be another component of emotional hide-and-seek games. Although both sexes do it, it's more commonly seen in women, who will very often pattern this behavior after what they saw their mothers do when they were growing up.

"I'll never forget hearing my mother go around the house making these huge sighs," says Betsy. "I would ask her what was wrong, and she'd just shake her head and say nothing, all the while looking at my father, who would usually have his head buried in the evening paper. He had long ago quit paying attention to her. Every so often, I'll catch myself doing the same thing around Ray, my partner, but he doesn't let me get away with it. He's much more confrontational than I am, and he'll drag things out of me, sometimes before I'm ready, but I always feel better after we talk."

Bad Habit #2: Being Critical

Grandma was fond of saying it, and it's true: You attract more flies with sugar than with vinegar. Unfortunately, the sweet nothings we whisper with such great regularity to our partners at the beginning of a relationship all too frequently turn into too-tart somethings as time goes on.

It's just as easy to say something nice about someone as it is to say something nasty. We know that. But we tend to say the nasty things anyway, often without realizing that we're doing it. The next time you're at a party or out with a group of people, turn an occasional ear toward the conversations going on between the couples around you. You might be amazed to hear them saying to each other things they would never dream of saying to someone outside of the relationship.

Being critical of our spouses, even if what's being said is meant to be constructive, often indicates a basic lack of respect for them. Respect may have been there once, but something happened to erode it. In other cases, it may never have existed. Strange but true, it's entirely possible to love someone and still treat him or her somewhat callously.

Affair Speak

Criticism is an unfavorable judgment or comment. It does not motivate anyone to change or to learn, and when regularly used between two people, it definitely doesn't create trust or build confidence between them.

Criticism Drives Love Away

There is no such thing as constructive criticism. For April, it was Mel's continual criticisms that motivated her to seek a relationship outside of their marriage. "Mel was always a little caustic toward me, but he's gotten worse over the years," April says. "At first, I was able to ignore most of it because I felt that he was just kidding around. But now, just about everything he says comes out as a negative comment about something I've done or said. When I try to talk to him about it, he truly doesn't understand what the problem is and claims he is only saying what he feels. Mel and I have a good sexual relationship, but I sure feel a difference in my self-esteem when I am with my lover, who is consistently upbeat and complimentary.

Dr. Lana's Secrets

A good way to tell the difference between humor and hostility is to see whether both people are laughing. If they aren't, it isn't humor; it's hostility. Hostility leads to hurt and ultimately to the end of the relationship. So if you're the only one laughing, take heed: Your target may not be around long. If you're the target of hostile humor and are laughing through your tears, it is time to move out of the firing range.

Be aware that criticism of your partner is not the only kind of critical behavior that can get him running. Art, who's been married to Cerisse for almost thirty years, has had multiple affairs and says he couldn't have stayed married to Cerisse without them. "My relationship with Cerisse is based on very traditional values, and I would never think of divorcing her," he says. "But there's nothing I can do about her attitude toward life. She doesn't complain about things, but she will criticize the least little thing, something that you or I wouldn't even notice. It got under my skin at a very early point in our marriage, and I've always searched out lovers with a more positive approach to life."

Dr. Lana's Secrets

Complaints should focus on issues or behaviors, not on a person. When you register a complaint, keep it specific and tell your partner how you view the problem and what solutions you would like to see happen.

Not the Gift, but the Gesture

A widely used textbook on marriage, published in the 1950s, advised young wives never to be critical of any gift their husbands bestowed on them. "Even if you hate the gift," the book encouraged, "smile sweetly and thank him profusely."

"O.K., so that was back in the 1950s," you're thinking. Endorsing this kind of behavior wipes out some thirty years of the fight for women's rights in this country, yes? Hardly. The point is to value the gesture and not just the object. Sometimes we get consumed with getting just the right stuff and forget about the meaning behind the gift. Sometimes, enjoying the moment and appreciating the effort is the best reaction.

Bad Habit #3: Living in a Rut

Comfy as an old shoe. Well-worn. Predictable. Broken in. Do these phrases describe your relationship with your partner? If so, you might be headed for trouble.

Human beings have a natural resistance to change, and our lives very often settle into routines that change little over the years. We get up at the same time every day, we eat at the same time, we even do leisure activities at the same times every week and see the same people in the same social settings. We wear our hair the same way year after year, and we even wear the same style of clothing. Comfortable, yes. Boring sometimes? Unless you're a garden slug, it has to be!

Routines are comfortable for everyone—up to a point. We need a certain amount of structure in our lives to make us run efficiently, to get us where we need to go when we need to be there. But too much reliance on the same old, same old can be the death knell of a relationship. A routine turns into a rut when it doesn't change because one or both of the people in it resist change.

Bumps Ahead

Security, which is freedom from danger, can be confused with predictability or, in other words, keeping things the same. However, people do change, both emotionally and intellectually. Thinking you are creating security for yourself by keeping your relationship the same is dangerous. If you don't create growth in yourself and in your relationship, you may be slowly killing the chemistry between you.

Constant Chaos, No Good Either

On the flip side, too much change and constant upheaval in a relationship can also create a rut. If you or your partner likes things to be changing all the time, your relationship can be just as vulnerable to an affair as a relationship that tends to be more sedentary.

After three years of a quick-changing, emotionally tumultuous relationship with Kris, Brad found himself extremely attracted to April, who led a calmer life. "Kris is like a bee, always flitting here and there, always changing direction," Brad says. "I found this very desirable in the beginning, but I'm ready to settle down just a little bit, and I've realized it just isn't in Kris's nature. I'm not sure she even realizes when I'm not around—that's how busy she keeps herself. April might be quieter, but the time I spend with her is so very pleasant and serene; it's time I spend clearing my head out from all the clutter created by my other relationship."

Too much of a good thing can be as damaging as not enough. The key is to strike a balance that suits you both.

Bumps Ahead

One of the top reasons people give for having affairs is that they're bored with their spouses. If you suspect that might be one of your problems, remember that it takes two to create a relationship, good or bad. Chances are, you both need to work on putting some spark back into what you have.

Bumps Ahead

Deathbed regrets are universally about not spending more time with loved ones, not enjoying special moments more, not following a dream, or not forgiving old grudges. Rarely are they about working more, mowing the grass better, or fixing a gourmet dinner.

Bad Habit #4: Putting Your Partner on Hold

"I can do it tomorrow," we often yawn to ourselves as we roll over to sleep without kissing our spouses goodnight. But what happens if tomorrow never comes? Awful thought, isn't it?

As hard as we work to improve our quality of life and prolong our existence on this earth, there's never any guarantee that tomorrow will come. This simple fact is the reason why it's so important to make the most of what we have now—not what we might have next year or the year after. Now. And that means not putting off your relationship with your spouse. Not for any reason.

Waiting for Perfection

"Now" is not an easy concept for many of us. We like to think about what happened in the past or ponder what may happen in the future, instead of dealing with the aches and pains of everyday living.

For some people, life gets put on hold until some point in the future. They don't know exactly where the point is, only that they'll get there after they've managed to achieve certain a set of goals in their lives. "I'll have more time for my kids," they think, "when I reach vice president at the firm." "I'll want to make love to my spouse more often when I lose those last ten pounds." The problem is, we often arrive at that future point without having achieved our goals, and we've missed out on a lot of life in the meantime.

For Carol, it took the death of a friend's husband to shake her out of her "future thinking." "I was always living in the future, telling myself I would do things at some point in the future when my life was on a more even keel, when I had more money, when I started to get into shape physically, whatever," she says. "Focusing so much on the future was putting my whole life on hold, including my relationship with my husband. I was always going to be more loving, more sexy, more giving...somewhere down the road, but not now.

"Then Sue's husband died, and I saw how much she regretted having not made him a higher priority in her life," Carol adds. "You really don't know what you've got until it's gone. I realized that life was too short to wait to live it until I reached some hypothetical point of perfection."

Bumps Ahead

The curse of perfectionism is wanting everything to be perfect before you can enjoy yourself or others. It means sentencing yourself to a sterile life. Perhaps it will be devoid of untidiness or mess, but it will also be empty of messy things like play, adventure, belly laughs, and giggles.

Work, Work, Work

Many of us, far too many of us, are more married to our work than we are to our spouses. Do we spend more time working than we do at home—or does it just seem that way because we don't have any energy left when we finally do get home? Long hours are expected of those who want to make something of themselves. We even brag about the time we put into our jobs and about how we can get by on four or five hours of sleep.

Virtual offices and new technology haven't helped the situation in the least. Yes, our workplaces are more flexible than ever before. But this flexibility has given new meaning to the concept of taking work home. Not only does the work come, the whole office comes with it! It's too easy, and too tempting, to sneak out of bed to put the last touches on that special report you've been working on for months. Far too many spouses are getting far too accustomed to the squeal of a modem making its connection and the sound of their partner's fingers tapping away on laptop keyboards late at night.

Too Much Exercise, Not Enough Sexercise

There's the aerobics class at 6:30 a.m. Maybe an after-work squash game with your law partner. In-line skating with your friends on Saturdays. Doubles tennis with your in-laws on Sunday.

We're not saying that any of this is wrong. In fact, getting a lot of leisure-time activity is an essential component of a happy, healthy lifestyle. Our bodies *are* our temples, and we are the ones charged with the primary maintenance responsibilities. However, it's so easy to let the things we do to take care of ourselves take priority over our relationships with our partners. A little couch potato time together is not necessarily a bad thing.

Tim puts it this way. "Marsha has a great body, but I wish she'd spend a little less time perfecting it and a little more time being intimate with me. She's always off doing something—running with her friends, going to the club for her aerobics classes—her energy level is amazing. I'll follow her lead, but with everything she does, there's little time for us to do anything else. Fitness is great, I don't deny that for a minute. But I feel like we're building up our bodies and wearing down our relationship."

Dr. Lana's Secrets

We know what's most important to us, but are you living by those priorities? Make a quick list of the five things that are most important to you. Now look at your calendar; have you scheduled time for them today? tomorrow? this week? If not, are you putting first things first?

Making time for intimate moments with your partner is one of the healthiest things you can do to keep your relationship alive. It doesn't have to be anything big and elaborate. Surprise her some evening with a back rub, instead of meeting your best buddy for a racquetball game. Stay in bed one morning and snuggle a little longer, instead of rushing off to your early morning aerobics class. Chances are, your body might even enjoy the day off...and one day away from the gym won't make or break your fitness routine.

Bumps Ahead

Scheduling elaborate activities for the children each and every day can cause problems for everyone involved. Keeping yourself so busy with your kids that you don't have time for your partner often leads to big trouble.

Kids, Kids, Kids

If you're a parent, you know all about that special little flip-flop that happens in your heart when you think about your kids. (If you don't have children, just read along and pay attention because you'll need to know this if you ever do become a parent.) There are times, certainly, when they should take priority in your life, especially when they first arrive on the scene. However, if you're consistently spending way more time with your little darlings than with your spouse, there may be big trouble ahead for you.

Apart from your relationship with your partner, your children are the most precious commodities in your life. The time you spend with them will be some of the most important moments in your life, good and bad. And it's the children that make you a family, not just a couple. However, many parents allow their children and their needs to take first place in their lives, overshadowing their relationships with their spouses.

Pet "Children"

For some couples, their pets play the role of children, and the same potential pitfalls exist. Sally, who breeds champion retrievers, spends almost every summer morning training her dogs for their water trials at a lake across town. The combination of early mornings and several hours of physical exertion in the water wears her out so much that she is exhausted by the time evening comes. Ken, her partner for many years and an avid hunter, was the one who got Sally interested in the dogs in the first place. Now he says he wishes he could wean Sally away from her canine companions.

"When we were just working with a couple of dogs, things were fine," he says. "Now, Sally's got a kennel full of them, and she trains for other people, too. Then there's the dog shows almost every weekend. I won't say she loves the dogs more than she loves me, but they sure get a lot more attention than I do."

Dogs, cats, or kids—here's one hard and fast rule when it comes to the role they play in your relationship. As much as you love them, they should come second to your partner.

Bad Habit #5: Failing to Communicate

As human beings, we have been given one of the most precious gifts in the animal kingdom. We have the ability to speak. We don't have to use an elaborate system of barks and whistles to communicate with our spouses, nor are we reduced to embarrassing displays of various body parts to show that we care (although it could be argued that we can and do do this at times!). We have the infinite beauty of language at our disposal. Too bad that some of us are not very good at using it to communicate with our partners.

The amount of time a couple spends in conversation with each other is infinitesimal compared to the number of hours that are in a day. We might spend more time talking to our pets than we do with our spouses. And it's a sure bet that we spend more time conversing with the folks at work than the ones at home. No wonder our coworkers often get to know us better than our partners do!

Talking is just one part of the communications equation. The other is listening, and we don't do well here, either. Funny, because it's such an easy thing to do, but for whatever reason, and there are many, we tend to listen to our partners with half an ear, if that. We hear what we want to hear, and we respond inappropriately.

Not listening to your partner again reflects a lack of respect or caring about them. Listening in the wrong way; that is, assuming we know what they're going to say before they say it, or always being on the defensive, shows this attitude as well.

Dr. Lana's Secrets

Researchers tell us that exactly how we communicate isn't important as long as we do it. Couples who communicate loudly are just as likely to have a successful relationship as those who seldom talk but often touch. The crucial issue is that your styles match and that the way you communicate is satisfying to both of you.

The lack of communication between partners is the driving force behind many affairs. More often than not, someone involved in an affair will think his or her lover is wonderful just for taking the time to listen. Fortunately, communication problems between partners are easy to correct if both people are willing to do it. The goal is to identify and work on those problems before it really is too late. One very easy and very quick fix: Turn off the TV and power down the computer. Go find your partner and look him or her in the eyes. And talk.

The Least You Need to Know

➤ Too much mental game playing can lead to a major timeout.

➤ Never criticize your partner. There is no such thing as constructive criticism.

➤ Never put your affections on hold until sometime in the future, no matter what the reason.

➤ Nothing stays the same: not you, not your partner, not your relationship. Seek change and encourage your relationship to grow as you both do.

➤ Talk may be cheap, but it's oh so valuable! You have to communicate to stay happily together.

Chapter 14

Reading the Warning Signs

> ## In This Chapter
>
> ➤ Identifying emotional signals
>
> ➤ The importance of paying attention
>
> ➤ What does it mean when a spouse is too nice?
>
> ➤ Signs that your partner's leading a double life

Like sex, knowledge is good if used in the service of life and love.

—Lillian Smith, *Killers of the Dream*

If you've been with your partner for any length of time, chances are pretty good that you know a lot about what makes him or her tick. He always runs a few minutes late because he never allows himself enough time to drive across town. You know you'd better pack a handkerchief if the movie you're seeing has an animal in it—your tough, independent wife even cried when Bambi lost his mother. If your sweetie orders eggs sunny-side up, it's a sure bet he'll dump ketchup on them, much as you've tried to discourage that nasty habit. And so on.

A certain amount of predictability is a good thing in a relationship. Not only does it give us a framework in which to function when we're together, it also helps us gauge the direction in which the relationship is going. Like the Dow Jones stock chart, there are bound to be lots of little peaks and valleys. However, like any investment, our goal is to have more up days than down days. We want to be ahead of where we started by the time we're done.

This chapter looks at the early warning signs, so to speak, of an affair, either one that's being considered or one that's probably in its early stages. And the next chapter, Chapter 15, "On the Trail of an Affair," explores what you may be seeing or feeling if your partner is engaging in a full-swing affair.

Emotional Distress Signals

One of the first and most subtle signs of trouble in a relationship is a sense of there being more valleys than peaks in your day-to-day life together. There may be an uncertainty in the air, and you don't quite know what to do about it. The signals you're getting from your spouse are mixed, and you're being more cautious about things than you used to be. You might even be putting off or rethinking plans that involve your partner because you're not quite sure where things between the two of you stand.

Affair Speak

Intuition, that sense of reality that we accept without reason or factual knowledge, has a way of alerting us to dangers.

What you're sensing are emotional distress signals being sent by your spouse. Something is wrong, and your partner is letting you know about it, consciously or subconsciously. The better you know him or her, the more likely you are to clue in on these signals at some level at a fairly early stage. If instead of just sensing that something is wrong, you can identify and understand your partner's S.O.S. calls, you have a better chance of addressing the underlying issues before they escalate.

Scoping Out the Signals

Some of these signals are deceptively subtle. Others are blatant. Obvious or not, they still can be easily overlooked by a spouse who's too busy to see them, doesn't want to see them, or doesn't believe them when she does see them.

What's behind these emotional calls for help? One, several, or all of the following emotions are likely to be fueling them:

➤ Guilt—over the affair, over contemplating one if it hasn't started yet, over hurting you or your kids

➤ Fear of what might happen and what may be lost

➤ Anger, especially toward the other spouse if blame is being placed in that direction

➤ Disappointment or a feeling of failure that the relationship hasn't gone as well as expected

We all experience emotions like these sometime during the course of a relationship. But such feelings can escalate during problem periods and are especially capable of getting the better of us when our needs aren't being met for one reason or another.

The stress and tension that results, if allowed to continue for any length of time, is guaranteed to put an enormous strain on your relationship.

While you realize you need to talk to your partner, knowing what you have to do is easier than doing it. You probably feel apprehensive and want to put off questioning your mate. Get a notebook and start making some notes to yourself about your feelings and changes you have noticed in your relationship.

Dr. Lana's Secrets

Behavior always makes sense when you have all the information. If your partner's behavior just doesn't fit, ask. Describe the feelings and niggling thoughts you've been having. Then simply ask him for the reasons behind his actions.

This is when your knowledge of your spouse's emotional patterns really pays off. Hopefully, you can recognize even the tiny blips on the radar screen and know how to react or respond. If you can't, then read on.

Something's in the Air

A stronger sign of a relationship that's struggling is a general feeling of tension. The comfort level that once existed between the two of you seems off. Instead of being in synch, you feel like you're living life in two different beats. You're doing the waltz. He's dancing the two-step. It feels like there's a thin film between the both of you and over everything you do that you can't quite penetrate, no matter how hard you try. Even worse, the person you know and love seems to be turning into someone else.

Dr. Lana's Secrets

If something feels wrong in a relationship, chances are that there is a problem somewhere. While it's possible to be overly concerned about the slightest things, it's generally a good idea to let your partner know you're concerned. Most affairs end when the affairee suspects her partner knows and she doesn't want to get caught.

Living a Double Life

Maybe there's no affair yet. Or maybe there is. In any event, something has happened to cause your partner's attention to your relationship to be pulled off-center. He may or may not be indulging in extramarital behavior, but he is experiencing emotions that are separate from your marriage. Even if he's not actually in an affair, he's still living a double life of sorts because there are things he either doesn't want to tell you or feels he can't tell you.

Under the Magnifying Glass

It is a good idea to be tuned-in to your relationship all the time, and at this time you want to be more observant than usual. Being observant means being attentive or watchful, noticing what is and isn't happening between you.

However, don't start searching every word and gesture for hidden meaning and then deducing that some sinister intrigue is taking place. Keep perspective; there is usually more than one possible explanation for your partner's behavior.

Little issues, silly things that were never a problem before can now seem like major evidence of wrongdoing. Abby noticed that Nate wasn't eating much at dinner but didn't seem to be losing weight. She wondered if he was eating another meal with someone else before he came home. As it turned out, he had a bacterial ulcer and after his doctor prescribed a course of antibiotics, his voracious appetite returned.

Words in a Bubble

Your actions as the observer also change the relationship. You may no longer be behaving naturally or reacting the way you usually do. But, some changes in your interactions are more indicative of an affair. Changes in the way you talk to each other can suggest something out of the ordinary is happening. Conversation doesn't flow as easily as it once did, and you find yourself measuring your words before you say them. When you do talk, you feel like your sentences are being displayed in cartoon word bubbles.

You may also notice that your conversations are dwindling down to what's absolutely necessary—the kids' schedules, who's going to pick up the laundry, what time you'll be home tonight, what you want for dinner. Even your nonverbal communication seems awkward. Where just a glance between you could speak a thousand words, they're few and far between now.

Too Good, Too Nice

Sometimes a wayward partner tries to manage their conflicted feelings by being kinder and more attentive than they have been in the past. Your partner might also be more interested in participating in social events than before. When you go out, you're showered with attention. Your kids may also be getting more affection and attention than ever before.

Dr. Lana's Secrets

A wandering partner may overcompensate because of their culpability. Overcompensation is a way of atonement, or of trying to make up for their transgression by being more generous than usual. This is a sign that while they may be having or contemplating an affair, they are also being protective of their relationship with you.

These spouses are feeling guilty, and their outward behavior is a study in sweetness as they try to convince everyone, including themselves, that there really isn't anything wrong between the two of you. It's important for them to have their family and friends see what appears to be a healthy relationship. One key reason is that showing such attention in a public place can make them look like the good guys if word should slip out about any marital difficulties.

Dr. Lana's Secrets

If you receive a grand prize winner's notice from Publisher's Clearing House announcing that you may have won a million bucks, you know better than to start spending the prize money. If he is suddenly eager to go to the grocery store or he starts to routinely offer to do the dishes so you can go to bed early, be appreciative but cautious. Go along with him to the grocery store and do the dishes together. Stay close.

It's tempting to allow this behavior to lull you into a false sense of security, especially if things have been strained between you for some time. However, don't let a sudden turn from distant to attentive fool you. How spouses act toward one another generally doesn't change significantly overnight. Unless the two of you are actively working on such issues, it's more likely that your spouse's suddenly sweet demeanor is actually an attempt to mastermind a cover-up.

An Increasing Sense of Dis-Ease

Marital stress at this level often causes general feelings of physical discomfort. One or both of you may feel vaguely achy, listless, or tired—like you're coming down with the flu or a cold. You're not sick, but you just don't feel up to snuff. You may even feel slightly blue or depressed.

These, again, are subtle signs, but they are important indicators. They can arise if you're denying the problems between you, and they also indicate anger turned inward. Because of the overall malaise that now exists between the two of you, whatever outlets you once had for talking about your feelings are most likely closed off and you're keeping things inside more than you're accustomed to.

Bumps Ahead

Some people feel things more physically than emotionally. Emotional pain can be felt as a chronically upset stomach, an unrelenting headache, or the proverbial pain in the neck.

Like any kind of stress, marital problems can exact a physical toll on your body. If you've been feeling punky for awhile, or your generally robust partner now seems tired and listless, it may be due to more than the bug that's going around.

As tension increases, the next stage of emotional distress sets in. Characterized by more obvious behavioral changes on the part of the errant or soon-to-be errant spouse, this stage also causes heightened discomfort for both parties that shows itself in a variety of ways.

Gimme Space!

What you'll most likely begin to notice is a feeling of greater distance between the two of you. Your spouse is even less interested in spending time with you than before, and the efforts to put space between you are more obvious as well.

Now is when discomfort turns into pain as your partner buries himself in the newspaper, watches television for hours on end, spends evening after evening working late, or loses himself on the Internet. Other distancing behaviors include:

➤ Going to bed early (this can also be a symptom of depression)

➤ Staying in bed longer than normal (so can this)

➤ Overeating

➤ Drug use, such as tranquilizers or prescription pain medication

➤ Long telephone calls at inappropriate times

➤ Overindulging in alcohol

Distancing serves a number of purposes for a straying or affair-seeking spouse as things continue to break down. It gives her more time to contemplate all the things that are wrong with you and your life together and to think about how the affair that she's having—or contemplating—might make things better. Emotional walls are being erected.

As one partner pulls away, the other starts to feel hurt or angry. When this hurt or anger is expressed as withdrawal or sulking, the straying partner uses this behavior as further justification for an affair.

"Frankly, My Dear…"

Another way to avoid dealing with emotional conflicts is to ignore the fact that they exist at all. This tactic is similar to distancing—but different. Instead of indulging in distancing behavior, a partner just goes about his normal routine.

Both partners can play this game. When it does take place, the other partner often feels hurt and abandoned at first. Soon, however, the response is "Fine. You want to be a jerk? I'll be one as well." Both partners can get so adept at acting like they don't care that the impression becomes reality, and they end up totally alienated from each other.

Walking on Eggshells

As tension and conflict continue to increase, your spouse might demonstrate some unusual and perhaps frightening behaviors. He may seem happy one moment and immensely sad or angry the next. Full-blown depression may set in. Tempers may flare where they never did before. If you have children, they may now be the target of some of these outbursts. If they sensed something was wrong before, they'll know it now.

The general feeling that develops during this period is one of hesitancy and fear. You're so far away from where you used to be as a couple that you don't know what you can do to bring things back to center. You're afraid that the smallest thing you say or do—or don't do, for that matter—might set off an emotional eruption, so you do your best to avoid saying or doing anything.

Bumps Ahead

Distress is damaging to your health in ways you may not expect. There are the obvious signs like headaches, insomnia, and increased heart rate, and there are more subtle and dangerous occurrences, such as higher blood pressure or lower blood platelet counts. Platelets cause the blood to clot, preventing us from bleeding to death following an injury.

Bumps Ahead

A good offense is often considered the best defense. And a common and effective defense for a guilt-ridden partner may be accusing the innocent partner of infidelity or dishonesty to deflect suspicion from herself.

What's sad about this situation is that both spouses may actually want to reach out to the other but are afraid to. It's the time when errant spouses in particular may want to be very loving, but feel they can't be because of guilt or fear over what they're thinking about doing or are doing outside of their marriage.

A Short Fuse

"I knew something was really wrong when Sherry pitched a fit over my not picking up her dry cleaning," Bryan recalls. "Usually, this wouldn't be a big deal, but Sherry just went off the deep end when I told her the cleaner had closed by the time I got there. She actually called me an inconsiderate jackass and threw something at me! Then she started to sob and ran into the bathroom. I didn't know what to do—she locked the door and wouldn't talk to me—so I just went into the other room and waited. She didn't come out until it was time to go to bed."

Bumps Ahead

Conflict is not something that can be avoided in life or in love. Ducking conflict in one arena means it will seep out in some other way, either in your physical, emotional or relationship health. While facing conflict is hard, avoiding it is worse.

Errant spouses that exhibit this behavior have often commenced an affair and are going through huge internal battles because of it. Their feelings of guilt and fear are literally going to war inside of them, and the process is wearing them down emotionally as well as physically. Headaches, muscle pain, stomach upsets, and sleeping problems are common at this point. Combine all this with the added pressure of living a double life, and you have a situation that can, and will, boil over when you least expect it to.

Picky, Picky, Picky

Sherry's conflicted emotions erupted into an attack against Bryan, and you may find similar emotions leveled at you, too. Where you once suspected your actions and behaviors were being scrutinized, you now know they are because you're being picked at or belittled.

"Sorting socks...that's what really broke me down," says Phoebe. "Jack's a little color blind, so I usually separated his socks into color groups for him so he wouldn't end up wearing brown socks with black shoes. One day, I messed up the sorting myself, and boy, did I hear about it. I was worthless, incompetent, not capable of running a home, and certainly not capable of keeping his sock drawer organized.

"It was so hurtful because it was so untrue, and I knew deep inside that Jack didn't mean any of it. But things were so strained between us that I didn't feel I could reach out to him and ask him what was really wrong. I just bit back the words and walked out of the room in tears."

Dr. Lana's Secrets

Reach out and touch someone is good advice. In times of alienation, when words don't work, actual touching may be the only bridge that keeps you connected.

Anger and disappointment often drive hypercritical behavior. Making a spouse feel worthless also helps to convince the affair-seeking spouse or affairee that he is justified in looking outside of the marriage. Once one spouse starts belittling or picking on the other, the criticism often continues and even escalates as the relationship breaks down.

Sex, Exit Stage Left

It is during this period that a couple's intimate life often suffers greatly. Sex, if it takes place at all, is perfunctory and mechanical. One partner often feels like she is just servicing the other. Or one may even refuse to have sex as punishment to the other. Suspicions over the likelihood of an affair are also enough for many spouses to put up the sexual skids.

"Our sex life had been on the wane for some time, but when we got together, we still enjoyed each other," recalls Naomi. "I had suspected that Frank had his eye on a woman he worked with for some time. I didn't want to know for sure. I kept telling myself, 'All men look at other women.' As the weeks went on, Frank avoided sex. A part of me knew Frank wanted to talk to me and I was afraid of what he was going to say, so I became more sexually aggressive. Finally, one Sunday morning when I reached over to touch him, Frank said with disgust in his voice, 'Get away from me.' I quickly got out of bed and tried to pretend nothing had happened. We didn't talk and we never had sex again."

Dr. Lana's Secrets

Sex is a powerful force in any relationship. In times of distress it can become a weapon used to destroy, function as a decoy to distract, or be a means to communicate feelings that cannot be expressed any other way. Sometimes, it is the only way to hold on to each other.

Is This the End?

By now, you're probably wondering if a relationship can erode any further. It's always possible to continue a downhill slide, and the behaviors will be similar to everything you've read about here. Some may worsen. Others may disappear. If they should disappear, don't take it as a sign that the underlying problems have gone away. The more likely scenario is that they haven't.

It's in our nature to want to avoid conflicts, but it's essential to take them on if you are dealing with a troubled relationship. Sooner is always better than later, which is why it's important to learn how to identify emotional warning signs when they're being sent to you.

The Least You Need to Know

➤ Gut reactions are usually right. If something about your relationship feels off to you, it probably is.

➤ Guilt, fear, anger, and disappointment are what fuel most emotional problems when an affair has started or is being contemplated.

➤ Early detection can prevent problems from escalating.

➤ Pay attention to what your spouse says and does. Even the most off-hand comment can yield a wealth of important information.

➤ Stay close. Enjoy his offer to help or to run an errand and join in and go along.

Chapter 15

On the Trail of an Affair

In This Chapter

➤ Spotting the signs

➤ Friendship...or more?

➤ Co-working or commingling?

➤ Finding out for sure

Why didn't I see it coming? Me, who had the foresight to buy Polaroid at 8¹/₂?

— Tony Roberts in *Play It Again, Sam*

Things seem strange around your house lately? Have there been changes in your partner's behavior (as detailed in Chapter 14, "Reading the Warning Signs") that don't square up? Does it seem like she's spending a lot more time at work? Does he act like he's living in another universe? Does money seem a little tighter than before? Keep sniffing the air and keep that magnifying glass trained to your eagle eye. Chances are very good that you're on the trail of an affair.

While it's true that none of these signs necessarily guarantee that an affair is at hand, they're some of the surest indicators that one is. There may be a legitimate reason for your wife's working overtime. Maybe your husband's emotional distance has more to do with problems at work than with problems at home. But you have every reason to worry, especially if you've spotted the signs of an affair in development and they seem to be progressing.

Although most spouses—about 68 percent—find out about an affair when their partner tells them, this percentage only applies to first affairs. Subsequent relationships are more often concealed. If you're feeling more suspicious than not concerning your partner's activities these days, this chapter should help you find out for sure if any indiscretions are going on.

Clueing into an Affair

Considering what you now know about affairs, it should be easy to identify one if it crops up in your life, right? Not necessarily. Depending on its nature and the people involved, an affair still can be difficult to spot, regardless of how aware of things you think you are and how well you think you know your spouse.

Your own intuition is more often than not the surest indicator that your sweetie is rubbing noses with someone other than you. Chances are, if something feels off to you regarding your relationship, there's a problem somewhere. But there are also a whole host of warning flags that can set off your internal alert signals.

The Subtle Signs

Any one of these behaviors or circumstances can signal the presence of an affair. The odds increase as you spot more of them:

➤ He's carrying a new wallet, and it's not the one you bought him for his birthday.

➤ She orders an entree that she never would have touched before.

➤ His credit card bills no longer come to the home.

➤ She starts reading magazines or books on topics that didn't interest her before.

➤ He starts wearing ties that you haven't bought him.

➤ You notice hang-ups on your residential phone line.

➤ There are changes in your sexual routine.

Dr. Lana's Secrets

High technology has increased the options when it comes to keeping in touch with lovers, but it's also provided new ways to catch cheaters. Curious about where your spouse just called you from? Try dialing *69 on your phone. Unless the number is blocked, your call will immediately go through.

The Not-So-Subtle Signs

Warning lights should be going off if you see or experience any of these:

➤ You call your wife's cell phone, and a man answers.

➤ A name other than your husband's is stamped into the collar of his freshly laundered shirt.

➤ She leaves for an early morning meeting, but when you call her office the secretary tells you there's nothing on her agenda.

➤ You have to change the adjustments on the passenger's side car seat more than just occasionally.

➤ He races to answer the phone before you do.

➤ He comes home wearing a different shirt than what he left with.

➤ You've been asked for the first time and without apparent cause to hold down your spending.

The Knock-You-Across-the-Chops Signs

These behaviors or situations are in-your-face indications of an affair:

➤ Perfume or cologne aromas other than yours or your spouse's.

➤ A significant diminishment in the time you spend together.

➤ A lack of interest in or outright refusal of any sexual or intimate acts.

➤ The bank calls you to confirm a large transfer of money from your joint account into your spouse's.

➤ He starts wearing a pager, but you know that no one he works with does.

➤ You contract a sexually transmitted disease.

➤ Your kids tell you they've been spending more time at the neighbors lately because Mommy's had a visitor during the day.

➤ You run into your husband and another woman in public, and they blush or stammer.

Blind Trust—or Blinders On?

Some spouses will steadfastly ignore the signs of an affair, even when they're painfully obvious. They think, for a variety of reasons, that their partner just wouldn't do such a thing or have any time to even consider an affair.

For Sally, it took her husband's confession after his nurse assistant Kayla died to believe that the two had been romantically linked for years.

"Kayla was always close to Ned," Sally says. "And she was a real helpmate to him at the clinic. They worked long hours together because of the nature of his practice; he's a veterinarian and there's often a last-minute emergency that keeps him at the clinic past closing hours. I really never thought much about the two of them being alone together so much. It never bothered me.

Affair Facts

In a sociological survey, only 10 percent of spouses were blindsided when their partner confessed to an affair. The rest were already suspicious or had been told by someone else.

"Over the years, Kayla became like another member of the family. She and I also were very close, especially after she was diagnosed with advanced colon cancer. When she died, Ned was more upset than I thought he'd be, and I did start to wonder where that was coming from. Several days after Kayla's funeral, we went for a long walk, and he told me how intimate their relationship had been. Only then did I recall some of the little signs that could have clued me in sooner, like some of the really personal gifts they exchanged or his taking Kayla instead of me to events such as horse shows, even if he wasn't the vet-on-call for the show."

Think No Evil, See No Evil

Sally's refusal to see the indications of Ned and Kayla's affair is different from those spouses who are fully aware of their partner's indiscretions but choose to ignore them.

Dr. Lana's Secrets

Denial can be a healthy defense mechanism when it is used to not think or feel about things that you cannot change or really are not important. You can just put them out of your mind and go on to things that do matter to you.

But denial is unhealthy and destructive if you deny or don't believe things that *do* matter and *are* important. Denial of an affair, or not allowing yourself to admit what you know because it would hurt or you are afraid of what it may mean or what might happen, is unhealthy and sure to lead to distress and dysfunction.

These women—and more often than not they are women—may have once taken their spouse's affairs very personally, but no longer do. Their rationales for staying with their roving mates range from the old boys-will-be-boys philosophy to preserving their status in the community. Often, concerns over financial hardship or worry about their children's well-being will also cause this attitude to develop. The blinders are on to protect the course these women have elected to take.

These women know what's going on; they just don't want to confront it for one reason or another.

When Business Is Monkey Business

Men and women mix freely in today's workplace, unlike the offices of almost a century ago where strict hierarchical structures kept women in their place and men far away from them. Today's business arena is fraught with possibilities for crossing the line into an affair. And with more women cracking the glass ceiling and moving into top management positions, the opportunities are steadily increasing.

"My wife would be suspicious of my relationship with Leigh except for one thing—she's my boss," says Dave. "Leigh and I started traveling together several years ago as part of our company's consulting team. Our relationship outside of the office is based purely on sex, and we confine our encounters to when we travel. I think if either Leigh or I were to leave our jobs, our relationship would end. It has had very little impact on our lives outside of our work."

Affair Speak

The Middle English term *cuckold* (pronounced "kukeld") is said to be an allusion to the cuckoo bird's habit of laying its eggs in the nests of other birds. Men whose wives had committed adultery were referred to as cuckolds; cuckoldry was the act of making a cuckold of a husband.

Affair Facts

The American Management Association says 80 percent of managers surveyed said they had been involved in an office romance or knew of others who had.

Dr. Lana's Secrets

Affairs are often with co-workers. Estimates are that 7 million Americans begin romances at work every year. Unfortunately, not all these romances are between two single people.

Be visible in your partner's work life. When there are events that include spouses, go along. Stop by the office now and then and introduce yourself to the office staff. Be sure to have a recent picture of the two of you proudly displayed near his desk.

Affair Facts

Not all affairees consider their relationship a success. According to British sociologist Annette Lawson, over 50 percent said their affair had a negative impact on them.

Affair Facts

About 30 percent of all long-term relationships start at work. And half of all office romances end in marriage or long-term relationships.

Spouses have traditionally been suspicious of the opposite sex in business situations, and they have every right to be. Most people spend more time interacting with their colleagues at work than talking to their partners at home. Business can easily turn into monkey business, and when it does, the results can be disastrous, as more than one divorced ex-affairee can attest. If neatly compartmentalized sex affairs like Dave and Leigh's, above, turn into love affairs, they can break up marriages.

Can Men and Women Just Be Friends?

That's the jackpot question. Is it even possible for members of opposite sexes to be friends? Logically, the answer is yes. Men and women should be able to interact without it leading to anything intimate.

But there's something about those interactions, no matter how innocent they are, that more often than not arouses our suspicions. There's a stigma about married people appearing in public with people other than their spouses for exactly this reason. It could be the most innocent relationship on the face of the earth, but if it's between a man and a woman who are married to other people, it's probably going to be suspect.

In the movie *When Harry Met Sally,* Billy Crystal's character believed there were two types of couples: people who were getting ready to "do it," and people who were "doing it." Men and women couldn't just be friends in Harry's book. The sexual undercurrent was too strong to overcome.

Crystal's character was talking about unattached men and women, but the same assumption commonly holds for married people as well. It doesn't matter who it is or what the situation is. It's almost a sure bet that someone will reach the wrong conclusion if a married person is seen out and about with someone of the opposite sex who's not his spouse or partner.

Whether the spouse or partner in question leaps to the same conclusion has a lot to do with the boundaries—or lack thereof—in their relationship. Some spouses aren't comfortable with their mates having anything to do with anyone of the opposite sex—except for them, of course. For others, it's only a problem when the friendship detracts from the primary relationship.

Dr. Lana's Secrets

Flirting or joking with a member of the opposite sex may be harmless fun. The fun stops and the intimacy starts when he begins thinking about her and talking about her on a weekly basis.

He may inadvertently start telling you little stories about what work he did with her, or what she said that he thought was funny, or he may share vignettes from her personal life. Whether he is aware of it or not, the fun is over and he has crossed the line into perilous territory.

Still others allow it but with a number of stipulations. Coffee at the local shop is O.K. Cocktails after hours at that cozy bar is not. Candlelight dinner for two at home when one spouse is away on business is definitely *verboten*.

Some people are capable of having purely platonic friendships with members of the opposite sex. If you're one of them, or involved with someone like this, you've probably already discussed it with your partner. On the other hand, an opposite-sex friendship cropping up out the blue is definitely cause for concern.

Dr. Lana's Secrets

It may be appropriate and essential to meet a co-worker, client, or friend after normal work hours, but my rule of thumb is this: After eight, it's a date. As the evening progresses and you start to relax and unwind, personal conversation begins and intimacy can easily evolve. It is often better to stay out of potentially intimate situations all together.

Satisfying Your Suspicions

You've come up with nothing when it comes to hard evidence. Your spouse has plausible excuses for her new work schedule. The wallet was quietly purchased because he lost the one you gave him and he didn't want to tell you (plus, he really didn't think you'd notice). When you've confronted your partner, there's been no apparent embarrassment. Your unexpected visit to the office yielded nothing more than a surprised spouse who forgot to let you know he'd be home late. Yet you're still suspicious for some reason or another. Things just don't seem right.

You have several choices at this point. You can:

➤ Relax and let things take their course.

➤ Intensify your efforts and get more aggressive at tracking your spouse's activities.

➤ Hire outside help.

Or you can…

Just Relax!

There's a chance that you may have conjured up a situation that really doesn't exist. This can happen for many reasons, but it's particularly possible if you (or your spouse) are going through some stressful times. If you're feeling insecure about yourself for any reason, your insecurity can spill over into your relationship and make you suspicious of any little thing that seems slightly off. It's like looking at the pores on your skin in a magnifying mirror when you're used to a regular bathroom mirror. You notice every little bump and imperfection, things that would escape the average eye.

The problem with situations like these is that they can easily become self-fulfilling prophesies, as in the case of Della and John. As John tells it: "Della was always very jealous of me and somewhat insecure about our relationship. Understandable, I guess, due to my work—I'm a male model. She thinks that women are always after me, which really isn't true. Women do hit on me sometimes, but I usually don't notice it unless someone else says something about it.

Dr. Lana's Secrets

To some extent we all do what is expected of us. If someone expects you to be polite, you are. If you hear enough times that you're always late, you tend be less careful about being on time. Hearing "I don't trust you" over and over can lead a person to give up trying to be trustworthy.

"For two years, I put up with interrogations from Della every time I came home from work a little late or spent too much time talking to a pretty woman at a party. Della would scream at me, then she'd end up crying about being afraid of losing me. She'd also say that she could understand why I would want to have affairs because I was so attractive and worked with so many good-looking women. It got to the point where I figured I might as well. It felt like she was giving me license to do it."

Maybe There's Another Problem Here

If your emotions concerning your spouse and your relationship seem to be taking on an irrational spin, try to identify other factors that may be causing them to do so. You, instead of your partner, might be the problem. Maybe you found one too many gray hairs or wrinkles on the same day you met your husband's new and very nubile administrative assistant. Maybe you're stuck in a dead-end job while your wife is getting choice assignments that put her on the road with her male coworkers.

We all have personal issues and insecurities, but they can cause major problems in a marriage when one spouse stands wrongfully accused of behavior that the other conjured up because of an unrelated problem. Instead of jumping to a conclusion, try taking a step back. Even though your suspicions are aroused, don't start flinging accusations if you have no evidence of improper behavior. If something is going on, it will most likely be revealed in time.

Dr. Lana's Secrets

Accusations lead to defensiveness not closeness, so be cautious about being accusatory. It is nearly impossible for anyone to prove he's not having an affair if his partner doesn't want to believe him.

I'm on Your Trail

Some partners decide to start tracking their partners' activities. They might do it casually, maybe planning to be at a certain place where they know they'll see their partner. Others literally stalk their mates, following them around town, even feeling the hood of their cars to see how long they've been parked at a certain spot.

If you decide to take this approach, be aware that it can backfire on you. There's nothing to match the embarrassment a spouse feels when he's tracked his partner, only to find that she's completely innocent.

Julie was suspicious of Dan's after-work appointments for several months, especially since they seemed to come out of nowhere. She asked him several times about what he was doing and received evasive responses. One evening she decided to follow Dan to his meeting spot. She was mortified to find that Dan was spending his time at a local garage, where he was lovingly restoring the car of her dreams—an early model Mustang. Embarrassed beyond belief, she decided to keep quiet about what she had seen. On her birthday, a month later, she woke up to see the Mustang parked in her driveway.

When I told Dan that I had spied on him, he was both hurt and angry. He said, "I am disappointed in you, first for not simply talking to me if you were upset and secondly, that you would assume I would lie to you." I had not realized how hurt and insulted he would be by my not having confidence in him. It took several years before he got over his disappointment in me and it tainted both of our feelings toward the beautifully restored Mustang.

Dr. Lana's Secrets

Before you go overboard collecting evidence of an affair, simply ask your partner what their behavior means. Talk to him about the feelings and thoughts you have been having. If you have been keeping a notebook of your feelings, read some of the excerpts to him. Let him know you are worried and frightened.

Talk about your feelings and your fears, tell him what you have discovered that is causing these fears. Allow him the opportunity to comfort and reassure you. Avoid deciding he is guilty when you really don't know for sure. Accusing a partner of lying is a serious and potentially damaging act.

Risky Business

The other way this approach can backfire is if the spouse under suspicion discovers that he's being tracked. Even if the suspicious partner's fears aren't confirmed, just finding out that he's being tracked can put a relationship in serious jeopardy.

Stephanie nearly lost it one evening when she saw Scott pull away from the parking lot at her ex-lover's condominium building. "I had gone to see Craig, my former lover, to pick up a piece of financial software I had loaned him," Stephanie says. "There is no chance that we'd get back together—he already has another person in his life, and they're thinking about getting married. Scott even knew about all of this; I'd told him everything about Craig at the beginning of the relationship. But Scott was always jealous of Craig's looks and just couldn't believe that things were over between us. He had to check up on me and see what I was doing. There was no other reason for him to be at this building or in this part of town.

"I was so angry I nearly couldn't see straight," explains Stephanie. "By the time I got home, Scott was there and he was trying to act like he had been home all evening. I laid into him the second I walked through the door, screaming, yelling, throwing things. I couldn't believe he didn't trust me more than this. I even met Craig in the lobby instead of going up to his condominium, which I felt would be inappropriate. It took months to repair my relationship with Scott, and we're still not really there. Scott's still suspicious of me, and no matter what I do or say he questions it. Sometimes it is just too much work to keep proving myself."

Hiring a Professional

If it's hard evidence of an affair that you're seeking, there's probably no more reliable way to get it than by hiring a private investigator. This may seem extreme, but it's really more commonly done than you think. And it's not just the private moments of the rich and famous that get recorded. Plain, ordinary folks hire private investigators, too. In fact, more and more private investigators and investigative firms are advertising such services as premarital background checks and spousal surveillance. They're easy to do and assured moneymakers for the investigators.

Private investigators are often asked to follow their suspects—a practice called tailing—but can provide other services as well. Investigators can look for patterns in phone usage and find utility bills and rent statements on apartments. Just a phone number can lead to an address and hard confirmation of an affair in the hands of someone who knows how and where to look for the evidence.

Victoria decided to hire a private investigator when several people told her they had seen her fiancé Alex out with his former lover. "He had sworn off her," Victoria says, "so you can imagine how I felt when I found out they were still being seen with each other literally weeks before our wedding." Victoria's p.i. followed Alex for a week and delivered a detailed report, with photos, soon after. "All the guy I hired had to do was park near her house," Victoria says. "Alex was going over there several times a week. When I found out, I called off the wedding."

Investigate Your Investigator

If you decide to hire a private investigator, be sure to thoroughly check out who you're hiring. Licensing requirements for private investigators vary by state, so you'll want to do whatever is necessary to hire a well-qualified person or firm. Ask for references and check them! Calling the Better Business Bureau also isn't a bad idea.

Get a firm estimate of what the fees and expenses will be and make sure that you've clearly defined the investigation's extent. And finally, be prepared to deal with the outcome. Chances are, it will only confirm what you've already suspected. Sometimes you just need to know for sure, one way or the other.

The Least You Need to Know

➤ Most spouses confess their first affair.

➤ If you sense trouble in your relationship, trust your instincts and investigate.

➤ Relationships and situations can appear to be more than they really are. Sometimes it's better to relax than stir up a tempest in a teapot.

➤ A professional can uncover even the most highly concealed affair, so if you absolutely must find out, you may want to hire a private investigator.

Part 4
When an Affair Happens

Maybe you thought it would never happen. Maybe you thought it only happened to other people. Maybe, just maybe, you thought wrong. The unthinkable has happened—there's an affair going on.

So…what are you going to do about it? Confront your philandering spouse and confirm your suspicions? Storm angrily out of the house, kids in tow? Throw him out? Ask your best friend for the name of the nastiest divorce attorney in town? Commit hari-kari?

Whoa! Put your speeding brain in neutral for a minute, take a good look at what's really happened and figure out what it all means. Part 4 is here to help. Chapters 16 and 17 are full of advice on how to cope, both when you first find out about the affair and then, if you end up having to live with it for awhile. Turn to Chapter 18 to learn why it's so important to take care of yourself during times of stress (which this certainly is!), and how doing so might make your relationship better in the long run. In Chapter 19, you'll discover why most affairs reach a less-than-happy conclusion and why it's not a bad idea to be waiting in the wings when it ends.

Chapter 16

The First Blush

In This Chapter

➤ Oh my gosh, it's really true!

➤ What his (or her) affair says about you

➤ How to stop the emotional merry-go-round

➤ Is retaliating ever a good idea?

➤ Don't even think about divorce right now

Everything happens to everybody sooner or later if there is time enough.

—George Bernard Shaw

Whack! You've just been hit square in the face by the ugly truth. Your lover, your paramour, your significant other, your better half is doing something that he or she shouldn't be doing.

O.K., it's time to get out the tissue box…even you guys out there, if you're so inclined. Have yourself a good cry. Or throw something (just be sure to fling it in the opposite direction of breakables, small children, and animals). Punch a pillow. Scream at the top of your lungs. Just do something to release the anger and hurt that you're feeling. Wallow in it. Get way into the depths of your despair. Feel real sorry for yourself. Swear revenge. (We'll wait until you're done.)

Feel a bit better? Good. Now…take a look around you. Things should look pretty much the same, save for maybe a few crumpled tissues at your side or a slight dent in the wall. The world hasn't ended…and it won't. Not because of this at least. No matter how awful you might feel right now, the sun will rise tomorrow.

This chapter and the next two, Chapters 17, "Coping with His (or Her) Affair," and 18, "Keeping Your Life Together," are designed to help you cope with your emotions and your life now that you've just learned that the unspeakable is true: Your loved one is involved with someone else. These chapters deal with helping you stay functional, address immediate issues, and work your way through understanding the thoughts and concerns you may be having. All the stuff about what happens next—in the months to come—is too much for you to think about right now.

Just keep in mind that there is a "next," and you don't have to go it alone. You *will* get through this trauma and move on to the next stage in your life. Part 5, "Creating an Affair-Proof Future," will help you.

Affair Facts

Affairees believe their affair is about themselves and not their partner. However, that does not mean that you, the betrayed partner, are unaffected by it at all. You most certainly are!

Shock Waves

Besides being angry, you might be in a state of shock, and understandably so, even if you've had premonitions about this sort of thing happening. Talk about stress! This tops them all. The realization that your partner has betrayed you is bound to throw you off center!

Even if you're not in shock, you probably feel somewhat numb around the edges. This perfectly natural response is your body's way of protecting you from more pain than you can handle right now. Or you may be feeling extremely anxious and nervous. If you are, that's your "fight or flight" instinct kicking in. This again is a natural response to acute stress.

Riding the Emotional Merry-Go-Round

After the initial shock wears off, you may find yourself feeling like an emotional food processor. The world hasn't ended, but it's clearly changed. What you've discovered has rocked the foundation of your relationship. And you're probably beginning to wonder if it was that steady to begin with.

When something as significant as an affair affects a relationship, it's easy to begin second-guessing just about everything. Maybe things were never as they seemed between you and your partner. Maybe you've been living a lie all this time. Maybe he's not as wonderful as you thought he was. Maybe you're a failure at relationships.

While thinking like this can be damaging to yourself and everyone around you if it continues unchecked, the jumble of emotions that you feel also indicates the beginning of the restorative process that you, and your relationship with your spouse, need to go through. If you're feeling conflicted, it's because you're heeding the wake-up call that the affair is sending you. You're realizing that you may have been operating under some false pretense or, at the very least, in some manner that either doesn't work or no longer fits your relationship with your spouse.

Like it or not, you have a role in what has happened, as a major or a minor player. This in itself can be tough for many people to accept or even understand, because it blows away some of the marital myths they may have concocted for themselves. But these myths must be exploded to find a successful resolution to the situation.

Although there's nothing wrong with allowing yourself some self-pity, what you don't want to do is chase your emotions and feelings to no end. To do so will just exhaust you and make you feel worse. Right now, you don't have the answers to the questions you're asking. You'll get them…but that will come later.

You also shouldn't spend your time beating yourself up over the fact that an affair happened. It's one thing to understand that you're partly responsible for it, but quite another to declare yourself an utter failure. For now, accept the fact that you're part of the problem…and that you'll be part of the solution.

Affair Facts

Shock is a normal reaction to trauma, and this situation is traumatic. It's the emotional equivalent of being in a car accident. You feel cut and bruised and shaken up.

What the Affair Means (or Doesn't Mean) About You

You take this affair personally. It's almost impossible not to. After all, the person you've loved and trusted has for some reason or another decided to spend intimate time with someone other than you. You feel less than desirable, less than loved, less than whole.

None of this is true.

An affair does not mean that you're a loser or that the life you've created with your partner is a sham. An affair, in and of itself, is not a reflection of your ability or inability to create and maintain a happy, healthy relationship. What it does indicate is that there are important issues in your relationship that need to be addressed.

Although you may be feeling like you're the only person to whom this has ever happened, you have now joined a large club of men and women who are very familiar with what you're going through. You're by no means alone.

So, what's next? How do you handle things now that your life with your spouse—at least in this regard—has changed forever?

Affair Facts

It is not true that if your partner is happy with you and your relationship that he would not have strayed. More than half of the men and a third of the women who had affairs said they were happy in their marriage.

Keep the Reins On

Only the rare spouse handles news of this magnitude calmly. Frankly, you'd be a little bit suspect if the information just rolled off your back. Even if you really want nothing more to do with your spouse, there will still be a bundle of emotions that will get unleashed when you face the reality that your relationship may be in serious trouble.

If possible, don't overreact about what you know or think you know. Although you may feel entirely justified in flying off the handle right now, there are some awfully good reasons for not doing so. First of all, anything you do or say when you're so upset is probably not going to be well thought out or in your best interest. Second, you really don't know enough about the situation to react appropriately at this point, especially if your spouse hasn't confessed the affair to you.

Should You Ask for a Confession?

If your partner hasn't disclosed an affair, but you're pretty sure that he's having one, should you confront him about it? Some people prefer to leave it up to the wayward partner to disclose or not. Others can't bear to be in the same house until things are out in the open. (For more help on deciding whether to force a confession from your partner, turn to Chapter 20, "Out in the Open.")

If you do confront him, be prepared for the consequences. There's a good chance that he'll deny it, especially if he's not ready to disclose the affair or doesn't plan to at all. Be firm with your feelings and don't let yourself be talked out of anything you know is true.

Dr. Lana's Secrets

Realizing your partner is having an affair is devastating. Beyond feeling betrayed and unwanted from knowing your partner has chosen to be intimate with someone else, there is another serious problem, lying. Lying can be more damaging to the relationship than the affair itself.

It is also hard to tell a painful truth, especially one that will cause hurt and could ruin your relationship, so if your partner is not forthcoming with the truth, realize it is a very difficult step to take. Give him time to think about what to say and how to say it.

If you're operating on suspicions or information provided to you by a third party, there's a chance that you or that other person might be wrong. And unleashing your tongue and making false accusations may cause even greater problems in the future if your partner is indeed innocent.

Face the Fear

One of the key reasons the discovery of an affair is so emotional is that it stirs up fear and insecurity. You're afraid that your relationship will break up. Even if it doesn't, you're uncertain about the effect the affair will have on you, your relationship, and your family. Will you have to face the world alone? Do you have the strength to do it? What will you do when your friends find out? What about the children? Financial support? The future? And on, and on, and on.

There may be no end to the questions in your mind. You may want to ignore the whole thing and hope that it all just goes away. But it won't.

Dr. Lana's Secrets

Allow yourself to feel your fear, your hurt, and your anger. These emotions are perfectly normal. But don't dwell on one feeling. You ought to be experiencing a whole range of emotions.

Ignoring the problem is denying that it exists. In the short run, this response might afford you some relief, and you may think it's a good way to avoid the fear you have of an affair. However, all you're doing is postponing the inevitable tough issues.

Sort Out Your Emotions

For now, one of the best things you can do is identify what you fear the most. For many people, it's losing their relationship with their spouse and/ or their children. Remember, though, that doesn't have to happen, no matter how bleak things look. If necessary, make a list of your concerns and sort them out. Which are valid and which are false? Then ask yourself which, if any, you can control. Chances are, you can't control the things that people might say if they find out that you're having marital difficulties. But you can decide how to manage your emotions concerning this disclosure.

Affair Speak

Going over and over what has happened in your mind is called *ruminating*, and it's a symptom of depression. To stop ruminating, write down an affirmation like, "I am a kind and loving person." Then anytime you find yourself ruminating, stop and repeat your affirmation ten times, out loud if possible.

Being afraid about things you can't control won't solve anything. It will only upset you further and might even make you ill. Once you've faced your fears, try to tuck the invalid ones and the ones you can't do anything about far away in your mind. Focus on what you can do and what's really important in your life.

Don't Let Worry Overcome You

A common problem for many people when they first face the facts about an affair is that they get wrapped up in a worry mode that doesn't go away. They ponder the same problems over and over, they worry about things that aren't even viable concerns, and they convince themselves that they'll lose everything because of the affair. The sad thing about this scenario is that they *will* lose everything if they don't change their thinking.

It's easy to let your worries overcome you when you really don't know what is going to happen next. One way to keep your emotions in check is to live in the moment as best as you can. Try not to project into the future. You may end up spending a lot of time worrying about things that will never happen. Stay as positive as you can. Franklin Delano Roosevelt said that the only thing to fear is fear itself. There's a lot of truth to that statement.

Affair Facts

More than 70 percent of people said that if their partner had an affair, they (the non-affairee) would end the marriage. But that's not what really happens; most people are willing to fight to save their marriage.

Don't Throw Him (or Her) Out!

In lots of movies, the betrayed spouse throws the errant one out on his or her ear the moment an affair is revealed. This behavior can make for great drama on the silver screen, but it's usually not such a good idea in real life. Stomping out the front door or insisting that your wayward spouse get out is going to cause a physical separation right when you really need each other most. It will also delay any efforts at reconciliation and possibly prevent them all together.

Maintain the Status Quo

It's a good idea to maintain the status quo as much as possible, especially if you have children in the house. And you may need to keep up other appearances as well. If you live in a small town and your weekly order at the local dairy shrinks significantly, your marital rift might become the topic of the day at a few coffee breaks.

"Our separation got out to people in town by the driver for our dry cleaning service," recalls Meredith. "He noticed he wasn't picking up men's shirts anymore and blabbed the news to everyone else on his route. My husband and I finally reconciled. We also made another big decision—we switched dry cleaners!"

Dr. Lana's Secrets

Don't send your partner away if you don't want him to go. This advice may seem obvious, but many times the betrayed spouse feels so much pain that she wants to get rid of the source of it. Unfortunately, that won't make the hurt go away.

Couples That Sleep Together...

Maintaining the status quo also means sharing the same bed. This may not mean having sex (although some couples have more sex immediately after an affair), but simply sleeping together. It's one of the most difficult things for some couples to do, especially if they're hopping mad at each other. But the physical act of sleeping close can go a long way toward healing a relationship that's in trouble.

Of course, the best idea is not to go to bed angry. If at all possible, put your emotions on hold when your head hits the pillow. You might be surprised at what happens.

Going on the Defensive

For some spouses, learning about their partner's affair brings out their fighting instincts, and they put up their dukes by retaliating. Counterstrikes can be pretty juvenile: There are stories of mature adults who've let the air out of their straying partner's tires when they're parked at their lovers' homes. Some people start affairs of their own, just to get even (see Chapter 17 for more on this topic)—*not* a good idea! Other retaliations are more serious. It might seem very appropriate to you when you're raving mad to clean out your joint checking account and run up the credit cards you're both liable for. But hold on a minute—just think of the problems it'll cause down the line.

If your mind starts to play games, tempting you to try such devious deeds, don't feel you're evil. You're not the first to think such malicious thoughts; many other injured spouses have been

Bumps Ahead

Things always seem worse at night. This is because your brain is not fully functional. Wait until daytime to think things through and make important decisions.

there. On the other hand, stop and think about all the possible repercussions of your plans before you act on them.

Confronting the Affairee

As uncomfortable as confrontations can be for everyone involved, they happen pretty frequently. It can be over the phone, in a public place, or by letter. Sometimes the betrayed spouse will do it to dissuade the affair from continuing. Others act out of anger or fear that their spouse will leave them for their lover. They may threaten their partner's lover.

Anna Jean called her husband's ex-lover, Billie. She says, "When I called I was going to tell her off, but we spoke for over an hour. She was very nice and I told her more than I intended to about Johnny and some of our problems. Later, my hairdresser told me she heard we were having marriage problems because I couldn't orgasm with Johnny. Of course, the source of this gossip was Billie—even though I had not told her anything about our sexual life, the fact that we had talked gave her more credibility. I was so angry at myself."

Sure You Want to Know?

Think twice before you confront your spouse's secret lover; most such talks don't go well. They can get nasty and be painful for both people. Taking the moral high road here can make you the classiest one in the affair triangle. If you need details, get them from your spouse.

Dr. Lana's Secrets

Put on your thick skin before you confront your partner's lover. Be clear about what you want to say and what you want to know. She may tell you things you're not prepared to hear, and her stories may not be true. She may intentionally say things to hurt you or undermine your marriage.

D-I-V-O-R-C-E

Don't even think about it right now! Getting rid of your spouse, as much as you might detest him at this moment, should be the absolute last alternative on your list. You need to find out a lot more about what's really going on between the two of you to determine whether a divorce is the best solution to your problems.

The reasons that a divorce isn't a good idea are legion: They take years to get over. Your kids will pay a high price. You'll probably take a big financial hit. This isn't to say that you should automatically write off divorce as an option. It's the only viable choice when some marriages go rotten. It's just not one that you should consider before you've tried everything else.

Affair Facts

Cosmopolitan magazine once found that nearly 80 percent of the men surveyed said they would remarry their former wife if they could. Don't prematurely close the door if you love your husband.

The Least You Need to Know

➤ What you do and don't do in the first few hours or days after you discover an affair can have a significant impact on the future of your relationship.

➤ Try not to make any rash decisions or say anything you may regret later; give yourself time to sort things out.

➤ Think twice about confronting your spouse's lover. It might seem like a good thing to do, but it rarely is.

➤ Divorce should be the last thing you consider.

Let's see..
Hinges,
Historical sites,
Hit men

Chapter 17

Coping with His (or Her) Affair

In This Chapter

➤ The importance of taking the long view

➤ Why a new "operating system" might be in order right now

➤ The value of keeping your personal life personal

➤ Is having a retaliatory affair ever a good idea?

➤ Deciding what to tell your children

➤ The issue of sex

You do not need to know precisely what is happening or exactly where it is all going. What you need to do is to recognize the possibilities and challenges offered by the present moment and to embrace them with courage, faith and hope.

—Thomas Merton, Trappist monk and spiritual writer

Courage, faith, and hope. They're three little words that can make the difference between success and disaster when faced with any life-changing situation. You may be feeling far from hopeful at this point and less than courageous. Your faith in many things may be at an all-time low. But when it comes to living through your spouse's affair, these attributes are especially important things to hold on to because they're vital to the survival of your relationship.

While the ultimate destiny for your relationship will be up to you and your partner to determine, how you approach the days and weeks to come will have a significant impact on how things will end up between the two of you. Do it halfheartedly or with a negative attitude and your chances of success will be far less than if you follow Thomas Merton's advice.

Taking the Long View of Things

Take a good look at your spouse when he isn't looking at you. Aside from what you know about what this person has done outside of your relationship, does he look any different than he did before you found out about the affair? Probably not. But in many respects, he's very different from what he once was. So are you. And so is your relationship.

Affair Facts

It takes between one and two years to heal from an affair and three or more years to heal from a divorce. Half of the women who divorce are still angry ten years later.

Now think ahead ten, maybe twenty years. Do you still want to see your spouse sitting across from you at the breakfast table? Can you envision a life together after you've weathered this event and all the other things that will affect your life? Is it too early to tell? Are you still too angry and upset to think clearly about such things at all?

If the feelings you had for each other were important enough to bring you together in the first place, don't throw it all away and declare your life together over just yet, or act in such a way that forces this outcome. Try to think ahead to the time when this trying period in your life will have faded to a distant memory. As difficult as it may be to believe that it will happen, it will.

Building a New "Operating System" (at Least Temporarily)

Externally, the landscape that is your life both apart and as a couple probably hasn't changed appreciably. Internally, it's another story. Your lives are going through a period of immense change. While the two are related, changes to the external parts of your lives are vastly more apparent than those that are happening privately to the two of you.

When your relationship is in trouble, it's often a good idea to build a new operating system, even if it's only temporary, that separates your private life from your public one and keeps your personal turmoils from spilling over into the public arena. What is happening to each of you individually and together as a couple is a very personal and very private part of your life, and it often works best in the long run to keep it that way.

Don't Air Dirty Laundry

Live your life—on the outside anyway—as much as possible as you did before you found out about the affair. It won't always be easy, but try to keep what's going on with you and your partner just between the two of you. You'll be much less worn out if you don't let your emotions color every other part of your life.

Dr. Lana's Secrets

It is hard to know how to behave during this chaotic period. Good manners can help you get through bad experiences. While saying please and thank you may seem contrived when you are hurt and angry, good manners are helpful. Sometimes, just putting aside your bruised emotions and being pleasant and polite eases the pain. Courtesy and kindness may keep your wounds from getting bigger and help with healing in the long term.

Keeping your personal life under wraps is a far better way to operate than in the emotionally charged arena that develops many times when couples are having problems. Things become so volatile between them that the smallest comment or look sets off a full-blown battle, often waged right in front of friends or children. Such demonstrations seldom help to move a relationship beyond its difficulties, and they can alienate feuding couples from everyone else around them. This behavior can also cause some serious embarrassment, as Gunnar and Nora sadly discovered.

Just Between the Two of You

"We were out to dinner at one of our favorite restaurants when something that Gunnar said really set me off," Nora recalls. "I tried to keep quiet, but something inside me just snapped, and I threw a very biting comment right back at him. Then he said something back to me that was even worse, and we were off. I don't think either of us realized how well our voices carried. We were still hissing at each other when the maitre d' came to our table and told Gunnar that he had a phone call. When they were away from the main dining area, he told Gunnar that there wasn't any call, but that our conversation was disrupting the other diners and he'd prefer that we leave. We were mortified. I know we'll never go back there again."

Affair Facts

In *A Garland of Love*, Daphne Rose Kingma writes that every interaction in a relationship leads toward or away from intimacy. Everything we do and say, she notes, sculpts the structure of the relationship.

The marks that words can leave on a relationship can be virtually impossible to erase, and they often become indelible when said in a public place. Work toward keeping your more intense interchanges with your spouse under control and away from the public's eye.

Putting the Affair in Its Place

What has happened has affected every fiber of your being, but you still need to keep functioning. And you might as well come out of this whole thing looking like a winner by doing the best job of managing things that you can. This means not giving the affair more power over your life than it deserves.

Put the affair in its place. Remind yourself as often as you need to that it doesn't mean you're a failure or any less of a person than you once were. It helps to write some personal affirmations on an index card and carry them with you. Develop your own mantra, such as "joy" or "beauty," and repeat it as often as you need to. Don't let your mind become overcome with negative thoughts driven by emotion. Fight them off by focusing on what is positive and true.

If you make a commitment to not allow the affair to have its way with your life, you'll find that many of the situations you were imagining are no longer really anything to worry over.

Dr. Lana's Secrets

This is a good time to count your blessings. While it feels like your life is a mess, everything isn't wrong. You have friends and family who love you. You are healthy and you have a good sense of humor. You can laugh as well as cry and you can enjoy the fragrance of a rose. You have all you need to live life well.

Telling Others

Many spouses spend countless hours worrying about what they should tell people about the affair. If you've decided to heed the advice above and keep your private matters private, you'll find that the best thing to tell them is nothing. You have no obligation to say anything to anybody, nor should you say anything until you really have something to say. It's too early to know what's going to happen to your relationship. If you're able to work through things together, you might not want the people who care about you to know or be concerned.

Dr. Lana's Secrets

It is necessary and important to be able to talk to someone about how you feel, but exercise discretion about what you say—and to whom. While friends may promise to keep a secret, bits and pieces of your story may have a way of spilling out.

Managing the Buttinskys

What if a friend or family member confronts you with what she knows or thinks she knows? Some people love to gossip, especially when the subject is something that might make them feel they're better and more "together" than others. Don't be surprised if a seemingly well-intentioned friend or family member decides to take you aside one day and whisper some things in your ear, all under the guise of "it's all for your own good."

Dr. Lana's Secrets

Generally, people are well intentioned, and if they want to talk to you about your crisis, you can be both polite and firm. Try saying, "Thank you for caring, but I don't want to talk about it now." Often people who have had their own affair crisis will tell you their story and offer advice. It can be helpful and reassuring to know other people have been through this experience, but be sure you set clear boundaries for yourself concerning how much you want to hear.

Men are also quite capable of tattling, and they don't restrict their comments to their buddies, either. More than one woman has found out about her husband's affair from her husband's best friend, who was probably sworn to secrecy but decided to blab anyway.

Stop 'em in Their Tracks

Remember, what goes on between you and your partner is no one's business but your own. Keep your focus on yourself and what *you* want, not on what other people want or what they think you should do.

Dr. Lana's Secrets

You are vulnerable right now and more sensitive than you would normally be, so be careful not to respond with hostility to people who are extending kindness.

While there are a few harmful people around, there are many more that will offer comfort, love and reassurance. They will want to support and console you.

What About the Kids?

What you tell or don't tell your children largely depends on their age and what you think they're capable of understanding. Regardless of how old they are, they will sense that something is wrong if there's tension in your home, and they'll know it for sure if you're suddenly spending a lot of your time apart from your partner. However, it's best to not say anything unless or until you have to. Whatever you do, don't put your children in the middle of your marital dispute.

Affair Facts

Children frequently report their childhood ended with their parents' divorce.

Don't confide in your children even if you're very close to them. This goes for adult children, too. It can put them in the middle of a situation that they most likely don't want to be in. It will be difficult enough to prevent them from choosing sides if problems continue in your marriage. You don't want to provide fuel for that fire.

If, horrors of horrors, your kids somehow find out about the affair, encourage them to talk about what they might be feeling. They need to know that the affair isn't about them and that their relationship with both of their parents hasn't changed.

Dr. Lana's Secrets

While you're in turmoil you may feel dependent on your children for emotional support, which is fine, but don't start confiding in them. Your children are your children, not your best friend or your therapist. Children have difficulty knowing what they should do because they want to protect both parents, and they will tend to take more responsibility for your situation than they should.

More Than They Can Handle

Liz came home from college a number of years ago to find the relationship between her parents vastly changed. Her mother seemed perpetually angry and had lost a great deal of weight. Her father, always somewhat distant and removed, now seemed very interested in Liz and her summertime activities. "I played a lot of softball when I was in high school, and I kept playing in a league with all my old friends every summer," Liz recalls. "Instead of ignoring me like he always had done, Dad started coming to my games. At first I thought it was great; he'd even go out with us after the game and buy us rounds of beer.

"One night he told me about the affair he was having with one of his coworkers. I had sort of guessed that he had had extramarital relationships for years. I didn't care; I still loved both him and Mom. But now that I knew for sure that he was involved with someone else, I had a hard time not blaming him for Mom's unhappiness. I ended up going back to school early. Now that I knew what was going on, I couldn't bear the tension between them. I never talked to either of them about it, and they ended up staying together.

"The next year was terrible for me. I lost twenty pounds and couldn't concentrate at school. My grade point slipped, and I couldn't sleep. I finally went to a therapist and sorted it out. I wish Dad had not confided in me. It was just more than I wanted to know."

Wait Until You Have Something Positive to Tell

The time to really talk about your affair with your children, if you are ever going to do so, is when you're putting your marriage back together. You'll find more information on how to do that in Chapter 24, "Next Steps."

Should You Retaliate by Having an Affair?

Some spouses cope with their partner's affairs by having one of their own. "I'll get you back," the thinking goes. Bad idea! Like doesn't cure like, at least when it comes to affairs. It won't even make you feel very good. Well, maybe it will at first. But the satisfaction you might feel in being able to say "gotcha" wanes very quickly.

If you're taking the long view, retaliating against your spouse by having an affair yourself is the last thing you want to do. But don't be surprised if you find yourself tempted to get even this way, especially if your spouse's affair has been going on for a long time, and don't be shocked if others suggest it to you if they find out what's going on. There are some marriages that work only because each spouse is having a relationship outside of the marriage. For most, however, an affair is not something that will benefit a relationship in the long run.

Affair Facts

About 7% of affairs are in retaliation to a partner's affair.

Bumps Ahead

The pleasure of revenge is short-lived. Be sure that whatever you do, it's not damaging to your self-esteem or your future. Hurting back does not end your hurt.

Crossing Your Spouse's Affair Wires

Living a life of normalcy while an affair is taking place can sometimes have an unexpected payback, especially if your efforts include such things as spending more time with your spouse or increasing the amount of time you all spend together as a family. Even if you didn't intend for them to do so, such efforts can provide your spouse with satisfying alternatives to his affair. Construct enough family activities, and you might even put the skids on the affair.

Change your schedule so you can join him at the club for those early morning workouts. Go on some of her business trips, even if you never have before. Go to that banquet and enjoy yourself.

Dr. Lana's Secrets

Make your wishes clear to your partner through your actions. If you want to continue your marriage, behave accordingly. Do things that bring your partner closer to you. Be complimentary about the qualities you like in your partner. Plan activities that you know you both enjoy, and have a good time together.

Dealing with Missing Persons

At this time you may find yourself flying solo when you thought you'd have a copilot. You might, for example, have planned on spending a quiet evening at home, with the assumption that your spouse would be there as well...but he isn't. Or she's either very late in meeting you somewhere, or she doesn't show up at all. There could be legitimate reasons for these things—or maybe not (they could be related to the affair). Because you don't really know the truth, give her the benefit of the doubt, no matter how annoyed you might be. Don't make a big deal of it.

Protect Your Children

If the situation involves your children, such as a soccer game you both planned to attend or a promise she made to read your son a story before his bedtime, don't play up her absence. Divert attention if you can or offer a plausible reason for her absence or delay. The time to hash out the matter, should you choose to do so, is later, when the two of you are alone.

You're Not Your Spouse's Keeper

If you're the one cooling your heels, don't make yourself into a doormat by waiting patiently for hours—unless you're the type of person who generally does this sort of thing. Set an acceptable waiting period and, the next time, tell your spouse what it is ahead of time. Many people think fifteen minutes is reasonable; your own fuse might be shorter or longer. Just make sure that whatever you decide is within your own comfort zone.

Dr. Lana's Secrets

It can be hard to strike a balance between being receptive to your partner and being a victim. This is a good time to call on friends who want to help. Ask your friends to be available for some spur of the moment entertainment. If your partner breaks your date or keeps you waiting too long, call your friend and go to a movie. Have a back up plan and you will feel less exposed and less upset.

When time's up, you can either move on to whatever it is that you're supposed to be doing together or change your plans. Don't feel guilty or that you owe anyone excuses or explanations. Although you may need to apologize for your own tardiness to others you may be meeting, your apology should end right there. You've upheld your part of the agreement; you're where you're supposed to be. If your spouse isn't...well, that's her problem.

The important thing to remember here is that you should always remain in control of the situation. You might feel sorely disappointed and let down, and you may feel anger over your spouse's lack of regard for you, but you'll feel less abused by the whole matter if you haven't wasted too much time stewing over exactly what is keeping him away.

Sex

Now we come to one of the most volatile issues facing all relationships affected by affairs: sex.

Regardless of what your marriage's sex life is like and your feelings about sex in general, don't make light of the sexual aspects of the affair. Sex plays a big role in most affairs, and the issue of sex will play an equally large role in your life now and later, whether you like it or not. If you suspect that the main reason for the affair is because of problems with intimacy in your marriage, reading anything even vaguely related to sex might be the last thing you want to do. But resist your inclination to turn away.

An affair can spoil even the best sexual relationship, turning beds into battlegrounds and once-intimate encounters into mechanical acts that involve no intimacy. Some spouses—whether they're the ones having the affair or not—withhold their affections completely, sometimes as a form of punishment or in anger. Or your spouse may be the type who tries to cover up the fact that she's having an affair by making it a point to have sex with you on a regular basis to try to convince you that there's nothing wrong between you.

What to Expect

How can you best approach this very delicate subject? If your sex life was already in trouble and has eroded significantly, there probably won't be much benefit in pushing now for more intimacy. Unfortunately, you're probably going to stay in a holding pattern until the affair and your relationship reach some resolution and you move onto the next stage. If you're feeling sad and lonely and in need of some snuggling with your spouse, give it a try, but be prepared for a rebuff. At the same time, if your spouse reaches out to you, don't throw up a cold shoulder just because you're hurt and angry if what you really want is a hug.

Dr. Lana's Secrets

While your sex life is stalled, try to maintain some degree of physical closeness. Since your usual non-verbal cues are not working, you will have to ask for what you want. Ask to be held or to cuddle. Be willing to snuggle or spoon, and always say goodnight.

Do you still have a sex life together? Then try to keep the pot boiling—or even try to turn up the heat (check Chapter 9, "Sex, Sex and More Sex" for suggestions). Look to the future. Is this person someone who once zinged you so much that your knees got weak every time you saw him? Well, you might just feel this way again, once you get past your current crisis. The key is believing that it really can happen again.

Be Here Now

If possible, put aside your problems and just live in the moment when you're together. Doing so may take some pretty serious resolve, especially if you're the type who tends to side with people like Lorena Bobbitt. Try to stay focused on what's happening between you right here, right now. Don't read more into things than you need to and don't get caught up in the kind of emotionally driven behavior that can make you ultrasensitive to anything that might be slightly different in your lovemaking.

Most important, don't play that awful mind game of thinking about your spouse's lover and how you compare. All you'll do is torture yourself with thoughts of the two of them in bed. Remember the old song "Love the One You're With"? You, not your spouse's lover, are in your spouse's arms now. Take that for what it's worth and make the most of it while you're there. This might just be the time to unfurl that fantasy that you never before had the courage to unleash. Why not? Remember, the rules have changed. You probably don't have anything to lose, and you might have everything to gain.

Sharing Life's Burdens

Being a couple in some respects and not in others can make you feel like you're living a deranged life, and in many ways you may very well be. At times you might even feel like you're sharing your house with an alien or with someone who's turned into a stranger.

Regardless of any feelings of distance that may now exist between you, keep your sights firmly fixed on the fact that you two share a history. You've made many good memories together that will never go away. Because of this, you both have a responsibility to your relationship, even if it's different from what it once was, and you still have a responsibility to each other unless or until one or both of you decide to end your marriage.

When a relationship has been affected by an affair, it's often difficult for either spouse to know exactly how to act toward the other. Conversations tend to be awkward, with the words dangling heavily in the air. Because of the strain, one partner—often the non-affairee—takes on more of the burden of the day-to-day relationship. This often happens silently and gradually, as the loyal spouse becomes reluctant to risk saying something that might start a confrontation or fight.

If you've been assuming this role, stop right now. Don't take on more than your fair share of responsibility. Regardless of what is going on in his life away from you, it's important for both of you to stay as involved in your relationship as possible. Take on too much of the responsibility that you once shared, and you'll make your spouse feel like he's an ancillary player in your life. That's reason enough for many partners to figure that they might as well keep their attention focused elsewhere.

Make a commitment to continue to share your life with your spouse. Keep the roles and routines between you as normal as you can when you're together. Talk to him about what's in your heart and on your mind in all areas of your life aside from the affair. While it'll soon be important to talk about the affair, don't do it right now. Wait a bit. Unless things are very bad between you, the benefits of keeping your spouse involved in your life will far outweigh the pain and agony you may go through in doing so.

The Least You Need to Know

➤ Do you think you still want to be with your spouse when you're old and gray? If your answer is yes, or even maybe, then make a commitment to repairing and renewing your relationship.

➤ Keep your personal life personal. Don't air your dirty laundry in public and be very discerning about who you confide in. Even the closest friends can make slips of the tongue, intentional or not.

➤ Don't let the affair overwhelm you. Put it in its place by not allowing it to affect every aspect of your life.

➤ Weigh carefully what you tell your children about the affair. Answer their questions briefly but honestly.

➤ Thoughts of retaliation are common, but are best left as such.

➤ Keep an open mind regarding your sex life. If overtures are made, don't turn away.

Chapter 18

Keeping Your Life Together

In This Chapter

➤ Ways to nurture the most important relationship in your life (you with yourself!)

➤ Determining your personal stress-management style

➤ The power of prayer, meditation, eating right, and more

➤ Volunteering is good for your mental and emotional health

There is a very unique relationship with a special person that most of us overlook: the relationship with ourself.

—Daphne Rose Kingma

Being your own best friend. It may seem silly, especially if you've never spent much time thinking about the relationship you have with yourself. You can't effectively love anyone else unless and until you love yourself. And that means taking care of yourself and doing the things you know you should do to keep healthy and happy.

Dealing with an affair and the effects it can have on your life can overwhelm you to such an extent that it takes precedence over taking care of yourself. That's the bad news. The good news is that, similar to its effect on your relationship as a whole, an affair can also shine a spotlight onto the parts of your life where you've maybe been a little negligent in the personal TLC department. If this is you, there's no better time than right now to put your very own caboose back on track and start taking care of your body, mind, and spirit.

Out, Out, Damned Stress

Much of what you'll read about in this chapter is in some way related to keeping your body and mind fit and sound and maintaining or regaining balance during what may be one of the most stressful times in your life. Some of the suggestions here are proven stress busters; others may not at first seem to be, but you may be surprised at what they can do for your body and mind.

Affair Speak

TLC means tender, loving care. This is a particularly good time in your life to remember to treat yourself with love, tenderness and care every single day.

You'll also find that for you some things will work better than others. We're all unique human beings; we all have different needs. The situations and issues that cause you to stress out might just slide off the back of your best friend. And what you find soothing and relaxing can put your spouse's teeth on edge. In theory, there are a thousand and one ways to knock stress right out of your life. Just keep an open mind until you hit upon the most effective ones for you.

Identifying Your Stress-Management Style

With so many different approaches to stress management available, how can you find the ones that will work best for you? Part of the answer lies in developing a better understanding of how you respond to stress. Are you a stoic who likes to keep everything in—or do you search frantically about for the support of friends and family when faced with the tough issues of life? Take the test below, choosing *a*, *b*, or *c* for each situation, to determine your particular stress response style.

1. You're hard at work on an important project when your computer crashes. Although you're able to get things up and running again, the revisions to the file you were working on when the machine died are lost, and you have to re-create them from scratch. You:

   a. Take a deep breath, cancel your evening out, and get settled in for a long, hard night.

   b. Throw the nearest handy object at the wall and start screaming bloody curses.

   c. Shut off the stupid thing for awhile so you can rest your hands and eyes and take a walk.

2. It's your big errand-running day, and you have lots of errands to do. You're a pretty good distance from home when you realize you've left your wallet and checkbook on the kitchen counter and there's no way you can pay for the dry-cleaning you need to pick up. You:

   a. Go back to your car and start the long drive home, mentally castigating yourself for being so disorganized.

b. Get on a phone and call home to see if your husband or kids are there and can give you the numbers off one of your credit cards.

c. Try to figure out a convenient time to come back for your clothes.

3. You get a tear-filled, emotional phone call from your mother, who tells you that your father has been diagnosed with Alzheimer's. After you hang up, you:

a. Pour yourself a big glass of wine and spend the evening turning the problem over and over in your head.

b. Immediately feel the need to talk to someone, anyone, who can help you feel better.

c. Realize you need to learn more about the situation and decide to contact whatever Alzheimer's groups are in the phone book, both for your own sake and your mother's.

4. You take your elderly in-laws to the airport after a nice visit. Since they have difficulty walking a long distance, you find a place for them to sit while you get them a riding cart. When you return to where you left them, they're gone. You:

a. Start walking up and down the concourse, calling out their names.

b. Call airport security and enlist the help of every ticketing agent in sight to try to find them.

c. Pick up a paging telephone and ask for them to be paged.

5. Your youngest comes home with a bloody nose and a black eye and tells you that his best friend hit him for no reason at all. Your son's best friend is also the son of your best friend and is not known for being much of a fighter. You:

a. Get your son cleaned up and wonder why he's fighting after all the discussions you've had about friendship.

b. Tell your husband it's time he had a talk with your son.

c. Put a bag of frozen vegetables on your son's eye and call your friend, both to apologize and to find out what really happened.

What Your Answers Mean

Mostly *a*'s: You're an *internalizer*, and your standard method of handling stressful situations is to go it alone. While you don't always internalize everything, you shoulder the major burden for dealing with life's ups and downs. You can also be critical of yourself when, in your opinion, you do a less-than acceptable job of it. You're not terribly aware of the stress in your life, and you tend to let it accumulate to the point where it starts to cause you problems.

Your stress-busting prescription: Meditation, not only to relax but also to help increase your awareness of your body and its needs; and exercise, perhaps something more vigorous than what you're currently doing. Internalizers tend to be loners, but you also may want to find a trusted friend, a counselor, or a member of the clergy member whom you can talk to.

Mostly *b*'s: You're an *externalizer,* and you tend to go off like a shotgun more often than not. While you generally take an active role in most situations, you sometimes look for others to assign that responsibility to. Your frenetic, scattered approach can drive the people around you crazy, but it also generally results in quick resolutions to most of the situations you have to deal with. Ongoing stress isn't much of a problem for you; however, developing a calmer, more focused approach will help you feel less frantic when faced with stressful situations.

Your stress-busting prescription: Meditation and other forms of relaxation, including such things as massage, aromatherapy, and exercise that emphasizes body movement, such as yoga, tai chi, or Pilates.

Mostly *c*'s: You're a *rationalizer,* and you tend to take a steady, balanced approach to most of what life throws at you. You try to not let your emotions get the best of you, preferring instead to respond and react once you have as much information about the situation as possible. You handle problems on your own when necessary and recruit the help of others when you feel you need it. In general, you're the sort of person others like to have around in an emergency because you usually keep your head on your shoulders. Because of this, you tend to be in demand and you sometimes take on more responsibility than you should, which causes you to forgo the things you would normally do to reduce stress.

Your stress-busting prescription: Pampering, including anything that makes you feel good; maintaining a proper diet; finding time to do things on your own and to be by yourself.

Are you a strong *a, b,* or *c*—or maybe a little of one and more of another? Once you've identified your particular style (or style combos) when you react to stress, it's time to take a look at some specific stress-management techniques that can help you.

Meditating

The idea of meditation often conjures up images of saffron-robed monks chanting in some strange foreign language, but meditation actually plays a role in many different religions and cultures. There are several ways to meditate, some easy, some not. All involve a clearing of the mind, which many people find both calming and enlightening.

The goal is to reach a quiet, thought-free place in the mind, as a way to relax, to pray, or to commune with nature and as a path to inner peace. People who meditate regularly say that the discipline helps them reduce stress and illness, improve their performance in the boardroom or on the playing field, increase their creativity, and gain a greater knowledge of themselves.

You don't even have to sit in the cross-legged lotus position to meditate, and you can do it for just a few minutes and still benefit from it. Here's a short, simple way to meditate that you can do just about anywhere:

➤ Find a quiet place or make the place where you are as quiet as possible. If you're in your office, close the door and turn off the phone and any other equipment that might be running. If possible, turn off the lights or draw the shades. You'll find it easier to relax if you don't feel like you're doing it under a spotlight.

➤ Make sure that you're not feeling restricted by your clothing. If something feels tight, such as a waistband, belt, or tie, loosen it. If you wear glasses, take them off. Contact lens wearers often feel more comfortable removing them, but it isn't necessary to do so if you don't have problems closing your eyes for a few minutes with them on.

➤ Sit in a good, straight-backed chair with your spine straight, both feet on the ground, and your hands either loosely clasped in your lap or positioned on top of each knee, palm up or down, as you prefer. Close your eyes and take a few deep breaths to center yourself.

➤ Then choose something to focus your mind on. Some people imagine a blank TV screen, which they then fill with the thought of something that makes them happy, say a beautiful sunset, a loved one, or an activity they particularly enjoy. Try to replace any negative feelings you may be having with some simple affirmations, such as "relax," "be happy," or any other short phrase that has meaning and power for you. Don't get frustrated if you feel your mind start to wander or thoughts begin to filter back in. Just move your thoughts back to your meditation focus. You may find that you have to work hard at first, but as you get more skilled at meditating, staying focused will be less of a problem.

Turn to Appendix B for more information and resources on meditation.

Affair Speak

Prayer is a humble communication in thought or speech expressing thanksgiving, praise, confession or supplication. Prayer may be to God, a higher being, or to the inner self.

Affair Facts

According to a 1997 *Newsweek* poll, not only do 54 percent of Americans report praying on a daily basis, 29 percent say they pray more than once a day. When asked if they believe that God answers their prayers, 87 percent stated yes, at least some of the time.

Saying a Prayer (or Lots of Them!)

Even if you think you don't pray much, you're praying every time you heave a deep sigh and say, "Oh, God"—which you may have been doing a lot lately!

Over the past few years, much has been written about the power of prayer, and if you're among the 54 percent of American adults who report that they pray on a daily basis, you already believe in its power.

Many people feel that they don't know how or that they need to have everything "just right" in their lives before they can pray.

Getting Better at It All the Time

In *Prayer: Finding the Heart's True Home*, author Richard J. Foster says, "Our problem is that we assume prayer is something to master the way we master algebra or auto mechanics." Praying can be as simple as taking a few moments to hope or dream.

In the words of one ex-affairee, "You don't have anything to lose, and you could have everything to gain by quietly reflecting on your thoughts and feelings."

Dr. Lana's Secrets

Prayer helps focus our hopes and is an expression of our faith. And hope and faith are important in all kinds of healing. Hope gives us positive thoughts about what we want, and faith offers us confidence in the future.

Experiencing the Power of Prayer

A number of years ago, Elena and her husband, Don, went through almost a year of turmoil in their marriage fueled by a chain of events that just didn't seem like it was going to end. It began when Don was forced to take a job in another city in order to maintain seniority in his company, leaving Elena behind for several months to sell their home and tie up loose ends. While both Elena and Don agreed that it would be the best move for them in the long run, there was no way they could predict the effect the decision would have on their lives.

"It really was torturous," Elena recalls. "Don was miserable being away from me and the kids. He hated his new job—he and his boss locked horns from the start. For me, it was a nightmare. Don sounded progressively more depressed and distant every time I talked to him, and we were having no luck selling our house. What we thought was going to be a few months of being apart stretched into a half year and then more. I took the kids and visited Don a few times while we looked for a new house, but money was tight and we didn't have our hearts in it as long as we were still tied to our old place."

Sometime during this period, Elena believes that Don had an affair. "We never spoke of it, and I don't think we ever will, but I'm fairly sure that Don turned to someone else out of loneliness, fear, sadness—you name it," Elena says. "I knew it had nothing to do with me so I wasn't angry, but I was sad and hurt because I felt so helpless. There really wasn't anything that I could do other than reassure Don that everything would be all right in the end."

After being separated from Don for almost eight months, Elena had her annual checkup, and the news wasn't good. Her physician found a lump in her breast and suggested immediate surgery. For Elena, it was almost the last straw. "I was alone and afraid, with my husband almost a thousand miles away, doing God knows what," Elena recalls. "I wasn't sure how much more I could take, especially when the oncologists found that the tumor had spread and that I would have to undergo chemotherapy in addition to losing a breast."

Praying for Peace (of Mind)

It was during this time that a friend of Elena's told her that she was adding Elena and her family to a prayer list at her church. "I appreciated her kindness, but I really didn't put much stock into it," Elena says. "Still, it felt good knowing that there were people who cared enough to spend some of their time focused on my needs in some way." Several members of the group visited Elena before she went into surgery, and they prayed for her then as well. "That was what touched me the most," Elena says, "their positive attitude and caring. It affected me in a way that I had never experienced before. Although I was still scared about what lay ahead, I also felt something else, almost a peaceful feeling."

Dr. Lana's Secret

If you are uncomfortable with prayer, set aside some time for positive self-talk. Yes, give yourself a talking to. Quietly review in your mind what you like about yourself or what you want for yourself. If it is a bit hard to think of anything that's good about you, ask friends to help you out by telling you what qualities they like in you; then write them down. Review your good qualities daily until they are firmly embedded in your memory.

While the next several months were some of the most difficult Elena ever faced, she began to approach her challenges differently. "I remembered how I felt when I was prayed for, and I decided to try it myself," Elena says. "It was so awkward at first, and I felt like a real dummy talking out loud to someone I couldn't see or hear, but I found comfort in my quiet moments and hope grew in my heart."

Don and Elena's house sold soon after Elena finished her final round of chemotherapy, and she and their children were finally able to join Don after almost a year's separation. "When I saw the look in Don's eyes as we got off the plane, I knew that what we all had been through was worth it," Elena says. "He was just so happy to finally have his family with him again. As for me, I was saying prayers of thanks for everything: for my wonderful husband, for being alive, and for my beautiful children and loving friends."

You'll find more about prayer in Appendix B.

Now, Just Take a Deep Breath...

It may seem pretty silly, but many people really don't know how to breathe correctly. They take small, shallow breaths from the top of their chests and never really expand their lungs as fully as they should. In the normal scheme of things, there's not much wrong with breathing this way, but it is a problem in times of stress. The lungs deliver oxygen to the bloodstream. Shallow, rapid breathing can make your blood become less than fully oxygenated, leaving you feeling short of breath, shaky, and light-headed.

If you've ever had any athletic, dance, or musical training, which teaches you how to "belly breathe," you're probably familiar with these techniques, but if you're still not sure whether you breathe properly, here's an easy way to find out: Just look down at yourself while you take a breath. If you see only your chest and shoulders rising, you're only using the upper half of your body to inflate your lungs. But if you see your stomach expanding as you breathe in, moving in and out as you take that breath, you're using both your sternum area and your chest cavity to breathe, and you're taking fuller, better breaths.

Here's an easy way to learn how to belly breathe:

➤ Stand or sit, whichever makes you feel more comfortable. Many people prefer to stand for this one, as it allows them to feel the action of their diaphragm and stomach more fully.

➤ Place your hands over your stomach, just below the waist. Lace your fingers together, but don't interlock them.

➤ Push your stomach out as you take a breath (through your nose if possible). Yes, this will make you look like you have a little bit of a pot (or maybe a lot of one!). You should see your hands move with your stomach, and a slight space may even develop between the fingers on each hand. If you don't see your hands move, you're still breathing from your chest. Expel this breath and try it again. Keep going until you see those hands move!

➤ To expel the breath, contract your stomach muscles and force it out through your mouth. Your hands should return to their starting position.

➤ Don't overdo it and take harder or faster breaths than normal. Just move the focus of your effort to your belly area.

Practice breathing this way for a few minutes as often as you think about it. Daily is preferable, but be realistic. Do it when you can. It will feel and look funny to you at first, but when you get the hang of it, you'll do it automatically. Any time you feel stressed, think about how you're breathing. If you've switched to your old shoulders-up, shoulders-down style, as many people do in such situations, get that tummy moving!

Finding Time to Be Angry

If you're a yeller and a screamer, you know what an excellent release for emotional tension being really verbal can be. It won't help your situation much, however, if your temper tantrums are aimed at those around you. If you need to unleash your lungs, don't do it at your kids, your friends, your coworkers, or even your spouse. Go find a mountaintop, row out to the middle of the lake, or lock yourself in the basement and let loose.

Affair Facts

Anger is hazardous to your health. People who feel intense anger or hostility have more serious health problems than people who are rarely or seldom feel angry. It doesn't matter whether it is expressed or repressed, it does damage to your body either way.

Finding a Sympathetic Ear

Although you read elsewhere in this book that it's generally not a good idea to do too much talking about the affair, don't deny yourself the positive benefits that having a good confidant can provide—if you really feel the urge to have one. Talking to a counselor, someone of the clergy, a doctor, or your trusted and wise best friend about your concerns and your fears can be excellent therapy and can provide a welcome haven at the times when you need it most. If you're concerned about leaks (of the personal information kind) choose a professional over your best friend. Turn to Chapter 24, "Next Steps," for more suggestions on finding a therapist or counselor. You'll also find more information on this in Appendix B.

Taking a Walk

If you're experiencing a lot of anxiety or tension, go lace up your sneakers and walk around the block. Do it as often as you need to. One injured spouse estimates that he logged several hundred miles during the early stages of his wife's confession.

Exercise is a renowned cure for tension, stress, the blues…you name it. While just about anything you do to move your booty will work, walking is one of the best forms of exercise you can choose. It's easy, cheap—and you already know how to do it!

Dr. Lana's Secrets

Exercise is one of the best tension relievers around. It releases endorphins, our natural "feel good" hormones, and that's what you really need right now. It doesn't matter whether you walk thirty minutes at a time or take 3 ten-minute walks, your mind and body benefit. If 30 minutes a day seems overwhelming, start with five minutes twice a day and gradually increase to 30 or even 45 minutes a day. You will feel better faster.

Pampering Yourself

More and more Americans are waking up to what Europeans have known for years: A little bit of pampering can go a long way toward making you feel like a new person. Day spas and other facilities that offer such services are now wildly popular, with dozens of new facilities springing up in cities across the country.

If you're the sort that melts at the mere suggestion of a long, fragrant aromatherapy bath, now's the time to indulge yourself. Go get a facial. Sign up for a series of massages. If you've never had a day of beauty, start looking through your local paper and check the Yellow Pages for listings under "spas"—even many small towns have them.

If you're living so far away from society that such lingo brings looks of bewilderment to those around you, plan your own spa day, or maybe a weekend. Even Wal-Mart now carries massage oils, facial masks, and other personal care products designed to make you feel like a princess—or a prince, for that matter. Don't think for a minute that such indulgences are designed only for women. Men comprise a steadily increasing proportion of the clientele at many spas; some even have specific services and treatment packages especially for their male clients.

Treating Yourself

That's right. Treat yourself to something nice. Maybe something you've put off for a long time. Call an old friend who lives far away. Go on that golf trip with the guys or on that antiquing weekend with the girls. Take an afternoon off from work to do something that pleases you, whatever it may be. Maybe you've always wanted to take a class on French cooking. Now's the time to book it. You deserve it.

Eat Right

It's your mother talking here, and she's telling you to eat your fruit and vegetables and drink your milk. "Ish," you say. "Eating is the last thing I want to do when my stomach's upset and I'm feeling miserable. And if I do get hungry, by golly I'm going to eat anything I want! Now just where *is* that big bag of spicy chips I've been hoarding?"

While a little indulgence in your favorite comfort foods during this time probably won't hurt you in the long run, don't lose sight of the role that proper nutrition plays in your life. Eating a balanced diet is always a good idea, and it's even more important during times of stress. If you lose much weight, you might just end up looking haggard. Gain weight and you'll feel even more miserable.

If you really find it difficult to maintain anything approximating normal nutrition, try eating smaller meals more often and focus on the foods that you find most appealing. There's really nothing wrong with making yourself a bowl of mashed potatoes if that's what Mom always made you when you were a kid and it's the only thing that soothes you now. Just don't eat the whole bowl in one sitting.

Other nutritional tips to keep in mind:

➤ Lay off the caffeine as much as possible. While it's always a good idea to limit your intake of caffeinated beverages, when you're feeling stressed, it's even a better idea to stay away from them because they can make you jittery and nervous, even if they don't usually have that effect on you.

➤ Select a nutritional program that gives you a varied diet. Eat small portions five or six times a day. This keeps your blood sugar more level than eating the typical three meals a day. Be sure to add in those vital fruits and vegetables, five to six daily, to give you the antioxidants you need, especially now. Vitamins are not a good substitute for healthy foods.

➤ Have a goodie when you want one. You don't have to deprive yourself. If you'd love to have a peanut butter cookie, have one and sit down and enjoy it. Don't chow down the whole box without really tasting a single one.

Get Your Rest

You'll be amazed at what a good night's sleep can do for you. If you're having problems sleeping, try a natural remedy. Herbal teas that contain ingredients such as kava kava and chamomile can help you fall asleep. Warm milk, mom's old standby, works for some, too.

Stay Away from Alcohol

Alcohol is a depressant. Although a glass of wine or a cocktail (or two) might make you feel better temporarily, it really only serves to mask your feelings.

Affair Facts

Six, seven, even eight hours of shut-eye are not enough. Sleep researchers tell us we should be sleeping $8\frac{1}{2}$ to 9 hours a night to allow our bodies to go through a complete sleep cycle.

You'll be just as blue, if not more so, after the effects of your imbibing wear off. What you may also find, especially if you're not sleeping or eating well, is that your usual tolerance for alcohol has been altered. Having even one drink may affect you more profoundly than before, and perhaps negatively as well.

Resist the temptation to drown your sorrow in your favorite brew. The same goes for other mood-altering chemicals (that is, drugs) unless prescribed by a physician.

Dr. Lana's Secrets

Antidepressant and antianxiety medications can be prescribed by your physician or by a psychiatrist for short-term use. They do work, they're not addictive, your personality won't be altered, nor should you feel drugged by them. They simply help you cope better during hard times like these.

Do unto Others...

This last bit of advice on keeping your life together comes from more than one injured spouse who found the benefits of volunteering during times of stress. These people discovered a great deal of joy and satisfaction—not to mention relief from the things that were stressing them—when they started to donate time to nonprofit agencies. Getting your mind off your own worries by focusing on other people's is a sure-fire cure to the blues, and it can definitely put a new spin on your own problems—maybe even convincing you that what you're dealing with isn't so bad after all.

Dr. Lana's Secrets

Each day set one simple attainable goal for yourself. For instance, do one nice thing for someone in your life, listen to your favorite CD all the way through, or clean out one messy dresser drawer. These simple and reachable daily goals give you immediate satisfaction and help build confidence in your ability to succeed in life.

If you've never volunteered and don't know what you'd be most interested in doing, start by thinking about the issues that are the closest to your heart. If you're a sucker for kids, maybe you'd make a good Big Brother or Big Sister. If you love nature, perhaps it's time to start planting trees or working with your local recycling program.

How do you find a place to volunteer your time? Try your local United Way agency, or other volunteer networks or clearing houses. You'll find them listed in the Yellow Pages under "charities," "nonprofit organizations," and similar headings.

The Least You Need to Know

➤ Keeping your life together includes learning how to be your own best friend.

➤ Learning how to manage stress is one of the keys to staying sane during the turmoil an affair can bring to your relationship.

➤ Meditation, exercise and a good nutritional program are essential to maintaining excellent health during this stressful time.

➤ Taking your mind off your problems by focusing on someone else is a great stress buster and can also have a positive effect on your community and the people around you.

Chapter 19

From the Outside Looking In

In This Chapter

➤ What an affair is like, from the affairee's point of view

➤ Why affairees get "buyer's remorse"

➤ Identifying the stages of an affair

➤ How your straying spouse's emotions, during and after, affect you

It was just one of those things,
Just one of those crazy flings.
One of those bells that now and then rings.
Just one of those things.
It was just one of those nights,
Just one of those fabulous flights,
A trip to the moon on gossamer wings,
Just one of those things.

—Cole Porter, "Just One of Those Things"

Songwriter Cole Porter, who penned these words in 1935, was supposedly reflecting the mores of New York's sleekly sophisticated cafe society when he called love affairs "crazy things." But the Depression years called for songs built on fantasy, not reality or nostalgia, and even Porter admitted that his flippant take on affairs was far from the truth. He knew all too well what it felt like to have a broken heart, and he also knew that most love affairs didn't end with a friendly wave and a cool, contained farewell, as he described in other verses of this popular tune.

Affairs really can send lovers over the moon, especially in the early stages, when they're riding their emotional highs, caught up in the giddiness of a new relationship that makes them feel so good. But affairs can also be a royal pain in the butt, not just for you, the one on the outside looking in, but for the affairees themselves.

Affair Facts

A 1985 study by Richardson showed that most affairs were between married men and single women.

If you're even the slightest bit interested in just what might be going on in your partner's little love affair (and it's really understandable if you are), this chapter is for you. Even if you think that too much knowledge is not a good thing, learning about the dynamics of an affair can help you gain a better understanding of your partner's reasons for having one. And it may help you understand some of your spouse's unusual or strange behavior. It can also help you recognize the different stages the affair is passing through, and hopefully, enable you to recognize the signs that the affair is drawing to a close.

Affairs—the Ecstasy

As you discovered in Part 1, there are many different types of affairs: love affairs, in-love affairs, sex affairs, revenge affairs—you name it. The players may know each other well, or they may have just met. The affair can be an addiction if it's motivated by the hormonal rush that happens at the beginning of a new relationship, or it can be driven by a host of other needs.

Regardless of the type of affair, almost all of them begin at an intensely emotional level, which may be hard to fathom if your spouse hasn't given a good yahoo over anything other than a football game for a long time. Rest assured, however, that this high doesn't last. In even the most emotionally charged affairs, it's not long before the feelings of ecstasy and euphoria downshift and reality sets in.

Affairs—the Reality

If the affair is to continue beyond anything but a brief, flash-in-the-pan encounter, it can't continue to be a fairy tale in fantasyland. It has to come down to earth, and when it does, it begins to assume a certain structure—both physically and emotionally—that governs the way in which it will function. Sometimes this structure is very similar to the relationship that the affair is supplanting, and other times it's not. Either way, the affairees begin to live dual lives, which can make for very tangled lives.

The Big Juggling Act

Think about all the responsibilities you have keeping just one relationship intact and multiply that by two. Is the sum total more than you think *you'd* want to handle? Probably.

Most affairees arrive at the same conclusion—that it's just too complicated—at some point during their liaison, which is why most affairs don't last forever. Not only is the straying spouse trying to conceal it from his family, but the expectations placed on him by his spouse and children haven't changed. At the same time, he now has a certain responsibility to another, perhaps equally demanding, relationship. It's truly a Herculean task, and most people find out after a time that while they may have once thought they were a giant action hero (or heroine), they are indeed only mortal.

Dr. Lana's Secrets

Affairs can intensify over time. I have spoken with countless people who thought they could handle their affair by keeping it separate from their everyday life. They planned to keep it light and fun and not get too involved; they certainly had no intention of falling in love. But emotions aren't rational and the best intentions don't always prevail against their biological and emotional drives.

Aside from the obvious necessity of keeping the affair secret—at least in most cases—affairees also have to juggle issues such as

➤ Their schedule. How often will they meet and where? And how will they keep in touch?

➤ Their social life together. Will there be one? Will they go places together or become friends with each other's friends?

➤ Setting boundaries, including determining how much they both want to know about each other's lives outside of the affair.

➤ Their future plans. Is making an exit from the primary relationship not an option, or is that a possibility? And if it's not, do both affairees still want the relationship?

➤ Protecting all the players, and not just from the birth control/infectious disease prevention perspective. It also means keeping emotions in check unless the affair is being conducted with the goal of breaking up one or both marriages.

And this is just the beginning! The longer an affair continues, the more complex it often becomes, and the risks it creates can substantially increase.

Maybe Hazardous Territory

An affair can destroy everything the affairees once held near and dear, and it's the rare wandering spouse who doesn't wake up at least once or twice during the course of the affair—even in the stages when it's the best it can be—with a cold feeling of doom over

231

just what the future might hold. The list of losses can be long, with the spurned spouse right at the top of the list, followed by children, job, standing in the community, self-esteem, house, car…and the list goes on.

Dr. Lana's Secrets

The people who were most likely to have an affair had premarital sex and lived in big cities usually on the East or West Coast. Affairees have a lower quality marriage and a lower quality sex life than people who are faithful.

"Buyer's Remorse"

If you ever spot your spouse taking a look around your house with a sad look in his eyes, or if he suddenly gives you a big hug and kiss and says he doesn't know what he'd do without you, chances are that he's reviewing such risks in his mind and asking himself if it's all really worth it.

Add to this a heaping dose of guilt—which is a pretty standard emotion for most spouses involved in extramarital affairs—and you have a spouse on your hands that may be deeply regretting having gotten himself into this position in the first place.

How these feelings may manifest themselves in your marriage will vary. Some straying spouses will distance themselves from their primary relationships, both physically and emotionally. Others intensify their efforts when it comes to their relationships with their spouses and bend over backwards to be solicitous and caring. While the extra attention can be nice, it also often doesn't ring true, which can leave both spouses feeling hurt and unfulfilled.

Affair Facts

While the decision to have an affair is a conscious choice, the swirl of feelings that engulf affairees are neither conscious, logical, nor easily controllable. Many lovers look back on their affair with disbelief, wondering how they ever got themselves into such a complex and convoluted situation.

"Although I suspected that Ben was having an affair, I really knew it when he gave me a super-expensive gift for Valentine's Day," says Corinne. "It was a beautiful watch—really the watch of my dreams—but it was so out of the realm of what he would normally give me that I just knew it was a guilt gift. It touched me because I saw it as a sign that Ben was sorry about what was going on, and it made me cry. Ben couldn't even look me in the eyes when he gave it to me, and he later said that my crying made him want to drop right through the floor."

Even so, many affairs keep on going, often on the premise that what the affairees stand to gain from the outside relationship outweigh the downsides and risks.

The Emotional Life Cycle of an Affair

Remorse is just one of the many emotions that mark an affair, and it can happen at just about any time during the life of an illicit relationship. Affairs go through stages just like other relationships, and each stage comes with its own particular set of issues and emotions. First, there's a beginning stage, with its obsessive thoughts and intense passions. Next comes the plateau, where everything is stable and passion simmers down. Finally, in most cases the affair becomes less important than other ordinary life experiences, and it ends.

Although all elements of the affair will affect you in some way, the affair's emotional side—including how things play out between the affairees—may have the strongest effect on you and your relationship with your spouse. Gaining a clearer understanding of the emotions that arise between affairees during the course of an affair may put you in a position to deal with them more effectively. This important knowledge can also help you determine what stage your partner's affair might be in…and you even might be able to use this information to help bring it to a close.

Dr. Lana's Secrets

One dilemma for affairees is where to have their affair. One-third have their affair at the woman's home and a quarter at the man's home. Another third use the home of a friend, their boat or camper, their office, or their car.

The Bloom Is on the Rose

The beginning of the affair is the most passionate and giddy period of all. If it's an emotionally based affair, this is when the feelings of being in love will be the highest. Sex is at its hottest in physical affairs. Desires run at fever pitch, and the affairees do their best to spend as much time as they can with each other.

Because of the priorities set by the affairees, disruptions often occur in primary relationships. Excuses start, and absences become more common. Straying spouses are often at their most distant emotionally during this time and tend to be very preoccupied with their own thoughts and feelings, choosing to keep them to themselves (or to their lovers, although you're not supposed to know this) and shutting the spurned spouse out of the equation. You may feel like you're being left in the dust, with your partner's emotions heading in the opposite direction from yours. Even when he's with you, it may seem like he's not.

Emotions on the Run

What you also might see are some incredible mood swings and some anger directed at you for absolutely no reason at all. These are caused by the emotional struggle your spouse is going through as she tries to balance her life with you and her life with someone else. If you try to get involved in this, chances are your efforts will be spurned or you'll be told that there's absolutely nothing wrong, or if there is, it's your problem.

Some affairees get jittery and excitable during this stage of an affair, especially if they're worried about their activities being discovered. You may notice your spouse getting nervous at what seems like inappropriate times, say, during a symphony concert or an evening out. There are several logical explanations for this behavior, once you put it in the context of the affair. He might be worried about running into his lover. Maybe he's supposed to be with her now, and instead he's with you.

Looking Different?

You may also notice some physical changes in your spouse. Many straying partners tend to lose weight and shape up during the first stages of an affair; they're trying to become even more alluring for their lovers. Changes in hairstyle, makeup, and clothing are also not uncommon. It could be argued that taking more interest in physical fitness and personal appearance isn't necessarily bad, but you may feel pretty lousy about the reason for it!

Getting to Know You

Affairs are at their best when they have few, if any, similarities to the affairees' marriages. Over a period of time, however, they will begin to take on many of the qualities of the marriage. The edges begin to soften on the sexual high the affairees felt so strongly at the start. The lovers start to settle into a routine.

There's still a lot of emotional and physical excitement during this stage, but the wonder of discovery has largely disappeared. The affairees have been together long enough to have a better idea of what to expect from each other, and the frequency of the trysts may begin to decline. This is also the point at which some physical affairs start to take on more emotional aspects. Affairs that remain based purely on sex begin to feel slightly old hat.

Sometimes, affairs at this stage move gracefully into friendships or more casual relationships with occasional sexual encounters, especially if the affair grew out of a long-term friendship. More often than not, however, they continue to wind down until they reach their end.

This settling period, which often lasts from about eight months to a year, can be somewhat of a good news/bad news scenario for both you and your spouse.

The Good and Bad of This Stage

For you, the good news is that the affair has settled into its own routine and may not be impacting your life as strongly, or as negatively, as it once did. Your partner may also be returning to a more normal mental state. Your sex life may even be picking up. For these reasons, this is a prime time to do what you can to begin rebuilding your relationship with your spouse—and to try to put skids on the affair (turn back to Chapter 17, "Coping with His (or Her) Affair," for more on this topic) if you're so inclined.

The bad news? Well, the affair is still taking place, and in many respects your life is in somewhat of a holding pattern until it concludes.

Dr. Lana's Secrets

When women choose to have an affair they usually think about it for a few weeks and even talk to a friend about it. Women also limit their emotional involvement and say they care for their lover but are not in love. At least that is their intention in the beginning.

Getting Comfortable

For your spouse, this period in the affair can start off by being very comfortable. So comfortable, in fact, that he may be thinking that he can keep it going on for as long as he wants. It's settled into a nice routine, and he's enjoying the best of both worlds—or so he thinks. Unfortunately, this phase usually doesn't last for long. Most affairs, if allowed to continue, will become more complex and will require a greater commitment from both players to go on. Pressure may start to build about making the relationship more than it is. It may become more difficult to keep it a secret, especially if spouses are starting to get wise. If a married lover starts spending more time with his family than before, his affairee may start to resent it.

Affair Facts

The number one reason men have affairs is sex. The number one reason women have affairs is to build self-esteem. As you would guess, men value the quality and quantity of their sexual relationship with their lover while women value communication the most.

Affair Facts

Often without a conscious thought, priorities shift. Things that seemed so urgent fade into the background, and new priorities take their place. Usually this process is gradual, and little by little, energy shifts away from the affair and back to normal living.

Instead of the affair being a wonderfully safe retreat from the world of married life, it starts to feel exactly like what the affairees have left behind. If your partner is in this stage of his affair, don't be surprised if you have a thundercloud on your hands, and a pretty angry one at that. He might be feeling like nothing is going right. It's a prime time for remorse to set in.

The Bloom Is Off the Rose

Affairs generally end when they outlive their reason for being. The sex may still be hot, the affairees may still feel a strong attraction to each other, but other factors change. Maybe they've received the emotional boost they needed. Maybe they've just gotten things out of their systems. For many affairees at this stage, reality has set in strongly enough to soften their emotions and make sex nowhere near as important as they once thought it was. The affair may also be draining them emotionally and physically. They begin to cancel dates with each other or see each other only occasionally.

Many lovers end their relationships, even if things are still going well, when the affair becomes more of an inconvenience than a benefit. It can become a hassle to see a lover. Schedules could change at work. Maybe the loyal spouse decides to disrupt a planned tryst by joining her partner for an early morning jog, and it happens more than once.

Distance Can Make the Heart Grow Colder

Long-distance affairs often end when the original hormone rush dies down, as was the case with Tom and Janet. Living at the opposite ends of a big city always made their meetings difficult. When winter set in and Tom began canceling more dates with her than he kept, Janet knew it was time to talk.

"Tom always called at the last minute to cancel, which would ruin my chances of doing anything else that evening," Janet says. "The weather made driving difficult, or he had to work late and was too tired to make the 120-mile round trip from his home to mine.

"As much as we enjoyed the time we spent together, we both knew it was just too hard to keep it going. Meeting halfway wasn't an option for us. So we stopped seeing each other. We never even talked about resuming our relationship after winter was over. I think we both felt the distance was too great an obstacle for a long-term relationship."

Recognizing the End

If you picked up on the telltale signs of the beginning of the affair, you'll probably notice those that mark its end. They may be silly things, like no longer having to make adjustments to the seats in your car. Or the signs may be blatantly obvious—in fact, they might slap you right across the face, especially if your spouse now decides it's time to tell you everything, or you are confronted by his lover.

Other signs that an affair is drawing to a close include

➤ Changes in his email address or cell phone or pager number, usually to divert communications from the ex-lover.

➤ Greater interest in family matters, like going to the kids' soccer games or planning trips together.

➤ A stronger desire for accountability. You may find your spouse telling you much more about where he's going and what he's doing and how you can reach him.

A Happy Ending? Probably Not!

Most affairs end on a down note; it's the nature of the beast. It doesn't matter how long the affairees have been together, the type of affair it was, or how mutual the decision was to part. The end of an affair is also the end of what was once an intense relationship in some shape or form. It's hard not to mourn such a thing and feel a great sense of loss. Eventually, one or both parties might look back in fondness.

For many affairees, ending their time together can be just as traumatic as calling it quits in a marriage. Karl felt depressed and lost for many months after he and Susan said goodbye. "I really felt like my life had come to an end," Karl says. "Susan was very loving about it, but I knew she was making a

Affair Facts

A survey of affairees conducted in England reported 60 percent of women and 48 percent of men felt pain from their affair.

renewed commitment to her husband and that made me feel rejected. I guess I had always hoped that things would work out between us and she would divorce him.

"She didn't even want me to call her after we were over—she said she couldn't handle it—and that made me sadder still, since I'd considered her a close friend. It took me six months, some antidepressants, and a lot of sessions with a good therapist to kick the blues and get my life back on track."

If your spouse has just called it quits with his or her lover, be prepared for some emotional roller coasters. The ups and downs are going to be there, no matter how or why the affair concluded. And, unfortunately, you'll get to ride them, too.

Coping with Postaffair Life

Most affairees feel a keen sense of loss when their extramarital relationship comes to an end. This feeling diminishes over time as all losses do, but it can affect you, your family, and your friends, especially if it's accompanied by some of the other feelings that often result when an affair ends—which can run the gamut from disappointment and loneliness to anger and resentment.

Dr. Lana's Secrets

The classic stages of loss—denial, anger, guilt, acceptance—apply to dead affairs just as they do to all relationships that come to an end for one reason or another. It's necessary to work through each stage in order to recover from the loss.

This is the time many affairees confess their affair, hoping to feel relief. If your partner confesses her affair and asks for forgiveness and reassurance, look out. It's tempting to deny your own feelings and sweep the whole thing under the rug. But if you wind up comforting her more than she comforts you, you can plan on her having another affair.

It's not uncommon for ex-affairees to want to withdraw from life for a certain period of time once an affair is over so they can sort through the emotional mess they've landed themselves in. Most will snap out of it on their own, and the most you'll see is some moping around or forced attempts at being happy when you know he's feeling anything but. You may also sense sadness, and possibly anger.

It may be hard to feel a great amount of compassion for your spouse after everything you've been through, and understandably so. But if you love the guy, maybe you can work up a little empathy. If nothing else, put the behavior in context and realize why it's happening.

If your spouse really seems to be having problems coping with life now, maybe it's time to take a more direct approach to the issue. Don't rush into a big discussion about the affair itself, but simply express your concern over his obvious state of distress. Doing so might lead you very naturally into the next stage of your relationship, where you can begin the process of building your affair-proof future.

The Least You Need to Know

➤ Affairs can appear to be nothing other than wonderful, but the reality is that they're often anything but. Many spouses end up deeply regretting the fact that they ever got involved in an affair.

➤ Your partner's emotions during the course of an affair will have an effect on your relationship. Be prepared by recognizing where they're coming from and put them into proper perspective.

➤ How your partner acts can often yield clues to what stage the affair is in.

➤ Most affairs affect the affairees deeply and are mourned at the end.

Part 5

Creating an Affair-Proof Future

Well, you've come through the eye of the storm. The tornado has swept through your life but you're still standing. You survived an affair.

Hopefully, your relationship did too. Chances are pretty good that it did if there was genuine love between the two of you to start with. But it's going to take some work. Lots of it, in fact. Holes to be patched. Cracks to be mended. Bruised egos to nurse and hurt feelings to soothe.

If your goal is to create an affair-proof future—and we hope it is—you'll find your game plan in this last part of the book. It will tell you what to do and when. Is it a good idea to air all the dirty laundry, or are some things better left unsaid? Should you seek counseling or can you go it alone? Can you prevent an affair from happening again? You'll find the answers to all these questions and more, and lots of good advice for rebuilding your relationship for the long-term.

What comes next may be some of the most difficult work you've ever had to do, but it can also be the most fulfilling. So roll up your sleeves! Let's get to it!

Chapter 20

Out in the Open

In This Chapter

➤ How to clear the air between you

➤ Why confession isn't always the best approach

➤ Nudging can be better than confronting

➤ The benefit of letting bygones be bygones

➤ Treat your spouse with the same respect and concern you would show a friend

➤ Some words of advice for your spouse

The death of the old is the birth of the new.

—M. Scott Peck

A new beginning. Do you like the sound of it? Are you ready to put the final touches on this particular chapter of your life and move on to what's next?

Chances are that if you've made it this far, you're more than ready. (Your spouse may or may not be, but we'll get to that later.) But you may not be sure of exactly how to get to the starting line. How do you put the affair behind you and move beyond it? What needs to happen right here, right now, to start your relationship moving forward again?

Clearing the Air

The fact that your life has changed somehow will have to be addressed if you are going to continue together successfully as a couple. Very often, this process begins with either a confession from the spouse who had the affair or a confrontation by the spouse who didn't. But it does not always. Some wayward spouses never confess their affairs, and some loyal spouses are never really aware that one has taken place. Others prefer to regard the affair as the symptom of a deeper problem and decide to address the issues behind the problem rather than the affair itself.

The fact that you're reading this book eliminates you from the unsuspecting/unknowing spouse category, so your focus is on deciding what you feel needs to happen to clean the slate between the two of you and give you a fresh start. Your options include:

Affair Facts

About half of both men's and women's affairs are never disclosed to the spouse, reports researchers Spanier and Margolis.

➤ Getting on with your life and addressing the issues at hand, not the affair itself

➤ Confronting your spouse with what you know and forcing a confession

➤ Aiding and abetting a confession

To decide which option is right for you, you must first answer a very fundamental question: Do you think the affair must be revealed?

Opening Pandora's Box

Maybe you think, "Yes, we've got to bare our souls; it's really the only way to save our marriage." But wait—this isn't necessarily so. A confession, while it can be significant, is actually a very small part of the process. In and of itself, a confession won't make a marriage better. In fact, it can make your marriage more difficult, and you both may end up feeling worse for it.

While many experts believe that complete disclosure is the best way to restore a relationship following an affair, it isn't right for every person or for every relationship. What can be said during a confession can actually be more damaging than the affair itself. Quite literally, you could be opening a Pandora's box if you insist on bringing everything out into the open or feel that you must.

Here are some questions to ask yourself to help determine whether a confession is a good idea for both of you:

1. Do you think that laying everything out on the table will move you to a resolution faster or better?

2. Will a confession open the door to positive communication?

3. Do you absolutely have to know what happened, even if the knowledge may make you feel worse for a certain period of time?

4. Do you believe that your straying partner would have a better shot at managing the guilt about the affair if it were confessed?

If your answer to any of these questions is yes, then it may be best to bring things out into the open. If not, then consider the other option: just getting on with your life and putting the unspoken affair behind you.

Dr. Lana's Secrets

Twenty percent of both men and women affairees said the confession of their affair made their marriage better. After that there was a big difference in how a man's confession of an affair affected his marriage and how a woman's confession affected hers.

When women confessed 70 percent said the confession had a negative impact on their marriage, while only 30 percent of men said the same. Most men said their confession had little or no impact on their marriage long term.

Letting Bygones Be Bygones

If you've suspected that your partner is having or has had an affair, you may be waiting for a confession that might never come unless you ask for it. Perhaps this isn't how you'd handle the matter if you were the wayward one—or how you'd like your spouse to do it—but your partner has a reason for his behavior, and sometimes it's better to leave matters alone and allow things to take their own course.

The reasons for not wanting to confess an affair are often related to feelings of shame over the affair or a desire not to cause further stress to the relationship. As quirky as it many seem, concealing an affair can actually be a kind of heroic act, since it's often done to protect the other spouse or out of respect for all the players involved. This reasoning might sound crazy to you, but put yourself in your spouse's position and see it from his perspective for a moment. While he can't erase what's happened, he also doesn't want to do anything more at this point that may hurt you. Only he will have to live with the shame and hurt that the affair caused if he can keep it away from you. This can be a big responsibility, and not everyone is up to the task. That's what makes it somewhat chivalrous.

Keeping the Past in the Past

Sarah, who weathered her husband Pete's affair without ever having direct confirmation of it, believed that discussing the affair itself amounted to reliving the past and was unnecessary to their future success. She never asked Pete for a confession and says she would have stopped him if he had tried to offer one. "To me, the thought of dealing with the affair was like beating a dead horse," she says. "It happened. There wasn't much I could do about that, but there sure was a lot I could do to try to prevent it from happening again. I felt that the affair would fade away by itself and that I would end up in an even better position if I avoided the strife and division that a confession might cause."

Rather than causing a huge upheaval in their relationship, Sarah ignored the obvious and turned her attention to the areas of her relationship with Pete that needed some work. "I did confront Pete," she says, "but it was along the lines of 'I think it's time to talk about what's going on between us.' I told Pete that I felt there were things that we weren't being very successful at as a couple and that it was time to address them and make them better. And that I wanted to do it in the context of looking forward, rather than looking back.

"In my heart of hearts, I think Pete knew that I knew," Sarah says. "But I also think that he was thanking his lucky stars that I hadn't confronted him. If anything, what I did do probably made him love me all the more. It sure seems that way now." There is no perfect way of resolving problems. If your normal communication style is non-confrontational and you typically acknowledge an issue but don't share emotions, that process can work for you now. A word of caution, be sure you are being honest with yourself about your needs and that they are being met. Accepting the reality of a partner's affair is complicated and emotionally draining.

Dr. Lana's Secrets

If you're in the confession process, be very careful about what you ask. It may feel as though knowing everything will make you feel better, but it won't. Once spoken, these tales of lovemaking, sex, lies, and injustices may haunt your memory and sicken your heart for years to come. Your spouse may feel that he should tell you everything to prove his sincerity, but take it slow. Ask for information sparingly and only for what you really need to know—things that clarify how the affair happened or offer insight into your partner. Don't ask for sexual detail.

Don't Sweep Your Problems Under a Rug

If you do decide to take the "let bygones be bygones" approach, be sure that you're not doing it just so you can sidestep the problems in your relationship. This response is not meant to be an avoidance technique. It's still important for you to work together to address the reasons that the affair happened in the first place.

It is possible to get your problems out in the open without bringing an affair out with them. Don't allow yourself to get hung up on having to know everything if you're not really sure that it's in your best interest to do so.

But…what if you think you do need to know?

Dr. Lana's Secrets

Moving on is not a one-act play. It is an ongoing process. You will have many conversations about your relationship, what works for the two of you and what doesn't. Have some short, simple conversations about changes you want to make. Also, talk about the good stuff in your relationship; don't let your focus lock on to only the negatives.

Laying Your Cards on the Table

Most affairs, if they aren't confessed willingly, are brought to light through a confrontation. Generally, it takes place between the spouses, but sometimes the lover is involved as well, often involuntarily. What usually propels a confrontation is the spurned spouse's feeling that she's either had enough, and just can't continue without a disclosure, or that she needs to know exactly where she stands in the relationship.

While confrontations are often the quickest way to cut to the chase and meet the affair head-on, they aren't always the best approach.

The Pitfalls of Confrontation

Demanding a confession can cause more problems than it solves. The resulting scene may be filled with anger toward you instead of remorse over stepping outside of your relationship boundaries. Your spouse may try to avoid the issue by lying about it or by telling you only what he or she thinks you want to hear. These are less-than desirable reactions, and they won't do either of you much good.

Some spouses orchestrate a confrontation around their need to make a strong point about their feelings concerning the affair, as Delia did when she found out about Frank's affair. He came home late one night after a tryst with his lover to find Delia sitting alone in a darkened room, lit only by one small lamp by her side.

"The second I walked through the door, I knew my goose was cooked," Frank recalls. "It was one of the spookiest things I had ever encountered. The way Delia had the light positioned made her look like Elvira of the Night. Any thoughts I had of beating her to the punch and confessing flew right out the window. She was loaded for bear and I mean that literally. We kept a revolver in the house for protection, and she had it sitting right next to her."

Whether Delia intended to or not, she created a situation that frightened Frank into confessing, instead of one that encouraged him to come clean on his own. "I don't know what she was thinking," Frank says. "Maybe she figured she could threaten me if I didn't tell her everything she wanted to hear. Maybe she was afraid of what I'd do if she confronted me. She was clearly furious, and believe me, the last thing I was going to do was take her on, physically or emotionally.

"I hadn't planned on confessing the relationship to her. In fact, I was in the process of winding it down. But Delia gave me no choice. I was so startled that I did a very poor job of telling her what she wanted to know, which only made her angrier because she felt that I was avoiding her questions."

Affair Facts

When people are cornered, they react to being trapped and usually make poor decisions.

Dr. Lana's Secrets

If you're confronting your spouse to save your marriage and he hasn't decided whether he wants to stay with you or leave to be with his lover, you have a challenge ahead. Proceed with great care, for yourself and your marriage. Talk to your partner about what you know and how you feel. Say, for instance, "I know you're having an affair, and I know you care deeply for her, but I want our marriage to survive." Don't force a decision from your spouse; it's not something you can make happen. He may say yes for the moment, but pressuring him may send him right into the arms of his waiting lover.

Staying in Control

If you do decide to force the issue, try to orchestrate the confrontation as calmly as possible. Choose an appropriate time and place—ideally, somewhere you both feel comfortable. Home is often the best choice. One of the worst is surprising your spouse and her lover when they're out together. Even if you know their activities like the back of your hand, resist the temptation to confront them in a public place. Yes, it's a great way of making very sure that your spouse gets your point. However, lots of things can go wrong in situations that you can't control, and you may end up embarrassing yourself more than them.

Try not to broach the subject in an adversarial manner. Keep the accusations in check as much as you can. Remember that you may be asking your spouse to do something she's either not ready to do or had no intention of doing. You're putting your partner on the spot, and she may really resent it.

Bumps Ahead

Forcing a confession on top of an emotional situation usually leads to disaster. If you've surprised your spouse and her lover by coming home unexpectedly, clear the scene before making any confessional demands. If at all possible, give your partner the chance to offer a confession first.

Dr. Lana's Secrets

When you ask your partner for information, limit it to what concerns the two of you. Ask about his feelings for you, how he feels about himself, and how he feels about his decisions. Keep the focus on the two of you, not on the other affairee and certainly not on the two of them. Getting more information about them will only hurt you, and it is hard to forget even after you forgive. You can always ask for more details about the affair later if it really matters, but you cannot "un-ask."

Dealing with a Buck Passer

Has your spouse been dropping tons of clues in the hopes that you'd be the one to bring matters out into the open? Any of these might be a sign that you're married to someone who wants to talk to you, but doesn't know where to start:

➤ Buying a book about extramarital affairs (even this one) and putting it in a prominent place for you to see, or even giving it to you. Talk about an open invitation! What your spouse is doing is planting a very obvious hint and looking for your reaction to it.

➤ Leaving a clue about his affair—like a picture of his lover or a note—in a place where you are likely to find it.

➤ Leaving email messages on the computer where you can read them.

➤ Acting sheepish and guilty around you or dropping verbal hints through open-ended statements or questions designed to lob the responsibility ball into your court.

Although it's really not very fair for one partner to transfer what should be her responsibility to her partner's shoulders, confrontations work well in such situations because the spouse is usually more relieved than upset when confronted and will show a great deal of remorse and contrition over her behavior.

Because you're the spouse who has been hurt by betrayal, you're really in control here. Just don't go too far with your authority. As much as you might want to berate your spouse while you have the chance, don't! If your spouse loves you, she's already miserable enough, and pouring salt into an open wound doesn't gain you anything.

Dr. Lana's Secrets

Being kind to your spouse is often your best bet in the long haul. Kind may be the opposite of how you really feel, but there's an added benefit to taking the moral high road in these situations, especially if your spouse is feeling very shamed and guilty. If you keep on acting like an angel, your spouse will put herself through her own mental purgatory as she grasps how wonderful you really are.

Aiding and Abetting a Confession

"Telling Audrey about my affair was absolutely one of the toughest things I had ever done," Ben says. "I expected her to explode. But she responded in a very gentle and sympathetic way. I kept on going, thinking she would eventually get angry with me. Maybe she felt it on the inside, but she just kept on asking me questions and listening to what I had to say. I finally felt so miserable that I burst into tears and threw myself at her lap. I couldn't believe what a wonderful wife I had, and I swore right then and there that I would never cause her this kind of grief again."

What Audrey had done was make it possible for Ben to confess to her in his own way and in his own time. She knew about the affair, and she wanted Ben to come forward with it without her forcing the issue, but she also wasn't going to wait forever. "I knew Ben would be reluctant to tell me, so I decided to 'nice' him to death," Audrey recalls. "I literally bent over backwards to be sweet and kind to him, and he finally ended up feeling so guilty that he had to tell me. By the time he did, the initial shock and anger I had felt when I first learned about the affair was long past, and I was ready to work with him on putting our relationship back on track."

It's not always necessary to lay on as much kindness as Audrey did; there are other ways to clear the path for a confession. An obvious one is to follow the let-bygones-be-bygones approach, but such leniency might just make it too easy for your partner to have another affair sometime down the road. Other approaches include:

➤ Rearranging your schedule so you spend more time together. If a confession is going to come, it's more likely to take place if your spouse doesn't feel as if he's always chasing after you or playing second fiddle to a career.

➤ Planning a vacation together. Don't make it a tour—be sure there's plenty of time for the two of you to be alone together. If you have children, leave them at home.

➤ Renewing your marital vows. Most wandering spouses find it pretty difficult to go through with an event of this magnitude with less than a clean conscience.

Giving a confession a gentle push may sound manipulative, but it's really much kinder than forcing a confrontation. The other nice thing about this method is that it usually makes wandering spouses feel as if they're in control of the situation, which usually makes them less angry and combative than if they're confronted.

Into the Confessional

Maybe you're ready for the release that a confession can bring. On the other hand, your spouse's behavior over the last few weeks or months may have made you so nervous and irritable that the last thing you want to hear is confirmation that you've been betrayed.

Dr. Lana's Secrets

Your role in the confession is to listen, and to ask relevant questions. Be thoughtful about what you ask. The purpose of the confession is to clear the air and reduce the tension between you. Don't ask leading questions to make a point when you know the answer, and don't create punishments for your spouse if you want the confession to end with more closeness between you.

251

Dealing with Dread

No one really likes to hear bad news, but you may be *really* dreading it. Dread indicates fear, and you can manage it to a certain extent by identifying what you're afraid of. If you need to, make a list. You may have some very legitimate concerns, but what you're most likely afraid of is the event itself.

Managing the Confession

Part of beating the fear involves knowing how to guide the situation toward a positive outcome. Even if you're forcing a confession, remember why you're doing it and what your ultimate goal is—to clear the air between you so that you can determine whether or not you have a future together. Remember that you're an equal player in this equation and have an active role in the process, no matter what. Consequently, you can have a certain amount of control over how and when the confession takes place.

Dr. Lana's Secrets

A positive step in moving your relationship to a better level may be making this confession a success. Treat your spouse with the same respect and concern you would show a friend.

Try to guide your spouse to a setting with as few distractions as possible. Make sure the television is off if you're at home and get the kids out of the way. Pare down the extraneous details until the focus is where it should be—on the two of you.

Bumps Ahead

While it's usually not a good idea to delay a confession, you should if you or the confessor is under the influence of drugs or alcohol. Strong emotions and mood-altering chemicals are never a good mix.

Don't Put Off or Avoid It

What you probably shouldn't do, as much as you may want to—because you're nervous or the time just doesn't seem right—is delay your spouse's confession once he's ready to make it. Maybe you've anticipated it for awhile, and you've gotten to the point that you really dread it. But there's really not much you can do to avoid it, so you might as well let it come.

Buying time only puts off the inevitable, and it could force your spouse into continuing a situation that he'd rather end if you'd only give him the chance. The sooner you face the reality of the affair, the better your chances are of repairing your marriage if you want to do so.

"I tried for months to find a time and place to talk to Dan about my affair," Staci recalls. "He kept on avoiding me and avoiding me. I finally realized that my need to confess didn't translate into his wanting to hear about it. Then I felt like he really didn't care what I did, so I kept my other relationship going."

Give your spouse a fair chance to do the right thing. Don't avoid his attempts to confess.

Handling the News

Once a confession is under way, try to sit back and let your spouse do it her way, regardless of how you feel. Listen from a neutral corner and reserve the temptation to jump to conclusions or make value judgments. Just open your ears and take in the information.

If the confession is causing you a great deal of pain, your natural impulse might be to stop listening after the first few words. If you weren't prepared for what you're being told, your emotions may overcome you and you actually might not be able to hear what your spouse is saying.

But it's essential that you keep your ears open and your focus trained on what your spouse is telling you. Overcome by emotion? Then just ask your spouse to stop for a moment. Get a glass of water or a tissue if you need one. If you can break the tension, you should be able to bring your attention back to the situation and avoid having to ask for a rehash of everything your spouse has already said.

Dr. Lana's Secrets

Expect to cry and expect to hurt. Even when you know what is coming, hearing it is hard. When you have absorbed all you can, stop. There will be another time.

Keep Your Defenses Down

As much as the confession may hurt you, remember that it's uncomfortable for your spouse to be making it. Don't put the stops on the process by getting defensive about what you're hearing.

A confession is probably going to arouse your anger in some way even if you're re-lieved that it's coming out in the open. With that anger comes the desire to defend your honor by lashing back at your spouse. While it's O.K. for you to express your emotions—and your partner should be prepared to accept your anger—don't go on the defensive and start pointing your finger at your spouse for all the grief and aggravation he's caused. Telling your spouse that you're angry is acceptable. What's not acceptable is saying that you'll never trust him or love him again because he's hurt you so deeply. These words are hard to take back later.

Dr. Lana's Secrets

The worst thing you can do is to say things you don't mean or insist on something you don't want—for example, "I'm calling your father, and you have to tell him what you have done," or "I am calling my attorney, and you will be getting the papers delivered to the office, so get out." As difficult as it is to simply listen, do it. Listen to your partner and try to grasp what's being said. Keep telling yourself that you don't need to make any decisions right now.

It's Not a Grudge Match

A confession is not the time to air all your dirty laundry. Try to limit your comments to issues directly related to the affair. If your spouse is significantly broadening the scope of your discussion, ask that it be narrowed to the issue at hand. The time will come later for digging into all the issues that led to the affair.

Withhold Moral Judgments

Maybe you're so virtuous and loyal and honest that you'd never ever consider the possibility of having an affair, no matter how unfulfilled or ignored or rejected you may feel. Haven't you yourself done something, some time, that was unethical? Maybe you didn't return the extra change you got when a cashier made a mistake. Or you took a few pads of paper home from the office on your last day of work. Although it could be argued that an affair is a higher moral crime than pocketing a few extra pennies or appropriating office supplies from your employer, elements of lying and deception are present in all such actions. You really can't afford to take a holier-than-thou attitude about your partner's indiscretions.

Don't Assume Your Partner's Blame

Affairs don't happen in a vacuum. In some way, shape, or form, you may have contributed to your spouse's extramarital activities, intentionally or not. But don't shoulder your partner's responsibility in the matter. You're not the one who chose to deal with your issues by stepping outside of your marital boundaries.

At the same time, don't treat the situation as if it's your spouse's problem and not yours. Accept the fact that you're both culpable for what happens between you, and you'll both have to make some changes in your relationship and in the way you treat each other to keep it from happening again.

Deciding What You Want to Hear

This may be the time when you want to hear every gory detail about your spouse's affair. And you may be the sort of person who thinks you'll feel better if you hear it all. Keep in mind that getting the gist of what happened is usually enough. Not knowing all the intimate details can save you from tormenting yourself over the situation.

Still, it's not easy to decide what you want to hear, especially when you have no idea what you're going to be told. So try to stay open to whatever your spouse has to say. If you're hearing more than you want to, you can tell him exactly that. On the other hand, if you need more information, ask for it. You may or may not get it at this point, but if this initial confession is constructive, your spouse may be willing to share more later.

Dr. Lana's Secrets

Some people communicate better nonverbally than verbally. Your partner may be showing you his love in physical ways, by doing things for you, touching you, bringing you gifts, or creating experiences he knows you like. He may be showing you that the affair is over and that he's committed to making it up to you. Accept and enjoy these gestures; they are just as legitimate as talk, and sometimes they are more sincere and more enduring.

For Your Spouse: Looking at Things from the Other Side

Let's turn the tables for a little while now and focus our attention on your spouse. This shift might at first seem a bit odd in a book that's really for you. But put yourself in his place and read this from his perspective. It's a good way for you to get a better grip on the big picture.

And when you're done reading it, give it to him to read, either after you've both agreed to sit down and talk about the affair (but really haven't yet) or just after you've talked a bit about the affair.

Ready? Here we go....

So you're the one who's had the affair. And you're going to talk about it with your spouse. Not an easy time for either of you, to be sure. But in the next few pages you'll read about some things you, the affairee, can do to make this experience the best it can be for both of you.

Why You Should Talk About It

Obviously, if you have this book in your hands, your spouse knows about your affair, whether or not you confessed or she confronted you. There's more for you two to talk about, and any one of these is good enough reason:

1. You are desperately sorry and have learned that you love and appreciate your spouse more than ever; if it takes the rest of your life to make it up to her, you will.

2. Your relationship is founded on intimacy and friendship, and based on past experience you know you can work through problems and become closer.

3. Your spouse is having a difficult time emotionally because he feels your marriage has been threatened and he is blaming himself.

Affair Facts

The top three reasons both men and women ended their affairs are they felt guilt to spouse, they were tired of lying, and they were afraid of being caught.

In these situations confession is healthy and has a good chance of helping your spouse and your marriage. The odds are in your favor that you can build a marriage that is better than ever.

Dim the Spotlight

Your guilty feelings might be nudging you to do something extra special for your spouse as part of your confession. Although you may think this gesture will help soften the blow, it usually has the directly opposite effect. It's a better idea to keep things as normal and low-key as possible. Making a reservation at the fanciest restaurant in town so you can confess is not going to go over well. Taking her to a public place will most likely make your spouse nervous and suspicious and leave her feeling exposed and manipulated. Few things match the comfort of being in your own home, even if things are very strained between you.

Bumps Ahead

Some times and places are better for confessions than are others. Two of the worst places: in bed late at night or in a public place after a few drinks.

Saying What You Need to Say

One of the greatest fears about making a confession is bungling the whole thing. Accept the fact right now that you probably won't be as eloquent as you'd like.

You're going to say some things poorly, and you're going to feel badly about what you say because you know it's going to hurt someone that you care about. While it's important to convey the message you need your spouse to hear, don't get too hung up on your delivery and the exact words you use.

That being said, here are some tips on ways to make your confession as good as it can be.

Dr. Lana's Secrets

How to start a confession? Begin with an "I" statement; for example, "I am asking your forgiveness for what I have done," or "I have had an affair," or "I want you to know I love you more than ever, and I have put that love at risk by getting involved with someone else." If it helps to write down what you want to say, that's fine. Just keep it brief.

The most you can cover in this first of a series of discussions is one or two points. Think about what will be the most important for your partner to hear—choose one or two from the list that follows.

➤ How you feel about her

➤ What you want to happen between the two of you

➤ What you did

For instance, "You are more important to me than anything else in my life; I want to be with you until the day I die, and I have made a terrible mistake."

No Pointing

A confession is a baring of the soul. It centers on the feelings and emotions of the confessor. So limit what you say to your feelings. Your statements should focus on what's on your conscience and in your heart, not on how your spouse made you feel or what he or she may have done to make you feel this way. Instead of pointing a verbal finger at your spouse and saying, "You neglected me," you're going to say, "I felt lonely."

Also avoid making "we" or "our" statements, such as "We never have fun anymore," or "Our sex life is unfulfilling." Making such statements implies that your partner feels the same way you do. There's a good chance that he or she doesn't.

Avoid Unclear Statements

Don't tell your spouse that "it" made you feel bad or angry. Vague, nonspecific statements put the burden on an already angry or upset spouse, as he now has to either figure out what you mean or ask you to clarify yourself. Be specific. If your sexual inactivity is part of the reason that you went to bed with someone else, say so. Don't try to protect yourself by calling something an "it" and hoping your spouse will figure out what "it" is.

Dr. Lana's Secrets

While being honest is important in your confession, don't go overboard with sordid details of what you did, how often, or in what position (either emotionally or physically). This kind of intimate detail is harmful, and although your spouse may ask for it, providing this type of information is not helpful; these images are hard to forget. Keep reassuring your partner about your feeling toward him, your desire to solve your problems, and your hope to build an affair-proof love.

Deciding How Much to Say

There may be some details about your affair that you should not disclose, maybe because they're too embarrassing or you feel they'll be too hurtful for your spouse to hear. Or you might be trying to protect your lover. You will have to make a judgment call. Be sure that the basis for your decision is what is best for your spouse and your relationship in the long term.

Bumps Ahead

If you're feeling too vulnerable or upset about disclosing your affair, the time might not be right for you to do so. Consider delaying your confession for a week or two, but no longer. There is no time that will feel good.

If you really don't want to answer a particular question, you might just tell your spouse that you're not prepared to talk about that aspect of your affair at this moment. Instead, you want to focus on the two of you. Also be reassuring that you are most interested in your spouse's feelings, not in those of your former lover. There's a chance that what your spouse asks now may not be something he will want to know later. Whatever you do, don't lie or be evasive. This is a time when you must be absolutely honest and candid. Any duplicity on your part will be painfully obvious unless you're a superb liar. And if you are, you probably wouldn't be making a confession.

Dr. Lana's Secrets

Your spouse will undoubtedly ask questions you don't want to and maybe shouldn't answer. Simply promise, "I will tell you everything that will help you to understand me and what happened to us, but I want to be sure I don't hurt you more. We can talk about the things you need to know now, and we can talk more later when you have had time to think about what you do and don't need." Then stick to your agreement. Confession is not a single session. There will probably be twenty to thirty emotionally revealing discussions throughout the next year before you find peace with each other.

Be Contrite

Admitting that we're wrong is something we never like to do. Regardless of how guilty or ashamed we might be over our actions, pride and vanity still get in the way when we have to make a painful admission.

A confession is an act of contrition. You're admitting that you've made a mistake. You are telling your spouse that you're sorry for what you did. But that's not enough—you also have to be sorry and willing to take action to resolve the issues. If you're confessing because you feel you have to and it seems superficial, it's not going to go very far in keeping your relationship intact.

Remember President Clinton's first televised apology? People sensed the lack of conviction and contrition behind his statement. It was hollow, and it angered the American people. They knew the president was apologizing because he had to, and not because he believed that he was wrong. If you want your marriage to survive, show your remorse and be more concerned about your partner than about yourself.

It goes without saying that you should make your confession in person and directly to your spouse. This is not a time for phone calls or notes, even if accompanied by a box of the finest cigars or dozens of her favorite flowers. Not only do you owe your partner the courtesy of a face-to-face encounter, it's best that you hear and see your spouse's reaction to what you say.

Dr. Lana's Secrets

Stay close physically as well as emotionally while you are talking. Touch each other and hold him in your arms while he sobs. Declare your willingness to keep talking over the following days, weeks and months.

Back to You, the Spurned Spouse: Deciding What You Both Want Next

The time is finally here to start giving some serious thought to the course you'd like your relationship to take. Is your marriage worth saving? Do you feel that you can work things out, or do you want to cut your losses and move on? Do you believe your spouse's sincerity, and do you want to invest the time and energy to improve your relationship?

Dr. Lana's Secrets

If you hear the words "I love you, but I'm not in love with you," stop right now! You need more help than this book can give you. See Chapter 24, "Next Steps," for finding and working with a marital counselor or therapist.

Knowing that the one you love loves someone else and deciding to stay and fight for your marriage is probably the hardest thing you will ever do. You will be working alone to improve your relationship. If you go this route, remind yourself of your great courage, tenacity, and devotion to your commitments and believe you are a brave person.

Unless your spouse has made her confession as a means of informing you that your relationship is over, determining what happens next is up to both of you. Although it's not yet time to make a final decision, the process starts now.

Always remember the affair-proof mantra. You can stay together if you're both genuine in your desire to do so.

260

The Least You Need to Know

➤ Confession isn't always necessary; be sure to weigh the consequences.

➤ Confrontation can get issues out in the open but can lead a spouse to feel cornered and defensive.

➤ Believe what your spouse is telling you during a confession.

➤ Stay open once your spouse begins a confession. Encourage a focus on the two of you and avoid the gory details of the affair.

➤ Confession is not a one-time event; have as many conversations as you need.

➤ Remember all the good things in your partner and not just this bad time. Everyone makes mistakes.

Chapter 21

Surviving the Storm

In This Chapter

➤ Will she or he cheat again?

➤ Learning from an affair

➤ The importance of forgiveness

➤ Fighting the fears

➤ The second-chance quiz

Only the strong of heart can be well married, since they do not turn to marriage to supply what no other human being can get from another—a sure sense of the fortress within himself.

—Max Lerner, *The Unfinished Country*

Feeling a bit black and blue these days? Somewhat frayed around the edges? So exhausted that you're not sure if you can climb the steps to your house at the end of the day? By now you have every right to feel like you've been through a war. An affair is one of the greatest challenges to a relationship, if not the greatest. And as hard as the battle may have been for you up to this point, it isn't over yet. In fact, some of your greatest challenges may still be ahead.

Has the Fat Lady Sung?

Has the affair been discovered, revealed, or confessed? Or are you both still dancing around the fact that one exists in your life at all? Depending on your particular situation, any of the following scenarios could describe your life at the moment.

How Are You Feeling?

As the betrayed partner, you could be:

➤ In a holding pattern, certain that an affair exists but uncertain whether to ignore it, confront it, or wait for a confession that may never come.

➤ Still pretty much in denial because it's hard for you to believe that your partner could possibly be having an affair (but you think it must be so because, after all, you are reading this book).

➤ So angry at your spouse that you can hardly see straight and ready to pounce the minute you sense a confession is on the way.

➤ Feeling like you're ready to crack under all the tension that's in your marriage and beginning to wonder if being married is worth all the heartache and agony after all.

How's Your Partner Feeling?

Meanwhile, your straying partner could be:

➤ In a holding pattern also. She is still involved in the affair and isn't really at a point where she wants to end it, but increasing pressure from you has her feeling uncertain about how long she can go on living a double life.

➤ Nearing the end of his extramarital affair and wanting to return to his marriage.

➤ Calling it quits with her lover and trying to decide whether she should tell you about the affair or keep it concealed.

➤ Feeling very guilty about his affair and praying that you discover it so he doesn't have to bear the burden of confessing it.

➤ Getting ready to let the chips fall where they may, expose the whole darn thing to anyone who wants to know about it, and take her chances on what happens next, regardless of the magnitude of the fallout that she knows will follow.

Where Things Stand Now

The list of possible scenarios is virtually endless, thanks to all the quirky little things that human beings are capable of doing to make their lives difficult. Describing them all could take years so, for the sake of discussion (and hopefully enlightenment), let's assume the following has happened:

➤ Your spouse has confessed to the affair.

➤ You've accepted the confession.

The fat lady has sung—Brunhilde has warbled her last aria. Now you're both looking at each other and wondering what's next. It's a pretty standard scenario for most affairs. If you're not there yet, you probably will be soon.

This Isn't the End...Unless You Want It to Be

If there's one absolute in the very nonabsolute world of extramarital affairs, it's that an affair, in and of itself, does not have to mean the end of your relationship.

An affair can be the end of what you two have, no doubt about it. If the affair began as a way to shatter your relationship, it probably will. However, if your relationship was once on solid ground and there was genuine love between the two of you, there's every reason to believe that you can learn from this experience, address the issues that lie between you, and move forward to build an even stronger partnership than before.

Learn from This? Surely You Jest!

Like it or not, an affair is a learning experience just like everything else in life. You may be wishing that you'd been given a completely different experience to learn from, but guess what? You didn't get to choose; this is the one you're stuck with.

You may be so angry or ashamed over the affair that you'd rather forget that it ever took place. Ignoring the lessons it could teach you or believing they're not of any value now that the whole messy thing is over and done with may help your memories fade a little faster, but it's not a very good idea. Doing so is like ignoring a toothache. Not only will the pain come back and hit you even harder sometime in the future, you run a good risk of losing the tooth because you didn't address the reason for the pain in the first place.

So open your eyes and ears, uncross your arms, and get down to work. Instead of resenting what the affair has done to you, your marriage, your kids, and so on, explore the affair's meaning. Look at the signals it has sent. The fact that one has erupted in

Bumps Ahead

Here's another sure thing (well, almost a sure thing) in the world of affairs. The discovery of an affair, or the confession of one, usually means the affair is over or winding down. Although it's possible to work on rebuilding a marriage while an affair continues, it's much more difficult than if the affairees have called it quits.

Affair Facts

Couples who go to counseling determined to rebuild their relationship usually succeed if both partners are willing to leave the past behind and learn new skills to become better partners.

Affair Facts

The book *American Couples* disclosed that men who had affairs usually had two or three, while women who had affairs normally had only one.

your marriage is a strong signal that there are issues you need to address and that there are needs that must be met. Don't ignore the warning signs.

Dr. Lana's Secrets

You are not powerless; in fact, you are responsible for your own life and your own feelings. Accepting that you have the power to shape your relationship and your life is an important step in making yourself happy. People who set simple goals they can succeed at to improve their relationship build confidence in themselves and in their relationship. Set a goal to be on time today or to make a loving phone call this afternoon, then do it. Compliment yourself on accomplishing your goal.

Addressing the Issues

What has happened between the two of you and why it happened needs to be analyzed and discussed. To do so, you'll have to reestablish communications with your spouse. For some couples, all this means is restoring what they had before the stress and tension caused by the affair silenced their signals. However, if poor communication skills or vastly different communication styles have plagued your relationship from the start, now is the time to learn how to understand what your spouse is saying and improve your speaking and listening skills as well.

Dr. Lana's Secrets

As you delve into the issues, don't keep going back to the affair or the affairee and asking more questions to get more details. Keep the conversation aimed at the two of you and what needs and issues you have to address to work through your feelings. Talk about your good times together in the past, discuss what is right in your relationship now, and start planning good times in your future.

Learning how to communicate clearly and how to listen effectively can be a challenge for even the most mature couples. But you don't have to go it alone. You'll find a number of suggestions for improving your communications skills in Part 2, "Secrets to Affair-Proof Love." If you need more help, you may want to seek out a marital counselor or therapist who specializes in this area; see Chapter 24, "Next Steps." In addition, several good books and other resources on the subject are listed in Appendix B, "Good Places for More Help."

Increasing the Odds for Success

The direction your relationship will take after the affair is out in the open will largely be determined by how the two of you handle things during the first few hours, days, and weeks to come. Your emotions are going to be running very high, and it's important not to let them color everything you say and do.

It's appropriate and necessary to vent your fear, frustration, anger, and anything else you might be feeling. But you'll wear each other out if all you do is yell and scream. Step back and be quiet if you feel that you're getting out of control. Remember that things are fragile between you right now. Words said in anger may cut much deeper than you'd like, and those wounds are sometimes very slow to heal. Don't say things you'll live to regret.

Dr. Lana's Secrets

Crises provide opportunities to change and to learn. Be sure you are spending as much time listening and learning as you are talking and venting. Ask questions to understand what changes your partner is asking you to make. Give your partner specific examples of behaviors you would like to see more of.

This is also a period when you might be reestablishing your physical relationship with your spouse. Get close if you can and want, but don't smother each other by feeling that you can't let your spouse out of your sight. Don't be afraid to give yourself and your partner some breathing room. This might mean forcing yourself to trust him to be away from you, even though you're not sure you're ready for it. If necessary, set some limits on how long you'll be apart or where you'll both spend your time when you're away.

Dr. Lana's Secrets

Reestablishing order in your life after chaos is difficult but necessary. Get together with friends, exercise, read a book, listen to music, go to work, and play with your kids. Do things that are usually pleasurable, even though you may not feel a lot of pleasure in them right now. Acting happy helps you feel happier.

Dealing with Depression

Feeling a little (or a lot) depressed? Maybe your partner is, too. Feelings of betrayal, failure, and anger can lead to depression for a spouse who's been betrayed. And the one who's had the affair often gets depressed when the affair ends and it's time to deal with the loss of something that was once enjoyed and cherished. Guilt and remorse over causing pain to you, your kids, or his lover can also have him singing the blues.

Affair Facts

During times of extreme emotional distress, your body releases natural opiates, known as endogenous opioids, as protection against stress and pain. These strong chemicals literally dull your senses, just like morphine and other painkillers do. They can also make you feel depressed and make it difficult for you to function normally.

A low-grade depression will make you feel weepy and sad and not terribly motivated to do anything positive for yourself or your relationship. It is nature's way of coping with a bad situation, of shutting down and closing off. A few days of depression can be a healthy coping mechanism, but it shouldn't go for more than a month. If it does, get professional help, because the longer it lasts, the harder it is to change.

At the same time, don't let working on your relationship become all consuming; also work on making yourself happy. Do something every day that brings a smile to your face. Get the focus off the affair, off your pain, and off your guilt. Take a break from the heavy discussions and do something else together to get your minds off things. Go play.

If you're experiencing more severe symptoms than just feeling a little blue, you may need professional help. Turn to Chapter 24 for suggestions on finding it.

Dr. Lana's Secrets

Some people are good at vocalizing their thoughts and feelings. Others find writing in their journal gives them relief. Many write letters they don't send.

Physical outlets such as tearing up a magazine or ripping a newspaper to shreds can give you a sense of release. Hitting helps, not a person, a ball. Get a tennis racket and hit that ball against the backboard as hard as you can, you'll feel better.

Coping with Anger

You've been betrayed. She's hurt because her needs weren't met in the marriage. You're angry at each other, and if you haven't made those emotions clear, it's time that you did—in a healthy way, of course.

Holding on to anger can cause physical and emotional problems. It can cause depression and anxiety, stomach upsets, neurological disorders, high blood pressure, and backaches.

Recognizing the Emotion

If you've stifled your anger for many years, you may not even realize when you're angry. You're so out of touch with your emotions that you've become immune to them.

Any or all of the following can indicate that you're angry and don't know it:

➤ Blushing or feeling like your face is hot

➤ Tingling or numbness in your hands or feet

➤ Ringing in your ears

➤ Diarrhea or stomach cramps

➤ An anxious, pins-and-needles feeling

Venting Anger Constructively

Even if you're good and aware that you're angry, shouting out your feelings at the top of your lungs

Affair Facts

Adrenaline and noradrenaline, the hormones that create our fight-or-flight response when we feel threatened, are believed to be the same chemicals that cue our brains to remember emotional moments with great clarity. Research conducted at the University of California-Irvine revealed two memory systems in the brain: one registers standard information, and the other ensures that we'll recall the events and behaviors that pose the greatest threat to our survival.

might not be the best way of releasing your pent-up emotions. Yes, sometimes you need to yell at the object of your anger. But doing it too often or at inappropriate times can drive your partner away at a time when you're trying to bring the two of you closer together.

Dr. Lana's Secrets

Constructive anger is healing, and destructive anger destroys. When you're expressing your feelings, make "I" statements, not "you" accusations. "I feel sad" or "I feel so angry I don't know what to do" are constructive. "You are a sick and selfish jerk" or "You've ruined my life" are destructive.

Here are a few venting techniques to try:

➤ Write out everything you'd like to say to your spouse. If you're a typist, you might get a higher level of emotional release by pounding it out on the keyboard. You might jot down your feelings and emotions. Let everything you're feeling pour out. But make sure you keep it to yourself. If you're working on a computer, erase the screen after you're done or store the page away for your eyes only. If you're writing longhand, keep your pad of paper where your spouse won't see it.

➤ Schedule a time to fight with your spouse. Acknowledge the fact that you need some time to yell and scream. Announce your needs and request an appointment to do what you need to do. Keep it brief—no more than a few minutes or so. You can request time to vent in one direction only, or you can both have at each other simultaneously. It may seem contrived to schedule time for a fight, but it really does work, and it can work at any stage in a relationship, not just when you're trying to recover from an affair. Some spouses even fight physically with pillows or with boxing gloves specially designed for this purpose!

➤ If you have an artistic bent, paint or draw out your anger. Tape big pieces of newsprint to a wall and fling your kids' finger paints at them. Or indulge in a little deconstructionist venting. Ever been tempted to dash a plate at the floor or against the wall? Do it right, and you'll create the material for one of those trendy mosaic mirrors or tables. You may want to buy some junk-sale plates for this one. And don't forget to protect yourself from flying shards. Glasses, gloves, long sleeves, and long pants are highly suggested!

➤ Confide in a close friend but keep it brief and focused on your emotions. Talk for an hour about your feelings, not about your partner. Stick to the one hour limit, then move on to other subjects or go do something together that gets your mind off your problems.

Can You Live Happily Ever After?

The answer is yes, eventually. Maybe later rather than sooner, depending on the amount of damage that your relationship has sustained and how hard you're willing to work at repairing it. But somewhere down the road, you can be happy together again. It will be a different happiness, most likely better and more honest than where you were in the past, especially if you do what you should to make things right.

The day will come when you realize, probably somewhat suddenly, that you're really quite pleased with where you are and you're very proud of yourself and your spouse for having the courage to keep going instead of quitting.

The Key Ingredient—Desire

Here's another absolute when it comes to approaching life after an affair: Both people must genuinely want to stay together. The enthusiasm doesn't have to be equal, but the desire must be there at some level on both sides to make a success of it.

This might be a tough one to get your head around, especially if you're so angry at your spouse that you'd just as soon close the door forever. You have every right to be angry, but remember, anger doesn't last forever, or at least it shouldn't. In any event, don't let the anger you feel now determine the future. Allowing it to do so is almost guaranteed to lead to regret later.

Dr. Lana's Secrets

Don't let your anger consume your life. We don't make our best decisions when we're embroiled in fury. Don't use what your partner has told you about the affair against her. If you throw it back at her, she'll stop opening up to you. And that will spell the end of a successful reunion because she'll not trust you!

Can You Forgive?

Love is the underlying strength of a relationship and it's what makes it worth fighting for. Trust can be earned and repaired over time. But you can't restore the love unless you can forgive each other for what has happened.

Both partners must be willing to enter the next phase of their relationship with a spirit of forgiveness. It isn't solely the responsibility of the injured spouse to forgive a wandering partner for his indiscretions. The wayward spouse also must be willing to forgive his partner for anything she did or said that contributed to the situation that fostered the affair—and forgive himself for breaking his marital covenant.

Forgiveness is essential for removing guilt and shame. Depending on your religious orientation, part of your forgiveness process may include turning to your faith, making a confession, and asking for forgiveness.

> **Affair Facts**
>
> We've become a nation of forgivers, according to religious leaders and scholars who track such things. And it's a good thing. Research shows that those who forgive have a better quality of life than their less compassionate counterparts and are less likely to suffer from high blood pressure, anxiety, and depression.

> **Dr. Lana's Secrets**
>
> It may seem contradictory, but you can forgive your spouse even if you're angry at him. Don't let anger, sadness, or fear stand in the way of accepting what your spouse did and moving forward in your relationship. Focus on what is, not what was. Talk about your feelings, your hopes, and your dreams. Don't keep going back and reliving the affair; it'll only do more damage.

Battling the "What Ifs?"

As you well know, the battles you're having with yourself and your partner are far from over. You may be wondering if your relationship is even worth fighting for, especially if you've been in the thick of things for a long time already. There's no real guarantee of success, and it's very easy to allow your fears to feed some second-guessing. What if your spouse wanders again? What if you achieve a state of reconciliation, only to have your partner decide that she really doesn't want to stay with you? What if you can't learn to trust your errant spouse again?

Tackling all these uncertainties is overwhelming and frightening, no doubt about it. But you have to face all these fears if you're going to move forward together.

Does She Deserve a Second Chance?

Still wondering whether it's worth the effort? Unsure whether you can ever trust your spouse again? The following quiz may reveal what's in the relationship cards for both of you.

Rank each statement on a scale of 1 to 5 as you think about your spouse's behavior, with 5 the highest mark (an overwhelming yes) and 1 the lowest (a definite no). If you're neutral or not quite sure, choose 3.

1. If your spouse confessed to the affair, was the confession genuine and complete? (Or if you had to confront your spouse, was she willing to admit to the affair honestly and openly?)

2. Has your spouse asked for forgiveness and expressed her forgiveness to you?

3. Does she seem to truly regret her indiscretions?

4. Has she accepted responsibility for the affair?

What Your Answers Mean

A perfect 20: Why did you even bother taking this quiz? Your spouse has clearly exhibited genuine remorse over what happened and is willing to do whatever it takes to get your relationship back on track.

16 to 19 points: Your spouse has done all the right things, and the indicators are good that you'll be able to forge ahead. Trust might be a key issue for both of you.

12 to 15 points: Your spouse may have expressed remorse about the affair but seems less than sincere about it and may be blaming you for what happened. You also might feel like you haven't been told the whole story or the real story.

8 to 11 points: Either your spouse is being very duplicitous about the whole situation or you don't trust her at all.

10 points or below: You probably caught your spouse and forced a confession. Either she wasn't ready to confess or didn't plan to, and what she said rang far from true. Your spouse is more angry than repentant, and you're suspicious of her every move. Forgiveness is still a possibility, but a lot has to happen for it to take place.

Will He Stray Again?

This is another big what-if question. No one wants to put a lot of effort into a losing proposition. How will you know whether there'll be another affair in the future?

Part of the answer has to do with how successful you were in addressing the issues that led to the affair. But affairs can still take place regardless of your best efforts to keep them at bay. Now might be a good time to go back to Part 3, "Danger: Affair Ahead!" to review the times in your life when affairs are more likely to take place and the bad habits that can lead to affairs.

For a quick read on the possibilities, take the quiz below. Answer each question with a yes or a no.

1. Is this your spouse's first marriage?

2. Is this his first affair?

3. Was the affair over before it was confessed?

4. Or did it end soon after the confession?

5. Does your spouse handle stress well?

6. Is your spouse a child of divorce?

7. Did your partner's parents or a close relative have an affair?

8. Does your spouse's family seem accepting of affairs?

9. Has your spouse strayed before?

10. Is the affair still continuing, even after it was confessed?

Scoring: If you answered yes to most of questions 1 to 5 and no to most of questions 6 to 10, the chances are slim that you'll face an affair with this spouse again. If the opposite is true, the likelihood of an affair happening again with this spouse is strong; you will have to actively work to protect yourself and your partner from infidelity.

Dr. Lana's Secrets

It is important that you have as much information as possible as you make a decision about repairing or abandoning this relationship. There are a few spouses who have numerous affairs. Around 25 percent of men and 15 percent of women who have affairs have more than four. A few spouses admit to hundreds of lovers.

There is nothing you can do to change the behavior pattern of these infidels. You can either decide to live with multiple infidelities or you can leave the relationship.

No Sure Thing

There really aren't many sure bets in this world, so if you're looking for firm assurance that an affair won't happen again in your marriage, you won't find it here. But don't let that be a reason to stop your desire to resurrect the relationship you once had. You've come this far; go ahead and see it through to the end. If you give up now, part of you will always wonder what would have happened if you had had the courage to work for it.

Reconciliation is a painful and excruciating process, but it also holds great promise for future happiness. Weigh the possibilities against the pain of separation and divorce and either staying on your own or having to do it all over again with somebody else. With luck, you'll believe that what is good between you and your spouse outweighs the bad, and you'll be willing to tackle the next steps on the road to rebuilding your relationship.

The Least You Need to Know

➤ When you talk about the affair, keep the focus on the two of you, not on the affair or the affairee. Don't ask for emotional or sexual details; it hurts too much and the pain takes years to forget, making forgiveness harder.

➤ There's a very good chance that you can restore your relationship to a level of happiness that is as good or better than what you once had.

➤ Venting your anger is essential and healthy, but there are other feelings to express also: hurt, sadness, hope, forgiveness, and love.

➤ Both partners must want to stay together and believe it is possible to keep their relationship moving forward for reconciliation to be successful.

Chapter 22

Love on the Mend

In This Chapter

➤ Lessons learned from an affair

➤ The relationship repair process

➤ How to tell whether it's worth the effort

➤ Why you need to restore trust and respect

➤ The importance of forgiveness

➤ Sex after the affair

And ruined love, when it is built anew, grows fairer than at first, more strong, far greater.

—William Shakespeare

If you're in need of some reassurances at this point, take Shakespeare's words to heart. You've weathered some tough times with your spouse. You've had something happen that you never wanted to face. But you faced it. And you survived.

You may now be wondering whether your relationship will survive, and if it does, whether it can really be better than it was. The answer to both questions is yes! An affair, in itself, doesn't mean the end of a relationship. And an extramarital relationship can make a marriage stronger by being a catalyst for change.

The lessons learned from an affair can be some of the most important you'll ever be taught. The result is very possibly a love that is stronger and deeper than you ever thought possible. It will take some time and energy, but it's an achievable goal.

Dr. Lana's Secrets

In counseling couples for more than two decades, I've seen the power of love, which can make you love your partner through your pain and build a relationship that is better and stronger than before.

What You've Learned So Far

An affair will rattle your cage and shake your foundation more than most life experiences. You found out that your relationship with your spouse wasn't quite what you thought it was. For whatever reason, good or bad, that old relationship is gone forever. You're now living your life A.A.—After Affair. You may be sadder, but you're also much wiser. Isn't it interesting that the things that don't kill you make you stronger?

The World Didn't End

There were times when it sure felt like you had reached the end and maybe you wished for it. But the sun kept on coming up, and you kept on facing each new day. If you haven't done so already, congratulate yourself for making it.

Dr. Lana's Secrets

Positive self-talk is important to keep your spirits up. Remind yourself daily of all the steps you have taken to make yourself and your marriage stronger. Compliment yourself for the times you have listened when you wanted to plug your ears, when you smiled through your tears, and when you were kind when you wanted to hurt back.

No One's Perfect

Any pedestals you may have erected for your relationship have most likely been smashed to the ground by now. You've learned that your spouse isn't Superman—or Wonderwoman. You both have some wonderful traits, but being a superhero isn't one of them. You're both fallible, just like everyone else. And you both made mistakes.

It Takes Two to Tango

You should have learned that no one's perfect by now. If not, and you're still pointing your finger at your spouse and blaming him for everything that's happened, you won't learn anything new about yourself or your partner. There are no perfect permanent relationships, and you can always be a better partner than you are. Did you have a part in what happened? Yes, most likely. Maybe there were needs or requests you ignored, time you spent unwisely, or perhaps you just weren't tuned in enough.

Dr. Lana's Secrets

If you are the faithful spouse, blaming your partner for everything that happened leaves no room for growth, understanding, or forgiveness.

What You're About to Learn

Perhaps the most important thing you're now going to learn is how the two of you got yourselves into this situation in the first place. You may or may not know what caused the affair. But either way, you can learn to understand each other better and to create stronger bonds between you.

Going through the steps to restore your relationship will expose any weaknesses in how you function as a couple and give you the opportunity to learn how to do things better. You'll also discover any problems in your abilities to address important issues, which may include:

➤ How well you're able to communicate your feelings and concerns

➤ How you resolve conflict, manage anger, and negotiate

➤ How willing you are to forgive each other

➤ How well you tolerate bearing the stress, pain, and anger that going through such processes can cause

If you're lucky, you'll also learn that you love each other enough to bear any pain necessary to make your relationship all that it can be.

Repairing Your Relationship

If things were fairly good between you before the affair, there's no reason to think that you can't put your relationship back together. It will take a good deal of time and effort, but if you're both serious and committed, you can do it.

Still, you might be wondering if it's worth the effort. Why go through all the work it takes to restore love and trust if it all gets shattered again? Although there's no sure way to factor the odds of this happening or assure you that it won't, the following are indications of a genuine desire to start afresh:

➤ A forthright confession, followed by such statements as "I'll do whatever it takes to make it right between us."

➤ A sincere apology.

➤ The expression of genuine remorse.

➤ Solid proof that the relationship with the extramarital lover is over and reassurance that you won't be threatened by this person's existence.

➤ Acceptance of responsibility for the affair itself. No blaming it on the wronged spouse or the former lover. It doesn't matter what contributed to the affair. The affairee, and the affairee alone, is responsible for breaching the commitment to his or her partner.

Dr. Lana's Secrets

Don't dig up dirt to fuel your feelings. Don't demand the retelling of the same stories of betrayal, lying, and sex so you can justify your anger or hurt. Forcing repeated disclosure as a punishment is bound to backfire. If you must hear your partner's revelation repeatedly, ask yourself why. How do you feel when you hear them? Do they make you feel relieved and reassured—or punitive and self-righteous? If your partner loves you and wants to be with you, keep the disclosures simple. Your partner will suffer enough seeing your pain; you won't need to inflict any more.

Put the Issues on the Table

Communication may be strained, but get the issues out anyway. Let your partner tell you about unmet needs that fed the affair. Very often these issues are related to sexual or emotional problems that have to be dealt with if you want to continue your relationship. Try to stop thinking about him and his lover and think instead about what you can do to help each other heal now.

Restoring Trust

Many spouses arrive at the tail end of an affair still in love with their partner but wondering whether they can ever trust their mate again. An affair creates such a significant breech of trust that it's easy to understand these concerns. However, it's important to restore the trust in a relationship for it to have any chance for survival.

There are two parts to the trust equation. The errant spouse must realize that his behavior has seriously injured the integrity of the relationship and must diligently work at reestablishing it. The injured spouse must learn to trust again by actively putting her trust into action. It doesn't work to keep your spouse on a leash and constantly monitor his actions until some unspecified time when you feel he's exhibited a sufficient amount of trustworthy behavior.

Dr. Lana's Secrets

The innocent trust you once had with each other is gone. It is shattered, and you will never have it again. This loss is one of the reasons an affair is so devastating. It will be a long time until you can just accept what your partner says at face value. When the former affairee says, "I'll be a little late," a chill runs through your whole body and like a shot, your brain sends a warning signal, telling you danger lurks. Overcoming your instincts to protect yourself from the pain you felt when you discovered the affair takes years of patient, unwavering reassurance from your partner.

"I had so totally trusted Phil before that I never felt I could restore those feelings again once he confessed his affair," Jodie says. "It wasn't until I realized why I was so distressed over his breach of trust that I was able to move forward on this issue. The problem was that I was embarrassed over trusting him so much. I refused to think that he would do anything to betray me, and I had completely ignored all the warning signals. I'm working on trusting him again, and he's certainly working at earning my trust. But I won't be so naive about it in the future."

Remember the comfort level that boundaries can establish in a relationship? The best way of restoring trust is by relying on them again. Redraw them if you have to. Once they're in place, the offending spouse must make sure they aren't broached. And the injured spouse has to cautiously believe that they won't be.

Forgiving and Forgetting

Forgiveness is one of the greatest acts of love that we can bestow on another person. It requires looking beyond the hurt and pain that the affair caused, past all the anger and all the negative feelings. One of the toughest things for a wayward spouse to hear is that his wife is so angry that she'll never forgive him. The words might be said in the heat of the moment, but there's often a ring of truth to them.

If you love each other and you want to stay together, you must both forgive the other for the part you each played in the affair, and you have to forgive yourselves for what you did to cause it. That's right. You have to forgive yourself, too. Remember the "it takes two to tango" thing? Very few people don't feel at least a little guilt over what they think they did to contribute to their spouse's unhappiness with their relationship or over how they took out their anger and fear on their spouse, kids, parents, or friends.

Forgiveness doesn't happen overnight. Like happiness, it's a process, and it unfolds as you work together through the aftermath of the affair. Forgiveness also doesn't erase the negative feelings you might have toward your spouse, nor does it wipe out the fact that the affair happened. Forgiving does not mean forgetting.

What forgiveness means is the desire to move past the immediate problem and focus on the future. That requires a willingness to stop dwelling on the past and on everything you both did wrong. You'll have to consciously shove those feelings to the deep recesses of your brain and allow thoughts about rebuilding your relationship to replace them.

Forgiving isn't forgetting, but it's about as close as you'll probably ever get to it. You'll never forget parts of what happened—the day you found out about the affair may be indelibly etched on your brain. In time even the most painful memories will fade, but you'll be disappointed in forgiveness if you expect it to speed the healing process along.

Dr. Lana's Secrets

Hope helps. Look forward to what you want, think about how you can get it, and then do it.

Rebuilding Respect

The discovery of an affair can also destroy the respect you have for your spouse. If your reaction was swift and strong and somewhat irrational, your spouse may have lost some esteem for you as well.

Respect is often restored as we rebuild trust. Being repentant about the affair can also go a long way toward improving your esteem with your spouse. Act honorably, and you gain honor. It's as simple as that.

Restoring Self-Esteem

How can an affair *not* be a blow to the ego? Your partner choose someone else over you and shared her feelings and affections with him. It's easy to feel pretty bad about that.

One of the fastest fixes for a damaged ego is to remind yourself that you're not the only reason that your spouse had the affair. Don't take on all the responsibility by yourself. You may or may not have contributed to it, but the fact that your spouse has strayed really has very little to do with your value as a human being.

Dr. Lana's Secrets

Make a list on paper of the qualities you like in yourself and post it in a place where you'll see it every day. When you read your list, think about what you can do to demonstrate those qualities that are the best part of you and then do it. Nothing builds self-esteem like being your best self.

If you know your partner's lover, you might be involuntarily comparing yourself with that person. If you're checking your butt to see whether it's better or worse than hers or thinking about dying your hair because his isn't gray, ditch those thoughts immediately! A little competition can be healthy (it might even prod you into doing some things that are good for you. Constantly comparing your attributes to another person's can erode positive feelings about yourself.

So...What About Sex?

Restoring intimacy to a relationship is one of the most difficult aspects of the rebuilding process for most couples who have let it lapse. While you might feel a strong need for physical closeness, you also may be very uncomfortable about being close to your spouse. The knowledge that she's been with someone else can also make it seem like there's a third person in your bed.

Dr. Lana's Secrets

If you suspended your sexual relationship with your partner, it has to be restarted. As scary as it is, it's an essential step. Start slowly, just touching, caressing, and holding each other for ten minutes each night without having intercourse. Do this for a week. Progress as you feel you can, little by little becoming lovers again.

The Rating Game

When you know that your spouse has slept with someone else, thoughts of how you rate compared to her lover are probably unavoidable. Are you as sexually skilled as he was? Can you satisfy her the way he did? Are you as sexy? And it goes on and on.

At the same time that you're playing the rating game, your spouse is probably going through some difficult times, too. Not only might he be trying to forget the memories of what sex was like with his lover, he's also trying to adjust to being back with you. And he might just be having trouble getting excited about sex with you again.

Whether or not he's using memories of his lover to increase his desire, any hesitancy on his part is going to send some strong signals that things aren't the way they used to be. Combine this prospect with the awkwardness caused by introducing any new sexual techniques that he may have picked up, and the whole situation can turn downright ugly.

Sex, the Second Time Around

But it doesn't have to. If you're working on rebuilding trust and you're going through the process of forgiveness, you can use the same emotions that fuel your actions in these areas to repair things in the bedroom. Don't focus your attention on the past. Shove your insecurities and anything else that can affect your relationship negatively to the back of your mind. Try to start anew.

Maybe you resent the fact that he picked up some new tricks with someone else, but you may enjoy those new tricks if you get over being angry about them. If you're not comparing new ways of making love to what you used to do, you'll have no basis for resentment anyway.

> ### Dr. Lana's Secrets
>
> Whatever you do, don't ask your partner for an intimate description of her relations with her lover while the two of you are in bed together. It's sure to put a damper on things!

More Fire Starters

Here are some other ideas for restoring intimacy:

➤ Be attentive to your partner's needs and emotions. There still might be a lot of mood swings going on when it comes to how she feels about you. If your sexual relationship seems to take a step backward after heading in the right direction for a period of time, it's time to talk about it and revert just to touching, holding, and talking for a while.

➤ Stay flexible. There may be times when your partner wants to have sex. You may also spend many evenings just holding hands and talking. You may want sex when he doesn't. Don't treat it as a rejection if your spouse's needs are different than your own. Both of you are still exploring your comfort limits. Along the same lines, don't push things. If you're able to maintain some contact with each other, you'll get to where you need to be in time.

➤ Focus on intimate things that don't involve sex. Take a bath together, give him a sensual massage, say "I love you" when she least expects to hear it…such personal expressions can go a long way to restoring those loving feelings.

➤ Reassure her of your love. Try to keep in mind that your partner's guilt feelings about the affair may be standing in the way of restoring your sexual relationship. Even if you've forgiven her, she may feel so badly about what she did to you that she doesn't feel worthy of your love or your attention in bed. The best thing you can do is to tell your spouse that you do love her and that you want to do everything you can to make your relationship better.

Addressing Sensitive Sexual Issues

If sexual problems were the primary cause of the affair, you have to deal with them or your efforts at reestablishing intimacy won't go anywhere. No one said it's going to be easy; in fact, it might be downright painful. But keeping your needs to yourself won't restore things between you. You'll also be robbing your spouse of the chance to work on them with you.

Dr. Lana's Secrets

Don't let sex drift back to its previous unsatisfying level. It may be difficult for you to talk about or seek treatment for sexual difficulties, but know that help is available. There are testosterone and estrogen patches, implants, and of course, now there's Viagra. Sex is important in maintaining your intimate bonds; don't try to convince yourself that cuddling is enough.

This is when you'll find out just how good you are—or aren't—at communicating with your spouse. Not only do you need to be able to communicate your needs and desires clearly and effectively with each other, you also have to be good listeners. And you'll need to keep your defenses down. If you're hearing for the first time that the way you've stroked your partner all these years really wasn't satisfying, it's easy to get your ire up. Either that, or you'll start thinking that you've never done anything right and wonder whether you ever can.

Affair Facts

Psychological issues are often not the cause of impotence. People over fifty, those who are overweight, and smokers may all have a physiological reason for their impotence or inability to have an orgasm.

Are your sexual issues so great that you don't know where to start? Then get outside help. This is no time to let a sexual standoff disrupt your marital repair work. Many very fine counselors and therapists can guide you through your issues and help you develop ways to solve them. Sexual counseling won't be any less painful than working on the issues alone, but it can be faster and more effective. You'll find more about marital counseling in Chapter 24, "Next Steps."

Falling in Love...All Over Again

It can take years for some couples to work through all the issues that came to light during and after an affair. Other couples recover more quickly. What keeps them all going is the conviction that their relationship is worth preserving. When two people are determined to rebuild what they once had, they can and do create something better than before.

During this process, you might discover some wonderful things that you never knew about your partner. The sheer effort expended when restoring a relationship can endear partners to each other in ways they never dreamed possible. You might even find yourself falling in love all over again. It's the best reward for all your hard work. And it's definitely worth setting your sights on!

The Least You Need to Know

➤ An affair can be a real catalyst to change and growth. Stay open, and you'll learn more than you thought possible about yourself, your partner, and your relationship.

➤ Being able to talk frankly with your spouse is an essential element of rebuilding trust and respect. Be protective of your partner and be sure you aren't just trying to make yourself feel better.

➤ Both spouses must forgive each other—and themselves—for the affair.

➤ Sex after an affair is bound to be awkward. Rather than obsessing about the past, stay focused on the moment.

➤ Love can wind up being stronger and deeper if both partners are willing to do the work involved to make it so.

Keeping Your Relationship on Track

By now, your knowledge of what affairs are, how they happen, and how to survive them is nearly complete. Given everything you know, you should be feeling very positive about your relationship's future and feeling very firm about not ever allowing an affair to affect your life again. Still, there's that little voice in the back of your head that keeps nudging at you. Can this all happen again? Sadly, the answer is yes, despite your best efforts to the contrary. But does it have to happen again? Absolutely not!

One of the best ways to keep an affair at bay and keep your life together moving forward is to make sure you've covered all the angles—both physically and emotionally—when it comes to putting your relationship back together. Is it time to redraw some of your relationship boundaries? Should you explore alternatives to traditional relationships as a way to add some excitement to your sex life? What should you do if extramarital temptations rear their ugly heads again?

In this chapter, you'll find advice from those with real experience—people who've had affairs and made it through with their relationships not only intact, but better. From dealing with temptation to rethinking relationship boundaries, this is their take on what works and what doesn't when it comes to reconfiguring your postaffair relationship.

Dealing with Temptation

Temptation might strike your partner again—or it might even strike you. While going through an affair is enough to deter some people from ever going near one again, many others find that the simple allure of the unknown can very easily draw them off course, no matter how hard they try to stay there. So…short of going through life with blinders on, what can you and your spouse do when temptation strikes? The "you" in this chapter is both of you (as is the "you" in Chapter 24, "Next Steps").

Dr. Lana's Secrets

Are fantasies about another person, sex talk on the telephone, or intimate email messages acceptable alternatives to a physical affair? These activities may qualify as an affair in your partner's mind. If you are being a bit risqué and think it's O.K., then talk to your partner. He may see your activities as harmless amusement, or he may be willing to play some of these games with you.

Just Say No

It's a simple, elegant response. Surprisingly, people say no more often than we think. They recognize that it's possible to be attracted to someone other than their mate and that it's even possible to acknowledge that attraction. But they choose not to act on their impulses. There are many different reasons behind that choice.

Checking Your Pros and Cons

Jean-Claude, a former affairee who often feels attracted to members of the opposite sex, runs through a mental checklist when he's tempted. "I remind myself of all the pros and cons of an affair," he says. "Once I'm done with my list, I'm usually thinking with my head rather than other parts of my anatomy."

It might help you to develop a checklist similar to Jean-Claude's. Such a list could include the following points:

➤ What's the attraction? Physical or emotional?

➤ What's going on in my life that could be fueling my attraction to this person? Am I stressed at work? Not spending enough time with my partner?

➤ What would this relationship accomplish?

➤ What do I stand to lose by pursuing this relationship?

➤ Knowing all the risks of an affair, do I want one anyway?

Dr. Lana's Secrets

One question is perhaps more important than any other. Ask yourself, "Do I feel O.K. about lying in order to have this relationship become something more than it is now?"

Your responses to these questions, and any others you might add for your own list, may help you identify why you're feeling the attraction. Often, we're more open to entering an affair when there are unacknowledged or unresolved issues in our lives.

Resisting the Devil

Feeling tempted? Is that little red devil sitting on your shoulder and whispering in your ear? Just this once, he's saying, "No one will know." Well, you can resist that temptation. Talk to him! Do it out loud if you have to. Pace around. Play each part.

Similar to working through a mental checklist, having a conversation with yourself on the matter may help dispel any thoughts you might have about acting on it. Confine your personal two-way communications to a discreet spot in your home or office. Another good place is your car, as long as you're the only one in it.

Being Accountable

Some people find success in coping with their attractions and desires by discussing their feelings with a very trusted friend when they're tempted to stray. Such discussions can be infrequent and informal, or they can be regularly scheduled and follow a set format—one person asks specific questions of the other and vice versa, based on issues that each knows the other has.

Redefining Emotional Boundaries

In relationships where just talking to a person of the opposite sex can be considered a violation, recasting boundaries might allow participation in a relationship outside of the primary one without endangering it. Generally, the redefined boundaries incorporate friendships, not sexual relationships.

Mikki and Steph became fast friends when Steph's husband went overseas for several months to participate in an archaeological dig. When Leo returned, Steph made sure that she didn't forget about her new friend and included Mikki, who was between relationships, in many of her activities with Leo. But when Steph overheard Leo call Mikki and ask her to meet him for coffee, she felt threatened.

"At first, I thought Leo would ask me to join them, but when he didn't, it was clear that he meant to meet Mikki by himself," Steph says. "I just couldn't understand what he wanted to talk to Mikki about that I couldn't hear or be part of. I didn't worry about what Leo may or may not have been doing while he was away, but when the possibility of his seeing someone other than me came up right under my nose, I had problems with it."

Getting Your Fears Out in the Open

Steph knew she had to tell Leo that his seeing Mikki bothered her. "He was surprised, as he had had many friendships with women he worked with on the dig," Steph says. "He really didn't see why having a friendly conversation with one of my girlfriends was such a threat to me. And, to be honest, I didn't know why I found it so disturbing. All I know is that I did."

What Steph may have been sensing was the attraction that Leo felt for Mikki. "There was no question that I was physically attracted to her," Leo says, "and I think the feeling was mutual. But what I really liked about Mikki was her willingness to listen to all my dry dull stories about my digs. Steph had heard about them for so long that she no longer paid attention to me. Mikki was real interested, and fresh ears were what I was looking for, not extramarital sex."

Dr. Lana's Secrets

There can be a fine line between friendship and intimacy with members of the opposite sex. Intimacy develops when we begin confiding our innermost secrets, our private thoughts, or personal musings. You are crossing the line when you are telling your friend something that you wouldn't tell your spouse. It's a good idea to keep descriptions of your sex life out of these conversations. Not only are you betraying your spouse's privacy when you do it, you may also send the wrong signal to the person at the other end of your conversation.

Steph voiced her concerns to Leo, and Leo told her why he was interested in Mikki. "Once he did, my level of concern diminished significantly," Steph says. "I realized I needed to pay more attention to Leo's stories, since what he did on his different digs was so important to him. But I really am tired of hearing about them, and I wasn't that interested in archaeology to begin with. Mikki loves listening to all that stuff. I think she sees Leo as an 'Indiana Jones' kind of guy."

A Comfortable Compromise for Both

Steph and Leo decided to modify their relationship boundaries to allow for his friendship with Mikki. "We agreed that it would be O.K. to meet during the day, in a public place, and for no more than an hour, two at the max and that Steph would always know about it ahead of time," says Leo. "Sometimes Steph joins us for part of the time, but she usually lets us yak away about bones and pottery fragments while she does something else. We might go see a movie at the natural history museum or visit an archaeology exhibit. But no lingering chats over a drink. We still do lots of things as a threesome. I consider Mikki a friend, but she and Steph are closer than she and I will ever be."

Dr. Lana's Secrets

Most affairs start just talking, so once you agree on boundaries, then be committed to abiding by them. Don't stretch it by adding extra time or forgetting to mention it to your partner. If you are deceiving your partner, there is a very good chance you are deceiving yourself.

Redefining Sexual Boundaries

Extramarital sexual relationships may indicate sexual problems between the couple but not always. Some couples simply have a different set of mores. Over the years, a number of models for making various forms of extramarital sex an acceptable part of a committed relationship have been developed and tested. Some, like the communal sex approach of the Oneida community (as discussed in Chapter 2, "What Makes Us Affair-Prone?"), have, for the most part, been discarded. Several others still exist and are explored by couples in search of something different.

Affair Facts

Half of the men who admitted having extramarital affairs said they were unhappy in their marriage, and 65 percent of women reported they were involved in an affair because they were dissatisfied with their partner.

Open Marriage

The concept of open marriage, which promotes independence and individuality in a relationship, was presented in the late 1960s and early 1970s by anthropologists Nena and George O'Neill. From their anthropological studies, the O'Neills developed an alternative model for contemporary marriage that they felt would be more successful, as it was closer to the true nature of humankind.

The O'Neills believed that marriage would have a better chance of survival if it didn't have unrealistic expectations. They felt couples should be honest about their needs for having other intimate relationships, rather than lying about it.

The O'Neills wrote a very popular book, *Open Marriage,* on their concept that was quickly embraced by many couples who were thrilled to find a marital model that endorsed extramarital sex. Finally, tacit approval for something that's been going on for years!

Dr. Lana's Secrets

Open marriage works best when a couple decides to try it with the belief that it could enhance what they already have in their marriage. It is rarely successful when it's used as a substitute for divorce or when it's forced on a reluctant spouse.

Affair Facts

No one knows how many open marriages are in operation today, although a study conducted over ten years ago estimated that less than 15 percent of all marriages are based on the open marriage model.

Understanding the Whole Concept

Unfortunately, rather than grasping the idea of individual independence and responsibility in a relationship, the belief in sexual openness was the bandwagon that most people jumped on, and the O'Neills' broader message of increasing equality, honesty, and intimate relationships between marital partners was overshadowed.

Many couples who decided to try open marriage focused on the sexual part alone, which gave them virtually no understanding of how the concept was to work. For this reason, they found the open marriage approach very difficult. Determining just how open an open marriage should be was a big issue.

Open marriage seemed to create more problems than it solved for these couples, and many of them went back to their former marital model. It was just too difficult to convert their traditional marriages to a new format that they knew little or nothing about and that had few prescribed formulas or boundaries.

Dr. Lana's Secrets

Is open marriage a viable concept in today's society? With the renewed emphasis on reconciling issues within a marriage, rather than looking to outside sources to compensate for what's lacking, many people question the viability of the open marriage concept because it pulls attention away from the primary relationship. Still, some experts believe the underlying concepts in open marriage—honesty, openness, and a balance of independence and interdependence—define the only way that a relationship can be truly successful.

Many other couples, especially those who tried open marriage instead of working to make their troubled marriages stronger, ended up in divorce court. Sophia and Richard divorced six months after they decided to give it a try. "When I look back on it, we should have addressed the issues in our relationship rather than entertain alternatives to it," Richard says. "When we started an open marriage, it forced us apart even farther because we lost what little intimacy we had left. The day came when we realized we were living in the same house, but we had become strangers. We didn't even try to resurrect what we had lost because it was so far away from where we were."

Dr. Lana's Secrets

Couples who have open marriages tell me the most important benefit they experience is not lying.

Mutual Consent and Respect

Nevertheless, some relationships thrive on the concept of open marriage. Steve and Brenda, married for more than ten years, have spent more time apart than together because of Steve's business, which sends him overseas for months at a time. They've had an open marriage, by mutual consent, almost from the start. They had a lifestyle that gave them separate friends, independent work, and divided activities.

Affair Facts

While they don't call it open marriage, many European couples have committed relationships that are not sexually exclusive. Forty percent of children born in France are born to unmarried couples.

As Brenda tells it, "Steve is a wonderful husband, but I would never expect him to be faithful to me when he's away. He's a very sexy guy—that's what attracted me to him in the first place—and he loves sex. Living without it for months would be next to impossible for him...and for me, for that matter. We talked about it early on, and he told me the last thing he wanted me to do was put myself up on a shelf while he was away. And, frankly, I'm just not the sort of person to patiently wait at home for my husband to return. We are both people people, and spending time with others is essential to each of us feeling happy with ourselves. Occasionally, one of our relationships becomes sexual, but not very often. We are one another's best friend and confidante."

Dr. Lana's Secrets

For open marriage to work, it needs rules and boundaries. Just like any other relationship, you need to know what is acceptable and what isn't and be willing to live by your agreement.

Many couples who have an open marriage go about their extramarital relationships very quietly, showing respect to their spouses by being discreet but honest about their other relationships. Other couples tell each other everything about their encounters.

Should We Swing?

The term is evocative of the open sexual lifestyles of the 1960s and 1970s, but make no mistake about it: Swinging, or "wife swapping," which involves sex between a couple and other participants, is still a popular activity for some couples. An estimated 5 percent of married couples have taken part in such activities at some point during their marriages.

Casual Sex

Swinging tends to attract people who view sex as a hobby and who want to explore it in as many forms as possible. Sometimes a spouse will suggest it as a way to add some spice to a dull relationship. Some couples, especially those who have been together socially for a number of years, will try it just to see how they might like it. Perfectly innocent social situations, as a matter of fact, can turn into swinging scenes when you least expect them to, as Carl and Lois found out when they had dinner with one of Carl's new clients and his wife.

"They wanted us to meet them at their mountain cabin, so we planned dinner for a weekend evening when our time wouldn't be as restricted," Carl recalls. "The cabin was gorgeous, with a six-person hot tub and lots of other amenities that Lois and I, quite frankly, were very turned on by. After a couple of drinks, we realized why the place was decorated as it was—it was where my client and his wife swung with the rest of their group. Because another member of that group had recommended me, my client assumed that Lois and I led the group's lifestyle as well."

Carl immediately made it clear that it wasn't something that Lois and he did, but they did join the other couple after dinner for a nude soak in the hot tub. "We didn't know these people at all well, but they were sure nice enough and they didn't try to force their sexual preferences on us, so we felt comfortable being nude with them," Carl says. "They just told us why they liked it, and they treated it like it was the most natural thing on earth. The next day, Lois and I talked about it a little, and while we both admitted some curiosity about it, we decided it really wasn't for us. We continued socializing, mostly in more innocuous settings, with this couple until he was no longer a client. The subject never came up again."

Affair Facts

Far from being society's biggest deviants or liberals, swingers generally are religious and political conservatives.

Sexless Swinging

Swinging often includes opposite sex and same sex couplings, which have led to some interesting discoveries by some of the couples who have tried it. Believe it or not, there also is sexless swinging. Following the outbreak of AIDs in the 1980s, several swinging clubs garnered attention for their elaborate safe sex plays based on dominance and sadomasochistic themes. Couples would decide which roles they wanted to play and who they wanted to play them with. They would then act their parts to the max, stopping when it came time to consummate the sexual act. Presumably, these activities are still going on somewhere, as some people are always ready to try something new.

Dr. Lana's Secrets

Typically men initiate the idea of swinging, but wives who are in agreement find they enjoy it as much as the men. If you decide to try swinging, go slowly and talk to each other about your beliefs as well as your feelings. You can say no at any point, so don't think that if you entertain the idea, you have to go through with it. You don't.

Of all the alternatives to having an affair, swinging is probably the least attractive to most people. More than one study has shown that swingers are happier with their sex lives and their lives in general than nonswingers are. More than one husband has looked at his wife in a new way after he's seen her do something he's only fantasized about. However, embarrassment and resentment can destroy the marriage if one partner gets pushed into it against his or her will.

The Least You Need to Know

➤ Saying no is a viable alternative to having an affair.

➤ If you're feeling tempted to stray, it's a good idea to try to figure out what might be prompting you to do so.

➤ Open marriages are based on independence and individuality and are not devoid of rules and boundaries.

➤ Swinging, although not very popular, is an alternative to conventional marriage with different boundaries.

Next Steps

Seldom, or perhaps never, does a marriage develop into an individual relationship smoothly and without crises; there is no coming to consciousness without pain.

—Carl Jung

This is the end of the road...well, it's the end of this book anyway. It's been quite a journey, wouldn't you agree? You started by learning about why affairs happen and how they happen. You learned how to detect the warning signs that an affair was near and then how to determine whether an affair is happening and how to respond to these signals. You learned how to restore your relationship and (hopefully) how to affair-proof your love. Now it's time to take a look at where you go from here.

Expectations, Great or Not

Couples who have weathered an affair often want to know what they can now expect from their lives together. "Will things really be that much better," they ask, "or will we just keep on bumping along because it's easier than not?" Other questions that are usually on the minds of couples like you include:

➤ How long will it take for us to really get back on track?

➤ What are our chances of staying together now that we've made it this far?

➤ What's the possibility of an affair happening again?

➤ How long does it take for the memories to fade enough so that they don't bother us?

If you've gotten this far in the book, then you know that affairs happen in many marriages and that most of these survive and many flourish. Researchers and counselors know many of the factors that can make yours either a success story with a happy ending or another sad tale of love lost. Here are some of them.

Dr. Lana's Secrets

Your commitment—to be continually involved in developing and rediscovering your relationship—will play the greatest role in determining how long you live happily ever after together. The best attitude is to see your relationship as a work in progress.

Getting Back on Track

For the relationships that survive affairs, the recovery period ranges from between one to three years. Obviously, it may take you a little less or a little more time. This period is not an altogether unhappy time; for many couples it is like a second honeymoon.

Dr. Lana's Secrets

Couples often comment that the first few years after the affair were great. It was a time when they were keenly aware of what they had almost lost, and they treasured one another and their relationship more than they had in many years prior to the affair.

Staying Together

The odds are that your marriage will make it if you want it to. Several counselors have published small studies based on their patients' reports, and most say that around 75 percent of those who are determined to save their marriage do just that. Very few affairees—less than 10 percent—divorce their spouse and marry their lover and are still married to each other twenty years later.

Dr. Frank Pittman, psychiatrist and author of *Private Lies*, found that although half of his patients who were involved in romantic affairs divorced, about 25 percent of them married their lover and 75 percent of these marriages ended quickly.

Affair Facts

John Gottman, Ph.D., author of *Why Marriages Succeed or Fail,* identified the four major marriage killers: criticism, contempt, defensiveness, and withdrawal.

Will It Happen Again?

The 1983 study American Couples, conducted by Philip Blumstein and Pepper Schwartz, determined that people (especially men) who have affairs are likely to have more than one. Of the twenty thousand people Blumstein and Schwartz surveyed, 65 percent of the men said they had had more than one affair; 25 percent said they had had four or more.

Reading these numbers on second or third affairs is probably enough to make you gasp in horror and decide to throw in the towel. Just give yourself a minute. It doesn't have to happen that way for you. The main reasons you read this book were to learn how to cope with an affair when it intrudes on your relationship and how to affair-proof your love. You can change the odds if you're willing to do the work.

Dr. Lana's Secrets

Many couples found the affair plunged them into new and exciting sexual territory. If that is true for you, keep those fires burning brightly and frequently. If the affair doused your sexual flame, get some help to rekindle it. Affairs are nearly always about sex in one way or another. Learn from this experience to keep the physical side of your relationship warm and glowing.

Good intentions and sincere promises are not enough to keep an affair at bay. You have to actively work to protect yourself and your relationship from another affair.

It may feel like a lot of work. You may be thinking at this point, "It's just too difficult and too painful, I don't want to work that hard. Starting over would be a lot easier." It's understandable that you would have those feelings, but the facts don't support you. Research shows that first marriages are the easiest and the most simple, second marriages harder and more complicated, third marriages harder still, and so on.

Forgetting the Past

While you cannot control every thought that passes through your mind, you have a choice about how to reflect on what happened and what you learned. If you dwell on the worst, you'll feel bad; if you highlight the best, you'll feel good.

The best way to put painful memories in the past is to create new memories in the present. Be intentional about creating them. Good times don't just happen by chance. Put some time and energy into thinking up some romantic playtimes, like you did before you got married.

Taking the Good and Leaving the Bad Behind

As you work through this next period of time together, your primary goal is to rebuild your relationship and move it forward. To be successful, it's important that you work through the issues that caused the affair. As much as you possibly can, leave the anger, the bitterness, the resentment, and the remorse behind.

The fact that one of you (maybe both) has had an affair won't ever go away. Don't let the emotions it created hold you back from experiencing what could be a really great relationship. Focus your efforts on your future together.

Dr. Lana's Secrets

There are many styles for resolving differences. It doesn't matter whether you are shouters; level-headed debaters; or the calm, smiling kind as long as you both feel your differences are acknowledged, validated, and reconciled.

Walking the Walk, Even When You're Not Sure

Even though you've made a commitment to stay together, there will probably be times when you question that decision. Maybe someone at work tells you that you're nuts to stay together. Perhaps another couple close to you finally breaks up after months of trying to reconcile. As much as you want to think that things will work out, you begin to wonder if they really will.

Don't give up just yet. Your relationship is in a fragile state, and so is your ego. Challenges to either of them can raise some doubts about what you're trying to do. Keep moving ahead, even when you really don't feel like it. It's important to keep the momentum going as much as possible. If you really are on the right course, you'll know it soon enough. But you have to keep going to make that determination.

During times of trauma, you cannot always trust your feelings: One day you may feel as in love with your partner as ever, and a day later you're wondering how you can ever trust him again. Right now, stick with your decision to move forward with your relationship.

Bumps Ahead

Although it's a good idea to ignore the little fears and doubts that get raised while repairing a relationship, that doesn't mean you should ignore repeated signals that things aren't going forward. Feeling less than optimistic at times is to be expected, but there should be progress. If there isn't, you may want outside help (see "Finding Help" later in the chapter).

Keep Talking

The road to reconciliation doesn't begin and end with the conversation you had at the point of confession. You have to keep the channels open at all times. Even if you feel you need a time-out because you've heard more than you wanted to or you need to gather your thoughts, make sure it's just a time-out, not a "power down."

Your conversations about the affair should continue for a long time. It's healthy if you're learning from these conversations and unhealthy if you are going over the same old, same old. If the conversation is repetitive, you are probably looking for reassurance rather than facts. Try teaching each other what words and gestures make you feel more confidant and more loved.

Dealing with the Children

If you haven't explained what happened between you to your children, you may be wondering if you should. There's a good chance they've detected the tension in your relationship even if you haven't been very demonstrative or vocal about your problems. When you talk to them, talk at their level. Reassure them that they are safe and that you are taking care of them. Telling them specifically about the affair is a bad idea because it takes them way beyond their emotional capacity, asking them to understand something that is a direct threat to their well-being.

Dr. Lana's Secrets

Kids are egocentric, which means they think everything is about them. It isn't until their late teens and early twenties that kids really understand the boundaries between themselves and their parents. This means that no matter how many times you tell your kids your problems are between the two of you and not them, kids cannot really integrate that distinction into their psyche.

Even if things are now going well between you, your children may have some unresolved issues. Even little spats between spouses can become huge fights in the minds of your kids if it is new behavior on your part. They can, and do, jump to conclusions very easily. You need to reassure them that everything is O.K. and that fighting is normal and healthy.

Dr. Lana's Secrets

Children learn how to handle conflict by watching their parents. Fighting with your partner in a way that resolves your differences and restores the family bond is one of the best lifetime gifts you can give your children.

Talk to Their Level

If you do decide to talk to your children, limit your comments to issues that will help them in their own lives. If they're very young, you can talk to them about how it feels when they expect something to happen and it doesn't, and what they can do to make themselves feel better. You can explain why fighting for things that are important to you is healthy, encouraging them to use their words and think about what they really want. The same applies with older children, especially if they're adolescents. They're already going through many changes and problems of their own, and they're looking to you for clues on how they should handle things. They need to be assured that they can depend on you. They need to know that problems can and do happen and that it's important to face them and find solutions that work for both parties.

If you have adult children, you may be better off if you don't say anything at all, especially if their exposure to your affair was minimal or nonexistent. Again, look at things from their perspective and try to determine whether there's anything you can say that will help them. Even adults don't want to see their parents having marital problems. Simple reassurance like "We were having a hard time but we are back on track now" may be good enough.

If adult children seem angry or suspicious or you're fielding leading questions from them, try setting boundaries. Mention that they seem angry or upset and ask them what it is about. It may not be what you think. If they know about or suspect the affair, ask them about their feelings and if necessary give a thumbnail version of the story. Then have them read this book.

Present a United Front

It's a good idea to present a united front with your children if they're upset. Agree ahead of time with your spouse what you are going to say. Keep the message simple and brief. Your children need to see that you're operating as a team and not saying anything behind each other's back.

The other reason for presenting as a team is that children will often take sides and blame one parent for hurting the other. It's easier for everyone if you talk about their emotions together and assure them that you love them and will take good care of them.

Dr. Lana's Secrets

When the parent's marriage is in trouble, childhood can end for the kids. The time of free exploration and discovery is over, and the serious work of fearing for their parents—and their family—begins.

Protect your children; reassure them that you will take care of them and they are not supposed to take care of you. Big kids need to hear this, too. Don't say anything critical about their other parent. Tell them Mom and Dad can be mad at each other and even hurt each other's feelings, just like when they feel angry with or hurt by their friends.

Reestablishing Social Contacts

Affairs often disrupt your social life and create strains in relationships outside of your marriage. It's very common for one spouse—usually the one not having the affair—to become very reclusive if she has knowledge of the affair and is worried about what her friends may know or think. Friends may have taken sides when your relationship was in trouble. They may even have had a hand in the affair, sometimes knowingly, sometimes not.

Reestablishing relationships with people can be awkward. Before you venture out as a couple, it's a good idea to talk about what impression you want others to have. Do you want them to see you happily reunited, or do you want to be open about the fact that you are struggling but surviving? It is up to the two of you to decide and declare whether you want to talk candidly about your relationship or not.

Be Up Front with Them

I have spent countless sessions with people trying to figure out how they should respond to their friend's marriage problems. It is a hard call. The best approach is to tell your friends what you do and don't want. If you want a lighthearted outing without a thought to your struggles, tell them ahead of time. If you want to talk about your problems, tell them about your successes, or make an announcement, make your intentions clear. And then, if you change your mind, let them know.

Mind reading is probably not an integral part of your friendship, so help them out and let them know how to help you. Friends who cared for you before the crisis still care for you; they just don't know what to do.

Choose Your Friends for Now

A few people may be very judgmental, and you know who they are because you have heard them criticize and gossip about others. Keep your distance from these people—they are not going to be different with you than they are with others. You're still vulnerable, and hurtful remarks are hard to slough off.

Finding Help

While it is entirely possible for many people to work through a marital crisis on their own, seeing a counselor or therapist can bring welcome support and direction to the process. Not only can counseling help couples cope with the aftermath of an affair, it can also aid them in better understanding their relationship and introduce or fine-tune relationship skills.

Counselors and therapists come in all shapes and sizes and with many different backgrounds. Those with master's or doctoral degrees in social work or psychology often focus more on the relationship itself, helping couples improve their communication skills and counseling them on how they can better understand each other's feelings and emotions.

For couples dealing with more severe problems—for example, affairs driven by addictive behavior or psychological problems such as depression—a psychiatrist or clinical psychologist may be a better choice. Psychoanalysts gear their efforts more toward helping individuals understand their past, whereas cognitive therapists focus on the present.

Counseling styles vary significantly as well. Some counselors focus on listening to and observing their clients and nudging them toward positive behavior. Others will synthesize what they see and hear and give direct advice. Some therapists will want to see couples together at all times; others will mix individual and joint sessions. Psychotherapists generally work with only one spouse, although they may ask to meet the other spouse at times during the course of therapy. They will often recommend that both spouses undergo some form of therapy.

Affair Facts

The single best way to find a therapist is a referral from a friend, especially someone you have seen make personal changes that you admire.

How to Find a Therapist

Friends are the best referral source, and your family physician is another resource for finding a therapist. If possible, get several referrals and talk to more than one counselor. Finding the right therapist is essential, and there are many things to consider when you're looking for someone to share your feelings with and to get advice from.

It's a good idea to meet face-to-face with anyone you're seriously considering, even though you'll be charged for the visit. You'll get a more complete feeling for the therapist's values and beliefs when you meet, and you'll get a better idea of whether or not you'll be comfortable—both emotionally and physically—with this person.

Dr. Lana's Secrets

When looking for a therapist, keep in mind that how you feel about him is as important as his credentials. Although it's important to find a qualified person, choosing someone you feel you can work with is even more important. Respect is an essential dynamic in any relationship; be sure you respect your therapist and that he respects you.

Ask those you're considering enough questions to know whether your values are the same. Be sure they know what you want to work toward and ask if they can help you move to those goals.

Counseling support can also be found through religious institutions. Some members of the clergy will recommend outside programs or counselors with whom they're familiar. Some churches or synagogues offer relationship seminars.

Your local mental health agency or United Way can also be a good source of programs in your area, especially if you're footing the bill entirely on your own or your health plan offers minimal coverage for such counseling. But don't let the lack of coverage or money deter you from seeking help if you feel you need it. Some agencies will ask you to fill out a financial affidavit and then charge you according to your ability to pay. You might also be able to find a therapist willing to work out an extended payment plan with you.

What to Expect

Although therapy and counseling don't carry the stigmas they once did, it's still difficult for many people to admit that they need help. Some couples feel a strong sense of shame or failure about it. Marriage is supposed to be easy, they think. So why did we make such a mess of things?

One of the first things you'll realize as you start seeking help is that you're by no means alone. Just take a look at the list of professional people in your local phone book who deal with marital counseling. It may take you several weeks to get a first appointment with a therapist. These people are busy, and they're busy helping people just like you. Couples often enter into therapy in a great deal of pain, and they want immediate relief. Unfortunately, there's no quick fix, no magic pill that dissolves marital anguish and strife. In fact, it's very common for couples to feel significantly worse about things for a few weeks when they start to open up to a counselor.

Dr. Lana's Secrets

A good litmus test for successful therapy is to ask yourself, "Am I learning something?" And the answer should be yes. While some of what you learn may be painful and lead to tears, some of it should also be joyful. If there's no laughter in any of your sessions, perhaps you or your therapist is taking everything a bit too seriously.

Hard Work—but Worth It

"We saw our therapist for almost a year, and I can honestly say at times we felt like giving up and just living with our problems," Adele adds. "But we stuck with it.

She was an advocate for our relationship. She worked us both really hard and made each of us face some things about ourselves that we would rather not have faced. She taught us new ways to think about our relationship and ourselves. In looking back, I'm glad we made the changes we made; I would not want to go back to the way we were."

It can take months to see substantial results from therapy, but you should feel like you are learning something new and making progress each time. Even when it's tough and painful, you should always feel that you're addressing the issues that need to be addressed. If you're being counseled as a couple, you should feel that the therapist is working for both of you. If not, you may need to find a different counselor.

Letting Time Pass

The saying "Time heals all wounds" is one to keep in mind as you cope with your feelings and emotions after the affair. While the passage of time won't in itself heal the pain that the affair caused, the pain will ease gradually.

Many couples who go through the experience of an affair talk about how much they want to get through the immediate crisis and fast-forward their lives to where the affair is just a distant memory. Unfortunately, this never happens. Time after an affair often passes very slowly. It's almost as if there's an invisible force trying to prolong your agony by holding back the seconds. This situation can be agonizing; you'd give anything to just skip over large chunks of your life. It can also make you anxious and nervous. You're tired of dealing with the strife. You want more than anything else to be two years ahead, right now.

So here's another old saying to remember: "A watched pot never boils." Hold back your groans…this is exactly what you're doing, whether you're aware of it or not. That force holding back the hands of time is you. If you saw the movie *Heartburn,* you might remember Jack Nicholson telling Meryl Streep (after she discovered his affair and confronted him) that they weren't going to get anywhere if she kept taking the temperature of their relationship. It's the same for you.

Focus on the Future

So quit paying such close attention to what's happening between you now. Look down the road a little. Force yourself into doing it if you have to. Think about where you'd like your relationship to be in six months, a year, two years. Make some plans. If you've always wanted to go to Europe and you know it will take two years to save enough to do it, start now. Do it together. Cast your dreams and aspirations into the future. Give yourself something concrete to shoot for.

Some spouses say they're afraid to think ahead after an affair because they don't know what will happen to their relationship. Guess what? You never do know. If there's one thing that you should have learned by now, it's this: Life can turn on an eye blink.

Shoot for the Stars!

There are very few sure things in this world, but this is one of them: Only you can determine just how much you want to accomplish in your life. Far too many people allow their fears to hold them back from living life to its fullest. They focus on "what if?" instead of "why not?" Think of the people who have accomplished really incredible things. They're probably not that much different from you. But what often sets them apart is their willingness to rise above their fears and doubts and press onward to their goals.

The legendary Winston Churchill used his superlative oratorical skills to encourage the people of the Allied countries during World War II. Even at the darkest of times, he took to the airwaves and spoke of such things as the flame of human existence and how it would never burn out. He told his listeners that victory must be won at all costs, for without victory there was no survival. He told them to "never give in...never, never, never, never—in nothing, great or small, large or petty—never give in except to convictions of honor and good sense."

Germany bombed London to smithereens during World War II, and there were surely times when Churchill's faith wavered. But he knew his country wouldn't survive Hitler's attack unless the people believed it could; Churchill was determined to not let fear of the future immobilize them.

Don't let it immobilize you either. Life is never easy. Don't live in fear of what might happen. Dare to dream. Believe that you can make your dreams a reality. Embrace all of what life has to offer and let it help you soar. You deserve nothing less.

The Least You Need to Know

➤ It can take anywhere from one to three years for a marriage to recover from an extramarital affair, but it isn't all bad times.

➤ Rebuilding a relationship is easiest if you can focus on the future and create new memories for yourselves.

➤ Telling your children about an affair is a bad idea and can cause difficulty for your kids. Let them stay innocent as long as possible.

➤ Marital counseling can be a great way to help move your relationship forward faster. Seriously consider it if you don't feel you're making progress on your own; there's always more you can learn.

➤ Don't let your fears hold you back from going as far as you can in this relationship or in any other part of your life. Don't just dream about what life can be. Make it so!

The Affair-Proof Love Blueprint

You've been through this book, and you've learned about the various aspects of affairs, as well as what it takes to protect your relationship from them. But it's one thing to have all that information cooped up in your head and quite another to turn it into action and really make it work. That's where an affair-proof blueprint can help.

There's no denying that relationships are impossible to pigeonhole. There's no one set approach that will provide the glue to keep you and the one you love together, humming along and moving in the right direction. But certain approaches to developing a healthy relationship have proven to be fairly consistent. I call these elements, when put together, an affair-proof love blueprint.

The following pages cover the key points found in Part 2 of this book, "Secrets to Affair-Proof Love." Use them as a starting point for creating and maintaining a wonderful, lasting relationship. Some sections prompt you to answer questions; others provide information to help you develop and follow your plan.

How to Create Your Blueprint

First go through the following material. If it's been some time since you've read Part 2, your review may reveal some areas you've pushed aside that need attention. After your review, you may find that certain sections apply more closely to the issues you're now facing. Still, it's a good idea to work through each section to make sure you're not neglecting something important.

Jot down your answers or any thoughts that come to mind, either in the space provided or in a small notebook. Pick a time and place when your attention is undivided. It isn't necessary to finish everything in one sitting. If you do take a break, try to do it at the end of a section rather than in the middle.

When you're done, go through your notes and highlight any areas of concern or questions you skipped or didn't answer for some reason. If you need more information in a particular area, turn to the appropriate chapter in Part 2 or check Appendix B, "Good Places for More Help," for additional resources.

Then think about what the exercise has shown you. Maybe you feel the need to discuss some relationship boundaries with your spouse. Maybe you've realized you could spend less time on the computer at night and more time doing things together. Use what you've learned to offer up some specific ways to make your relationship stronger.

One last point: The blueprinting exercise is meant to help you get a firmer sense of your feelings and beliefs in the areas that have the greatest effect on your relationship. For this reason, it's meant to be done solo, with the exception of the section on boundary setting. If it's appropriate and it works for your relationship, by all means encourage your spouse to work through the rest of the blueprint, too—but don't do it together.

You can use your notes as a starting point for conversations concerning your relationship. But keep in mind that the primary purpose of the blueprint exercise is to help you determine your feelings about your relationship and how you can work with your spouse to build a long-lasting, long-loving union together.

Finally…while it's a good idea to have a blueprint, don't get too formal or legalistic about it. Blueprints, like relationships, must be flexible and giving. Don't use this exercise as a fallback in an argument over boundaries or when you don't feel you're getting enough attention from your spouse. Use it as a road map to identify the good points in your relationship and the areas in which you feel there's some room for improvement.

The Custom-Made Relationship

The custom-made relationship has at its foundation a set of core beliefs or values, including:

➤ A basic respect and trust in each other

➤ Knowledge of our own values and our spouse's values and the desire to live by these values

➤ A commitment to knowing and meeting each other's needs

➤ The willingness to take responsibility for our own happiness

➤ The desire to support our partner's growth

Ask yourself:

1. Do these core beliefs and values form the foundation of your relationship?

2. Do you agree with all of them? Disagree with some? Agree with some, but don't feel they're feasible for relationships in today's world? Have some of your own that you'd like to add?

3. Do you feel that you once had these beliefs and values at the center of your relationship, but no longer do? If so, why do you think you've drifted away from them?

4. If you have drifted away from these beliefs and values, do you feel your relationship would be stronger if they were reinstated? What would it take to do so? Do you think your spouse would be open to the idea?

The Work of Attention

Relationships never just happen. They have to be created. They take time and energy, and they take attention. Just like other parts of your life, relationships flourish when you focus on them and flounder when you neglect them.

Finding Time

A key argument I hear from many couples is that they don't have the time to pay more attention to their relationship. Generally, we think we are busier than we truly are, so finding time boils down to managing our time better.

Go back to Chapter 7, "Paying Attention to Your Love," and answer the quiz on time gobblers there. If you've already taken the quiz, review your answers to see which category you fell into. Then review the specific recommendations for your category—all are repeated below—and determine which suggestions will work for you.

Remember, it will take time to make these changes. Try tackling them as part of an ongoing process, especially if you have many changes to make. Breaking your goals into smaller objectives and tasks will make them easier to achieve.

High Time Demands

Your goal: to off-load some of your responsibilities or eliminate some of your obligations. Try:

➤ Hiring someone to clean your house

➤ Eating out instead of in (with your spouse, of course!)

➤ Saying no to chairing the next volunteer event

➤ Getting a handyman to come by to take care of the "honey-dos"—the little things around the house that you need to get done but you never find the time for

➤ Having your own kids, or the neighborhood kids, mow and rake your lawn

➤ Taking your car to the car wash instead of washing it yourself

➤ Having your laundry picked up and delivered

➤ Hiring a bookkeeper to pay bills and reconcile your bank statement

People with high demands on their time often have to get very creative with their time. Here are a few suggestions:

➤ Call your spouse during the day. You don't have to have a lengthy conversation; just a fast warm hello, thinking of you, is good.

➤ Don't rely on home-cooked meals. Even if you're a health nut, you can find healthy take-out. Use the time that would have been spent on meal preparation to relax and enjoy your time together.

313

➤ If you travel for business, find ways to take your spouse with you. Plan your schedule so you can stay away over a weekend with your spouse.

➤ Change your exercise routine if you generally do it alone. Find an activity that you and your spouse can do together, even if it's not something you'd usually want to do.

Since your life is so full, don't leave things to chance. You will have to schedule time to be with your spouse, especially if your spouse's life is as hectic as yours.

Busy but Not Crazy

Your goal: to pay more attention to the distractions in your life and determine whether they're really worth your time.

People in this category generally have time to devote to their spouses but need to cut down on time wasters, including:

➤ Watching television. More than two hours a day in front of the tube, even in the company of your spouse, is too much. Try to limit your viewing.

➤ Working on the computer at home. The computer is another wonderful distraction, and it's easy to spend hours doing an information search when you expected to spend a few minutes

➤ Volunteering, taking classes, or participating in other activities away from your home and your spouse. Try cutting back on your volunteer time or find things the two of you can do together.

➤ Cooking and housekeeping. Streamline your meal preparation time. Do a weekly menu plan and stick to it. Learn how to work take-out and convenience items into a balanced diet. Spread out your housekeeping duties rather than saving everything for one day.

This is a shortened version of the list in Chapter 7. If you would like more detail or more explanation, please refer back to Chapter 7.

Low Responsibility

Your goal: to learn how to spend your leisure time wisely. Now is the time to develop good relationship skills—you'll be glad you did when your responsibilities increase. Focus on:

➤ Spending less time with your friends and more time with your partner. If the two of you regularly go out as a couple with a group of people, try leaving the group behind occasionally.

➤ Developing mutual interests. Try to find activities that you either both enjoy and want to do together or that will make your spouse happy if you join him or her.

➤ Managing your money together. This is a prime time for developing a budget and learning how to live with it.

➤ Limiting the amount of time you spend watching television, working on the computer, and talking to friends on the phone.

Off Balance or Out of Focus

Your goal: to equalize relationship responsibilities and develop an appropriate focus on life by:

➤ Setting strict limits on the amount of time you spend at work

➤ Seeking assistance for taking care of children, parents, and other obligations if you devote a lot of your time to any of these responsibilities

➤ Limiting the time you spend volunteering, taking classes, or exercising on your own

Boundary Setting

The best relationships have mutually agreed-upon boundaries in a number of areas. Since agreement is necessary, plan on discussing your findings with your spouse once you've worked through this section. Or you may choose to work on this section together.

Finances

➤ Budget. Do you feel you need one? If so, do you want to develop it together or separately and then compare notes? How accountable do you want to be concerning your budget?

➤ Long-term goals. Try to envision where you'll be in twenty, thirty, or even forty years and how you think you'll get there. Include issues such as how and where you plan to retire and how much money you'll need, saving for your children's education, and being able to help your parents. Think about how your career and your spouse's career will support these plans and consider what kinds of investments you'll need to get you to where you want to be.

➤ Significant versus insignificant purchases. Is there a dollar amount that determines when you feel a purchase should be discussed?

➤ Responsibilities. Who pays the bills, and who balances the checkbook? Do you want to share this responsibility? How much information sharing do you feel is necessary? Do you think a personal financial program on your computer is enough, and if so, who should have responsibility for keeping it up to date?

Relationships with Others

Gauge your feelings about your relationships and your spouse's relationships with other people, even your pets. Be very specific about key factors, such as the depth of past relationships, certain settings and time periods, frequency, and so on. Add your own issues to the list below as appropriate.

- ➤ Time spent with family members
- ➤ Time with the kids
- ➤ Time with pets
- ➤ Volunteering
- ➤ Relationships (if any) with old boyfriends/girlfriends, ex-spouses, and so on
- ➤ Time spent with friends of the same sex
- ➤ Time spent with friends of the opposite sex

Points to keep in mind when setting boundaries:

- ➤ Be flexible.
- ➤ Be specific. If certain situations are a problem when others aren't, say so.
- ➤ Keep the egos at bay.
- ➤ Recognize when it's a good idea to compromise your position and do so.
- ➤ Revisit boundaries as necessary to redraw and redefine any that aren't working for you now.

Maintaining a Good Sex Life

Sex, more than anything else, is the fuel that fires our love and keeps our relationships going. It's the rare marriage that fails because the sex is good and plentiful. When sex is absent, it's almost always a sure indication that something is wrong.

Review the points below and determine how your sex life is doing. Are you satisfied? Could things be better? Are some areas of your love life dead in the water? What can you do to make them better? What do you want your partner to do?

	In Good Shape	Could Be Better	Dead in the Water
➤ Making intimacy a priority			
➤ Scheduling your intimate time together			
➤ Treating your partner like a lover			
➤ Making time for foreplay			
➤ Maximizing your opportunities for intimate encounters			

	In Good Shape	Could Be Better	Dead in the Water
➤ Staying creative and flexible when it comes to finding time for sex			
➤ Keeping the sparks flying through the use of sensual items, sexy lingerie, erotic books, magazines, videos, sex toys, acting out fantasies, and so on			

Tips to keep in mind:

➤ Almost nothing is out-of-bounds when you love each other.

➤ Intimate urges can fluctuate a great deal without any diminishment of the love you feel for your spouse. It's important to separate temporary glitches from long-term problems.

➤ Bodies age but passion need never die. Don't let some sags or wrinkles stand in the way of a great love life.

Keeping the Magic Alive

Sex, while very important, is not enough to keep an intimate relationship healthy. One of the surest ways to keep it strong is to maintain or strengthen the emotions you felt when you first met each other.

This section is a checklist of things you can do to keep romance on the front burner in your life. Use it as a reminder or for tips if your imagination wanes. There can never be too much magic!

➤ Make romance a priority.

➤ Say "I love you" at least three times every day.

➤ Turn that quick goodbye kiss in the morning into something deeper and more meaningful.

➤ Tuck an "I love you" note into a pocket of his suit.

➤ Do an unexpected chore. If it's your spouse's responsibility to empty the trash, do it yourself once in awhile.

➤ Leave a voice message for your spouse that just says "I love you."

➤ Spend an extra few minutes in bed with your partner in the morning, or go to bed together a few minutes earlier than usual.

➤ Don't just welcome him home after a busy day. Pretend that he's been away for a month and really show him how much you missed him.

➤ If you wind down in the evenings by watching television, don't sit on opposite ends of the sofa or in separate chairs. Use the time to show some physical affection. Almost everyone enjoys a neck and shoulder rub or having their feet massaged.

➤ Polish her shoes. Don't ask. Just do it.

➤ Stay in the dating mode.

➤ Find new places to go that you think your spouse might enjoy.

➤ Expand your horizons. Planning an overnight stay at a bed and breakfast in town can be very romantic, but how about planning one in a city where you've never been?

➤ Limit your dates to the two of you as much as possible. The key idea here is romance, right? Leave the double dating to the teenagers.

➤ Call each other frequently. Daily might not be practical or necessary if you're apart for any reason, but be sure you hear each other's voice on a regular basis. If you can, call and say goodnight to each other at the end of the day. Faxes and emails work too.

➤ Send romantic cards. Do it even if you're not usually the type to send anything gushy. Go to the card shop and buy an assortment so you have a good supply on hand. Don't let a hectic schedule or the excuse of too little time get in the way.

➤ If you're apart, plan time for reunions. You may not get the chance to see each other as often as you'd like, but it's better than not at all. If time, convenience, or expense is an issue, maybe you can meet halfway.

➤ Make sure you express your emotions. Don't assume that your spouse knows how much you love him. Tell him. Reassure him that what you have is real and true and will withstand the test of time and distance.

The Affair-Proof Love Action Plan

Remember, change doesn't happen overnight. However, it's a good idea to get the ball rolling by having a plan.

But don't make your plan complicated. Start by identifying four things from your blueprint that you can do right now—and do them. Here are some examples:

➤ Plan a special night out.

➤ Treat her to a foot rub.

➤ Send him flowers at work.

➤ Offer to take over the bill paying for a month.

It doesn't matter what you choose. The idea is to get yourself into the action mode by identifying specific things you can do and then doing them. Sometimes our best intentions end up remaining just that—things we intend to do someday, when we get the time or when we get around to it. Don't rob yourself or your relationship by keeping your actions in the "intention" mode. Take action! Make affair-proof love a reality.

Good Places for More Help

The list below highlights additional sources of information on the various topics discussed in this book.

Anxiety

The National Mental Health Association sends free pamphlets on anxiety, depression, and other mental health issues and will suggest services and support groups. Call 800-969-6642 for a twenty-four-hour recording or call 703-684-7722 Monday through Friday, from 9 to 5 EST to request information.

Communicating

For help on improving communication skills, try Doyle Barnett's *20 Communication Tips for Couples: A 30-Minute Guide to a Better Relationship* (New World Library, 1995), a concise and simple guide to improving how couples talk and listen to each other. Each commonsense tip includes a short explanation and examples. Barnett's subsequent book, *20 Advanced Communications Tips for Couples: A 90-Minutes Investment in a Better Relationship* (Crown Publishing, 1997) expands on the original book with advanced strategies that address such issues as learning to be wrong and being right or being fair.

Author Jonathan Robinson believes that most couples get stuck in blame and anger, which prevents them from learning simple methods of communicating with love. His short book *Communication Miracles for Couples: Easy and Effective Tools to Create More Love and Less Conflict* (Conari Press, 1997) presents simple and practical ways to avoid arguments as well as communication methods designed to solve problems without resorting to blame.

Counseling

The American Psychological Association (APA) can assist in finding professional help.

American Psychological Association
750 First Street NE
Washington, D.C. 20002
202-336-5500

Depression

The National Mental Health Association (listed above) also provides information on depression. The National Institute of Mental Health offers free brochures on depression. Call 800-421-4211 for a twenty-four-hour recording or go to its Web site at 222.nimh.nih.gov and click on Public Information.

You Can Be Happy No Matter What: Five Principles for Keeping Life in Perspective, by Richard Carlson, Ph.D. (New World Library, 1997) is a practical, easy-to-follow guide to finding happiness now, not when all of life's problems are solved. Carlson's upbeat, commonsense approach focuses on removing mental barriers to happiness by using each individual's unique ways of thinking and emotions as a biofeedback mechanism to stay in touch with the causes of unhappiness.

Another book by Carlson, *You Can Feel Good Again: Common-Sense Therapy for Releasing Depression and Changing Your Life* (Plume, 1994), addresses depression more directly, also with an upbeat, commonsense approach.

Exercise

Resources on exercise are almost limitless, but if you're in need of a jump start, try this book: *Real-World Fitness* by Kathy Kaehler and Cheryl K. Olson (St. Martin's Press, 1999). You may know Kaehler from her twice-monthly appearances on the *Today* show; she's also a trainer to the stars, and she peppers her book with examples of routines she's developed for such clients as Michelle Pfeiffer, Alfre Woodard, and Peri Gilpin. This interesting and enjoyable book is based on Kaehler's popular *Today* show spots and includes an easy-to-follow eight-week shape-up program that can breathe new life into even the most long-forgotten exercise habit.

Life's Journeys

One of the classics on what love really means and what it takes to build a solid relationship is *The Road Less Traveled* by M. Scott Peck (Touchstone, a division of Simon & Schuster Inc., 1978). Although published more than twenty years ago, Peck's words are as relevant today as they were then—and as they will be tomorrow.

Meditation

If you've never meditated, *Joy Within: A Beginner's Guide to Meditation* by Joan Goldstein and Manuela Soares (Prentice Hall, 1992) is an easy-to-understand and practical book that can get you started pretty quickly. It's a guide for everyone—and one that doesn't promote any specific religious or spiritual point of view.

For an overview of the basics of meditation and tips on how to incorporate it into your lifestyle, try *The Complete Idiot's Guide to Meditation* by Joan Budilovsky and Eve Adamson (Alpha Books, 1999).

Pampering

Spas are great places for pampering and relaxation, and there are many to choose from. Overnight spas can be beyond the budget for many people; day spas, which offer a variety of different services in many price ranges, are a popular alternative. A good source of information on both types of spas is Spa-Finders (800) ALL-SPAS, which lists a number of overnight and day spas located across the country. Go to their Web site at www.spafinders.com for a searchable database of spas and a gift certificate service that allows you to order spa certificates online.

Many companies are now making products that can provide spa luxury in the privacy of your own home. One online resource to try is the BASU Spa-of-the-Month Club, which offers a number of prepackaged spa therapies based on various treatment regimens—seaweed, aromatherapy, and so on. Call 888-227-8772, or visit the BASU Web site at www.basu.com.

Positive Thinking

There are many books on this subject, but Norman Vincent Peale's, *The Power of Positive Thinking* (Ballantine Books, 1996), is the classic, having sold more than 7 million copies in fifteen languages. A newer book by Peale, *The Positive Principle Today: How to Renew and Sustain the Power of Positive Thinking* (Ballantine Books, 1996), builds on Peale's earlier writings and shows how to apply the "Positive Principle" to the challenges of today's world.

Prayer

There are probably as many resources on prayer as there are on meditation, which says two things: Prayer is popular, and many people find it difficult. Richard J. Foster's *Prayer: Finding the Heart's True Home* (HarperCollins, 1992) is a book to pick up if you want to learn more about different kinds of prayer and how easy it really can be.

The Art of Prayer: A Simple Guide by Timothy James (Ballantine Books, 1997) is a helpful guide to prayer that answers many questions about praying, such as whether it's all right to ask for help on little things and whether it's O.K. to get mad at God. (The answer to both questions is yes.) This book has a selection of nice quotes from religious leaders, philosophers, and poets, as well as specific suggestions for prayers.

Timeless Healing by Herbert Benson, M.D. (Fireside, 1997) isn't about prayer per se but is a good treatise on the effect that faith and positive thinking can have on life. Benson is the founder of Harvard's Mind/Body Institute, which studies the relationship between health and well-being.

Romance

If your imagination starts to run dry as you're looking for ways to romance your partner every day, you need *10,000 Ways to Say I Love You* by Gregory J.P. Godele (Casablanca Press, a division of Sourcebooks, 1999). Some of his suggestions can border on the silly, but they'll definitely get your mind working. An earlier book by Godele, *1,001 Ways to Be Romantic*, is more of the same but a lot less daunting.

Sensual Products

Massage oils and other sensual products can be found at many specialty retailers (and they can be fun to shop for together). If you'd rather shop at home for such products, try The Kama Sutra Company's Web site at www.kamasutra.com. This long-established company makes a very enjoyable line of edible love oils, creams, powders and other sexual potions that are enjoyed by lovers all over the world. If you're interested in sampling several products, take a look at The Weekender Kit, which includes travel sizes of some of the company's most popular products, including Honey Dust, Pleasure Balm, and the Original Oil of Love.

Another discreet source of sensual products is the Xandria Collection, which offers an extensive collection of sensual toys and other products designed to add some spice to intimate encounters. Contact Xandria at 800-242-2823 to request a catalog.

Stress

The National Mental Health Association (listed above) also provides information on managing stress.

Index

A

accepting self appearance, improving self-esteem, 139
accountability, 291
acting out fantasies, spicing relationship up, 119
active listening, 98
adapting boundaries, 38
addressing issues surrounding affair, 266
adultery, 7, 25
affair-prone quiz, 14
affairs
  addressing issues behind affair, 266
  affairee's perspective, 230, 235, 238
  as addictions, 55
  biological factors, 19
  bridge affairs, 58
  cheating again quiz, 273
  confessions, 196, 244, 246, 249-251, 254-258
  confronting affairee, 247
  coping strategies, 194, 198-199, 215
    confiding in others, 223
    deep breathing, 222
    exercise, 218, 224
    expressing anger, 223
    keeping situation private, 205
    living in the moment, 213
    maintaining perspective, 206
    meditation, 218
    pampering self, 224
    prayer, 220-221
    proper diet, 225

retaliating by having an affair, 210
  sex issues, 212
  taking long view, 204
  taking over responsibilities, 213
  telling children, 208
  telling others, 206
  volunteering, 226
  walking, 223
crucial periods in marriage, 149-151
discussing
  with children, 208
  with others, 206
elements, 56
emotional life cycle, 233-235, 238
evening the score as reason, 60
expectations after, 300
family behavior as factor, 10
financial success as factor, 10
forgetting the past, 302
forgiveness, 282
habits that lead to affairs, 159
  chaotic lifestyle, 163
  children coming first, 166
  criticism, 161-163
  emotional hide-and-seek, 160
  exercising excessively, 165
  failure to communicate, 167
  future thinking, 164
  living in a rut, 163

pets coming first, 167
  putting partner on hold, 164
  working too much, 165
ignoring signs of affair, 181
Internet affairs, 62
jealousy, 19
keeping in perspective, 206
keeping situation private, 205
learning from experience, 278, 283
long-distance affairs, 61
love affairs, 6, 56
loving affairs, 57
men's views, 6
not-so-subtle warning signs, 181
obvious signs, 181
potential outcomes, 7
potential positive effects, 46
reactions to disclosure, 264
recurring, 301
repairing relationship, 271
resolving situation, 264
retaliating by having an affair, 210
risks and dangers, 63
  casual becomes more, 65
  children, 66
  obsession, 64
  sexually-transmitted disease, 63
sex affairs, 6, 59
sexual experimentation as cause, 59
socioeconomic factors, 9
statistical variation, 8
subtle warning signs, 180

T–U

V

W–Z